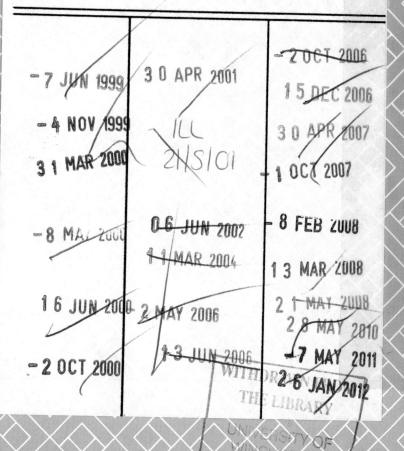

Identity in Adolescence

The second edition of the very popular *Identity in Adolescence* overviews the contributions of five developmental theorists in considering how effective intervention with adolescents can be a planned event rather than a chance occurrence.

Jane Kroger examines the key concepts and practical implications stemming from the theoretical models of Erik Erikson, Peter Blos, Lawrence Kohlberg, Jane Loevinger and Robert Kegan. All these theorists point to distinct stages through which ego organization shifts to a more differentiated self–other balance and from which identity development proceeds. It is our ability to recognize and respond to these stages of adolescent identity development that defines the limits of effective intervention, in either the facilitation of normative maturation or the alleviation of developmental arrest.

From the author's own experience working with young people in both clinical and natural settings *Identity in Adolescence* offers a unique blend of theoretical insight and practical advice which will prove invaluable to academics, professionals and parents.

Jane Kroger is at present Reader in Education at Victoria University of Wellington, New Zealand. Her previous publications include *Discussions on Ego Identity* (1993).

Adolescence and Society
Series editor: John C. Coleman
The Trust for the Study of Adolescence

The general aim of the series is to make accessible to a wide readership the growing evidence relating to adolescent development. Much of this material is published in relatively inaccessible professional journals, and the goals of the books in this series will be to summarise, review and place in context current work in the field so as to interest and engage both an undergraduate and a professional audience.

The intention of the authors is to raise the profile of adolescent studies among professionals and in institutes of higher education. By publishing relatively short, readable books on interesting topics to do with youth and society, the series will make people more aware of the relevance of the subject of adolescence to a wide range of social concerns.

The books will not put forward any one theoretical viewpoint. The authors will outline the most prominent theories in the field and will include a balanced and critical assessment of each of these. Whilst some of the books may have a clinical or applied slant, the majority will concentrate on normal development.

The readership will rest primarily on two major areas: the undergraduate market, particularly in the fields of psychology, sociology and education; and the professional training market, with particular emphasis on social work, clinical and educational psychology, counselling, youth work, nursing and teacher training.

Also available in this series

Identity in Adolescence

The balance between self and other

Second edition

Jane Kroger

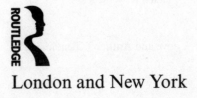

London and New York

First published 1996
by Routledge
11 New Fetter Lane, London EC4P 4EE

Simultaneously published in the USA and Canada
by Routledge
29 West 35th Street, New York, NY 10001

© 1996 Jane Kroger

Typeset in Times by Datix International Ltd, Bungay, Suffolk
Printed and bound in Great Britain by Clays Ltd,
St Ives plc

British Library Cataloguing in Publication Data
A catalogue record for this book is available from the British Library.

Library of Congress Cataloguing in Publication Data
A catalogue record for this book has been requested

ISBN 0–415–10678–8 (hbk)
ISBN 0–415–10679–6 (pbk)

You observe the carven hand
With the index finger pointing heavenward.
That is the direction, no doubt,
But how shall one follow it?
It is well to abstain from murder and lust,
To forgive, do good to others, worship God
Without graven images.
But these are external means after all
By which you chiefly do good to yourself.
The inner kernel is freedom,
It is light, purity –
I can no more,
Find the goal or lose it, according to your vision.

'Marie Bateson', in Edgar Lee Masters' *Spoon River Anthology*

This book is again dedicated to those who search and to those who assist along the way.

Contents

Preface to the second edition

When I wrote the first edition of *Identity in Adolescence* some six years ago, the interests of social scientists in researching issues of adolescent development were just beginning to expand. Textbooks for tertiary courses on adolescence certainly existed, covering a broad range of issues in normative adolescent development and sometimes including sections on adolescents in crisis. In the interval since that time, there has been an enormous increase in research attention directed to issues of both normative and non-normative development during life's second decade. Overview textbooks on adolescent development continue to flourish, but there has been an additional demand for more specialized texts dealing with specific issues of concern during the adolescent passage. The present volume and others included in the Adolescence and Society series edited by John Coleman reflect this important trend. Additionally, there has been an increasing attempt by many social scientists to integrate their varied theoretical models and research findings with some discussion of practical implications for social response to adolescents in the transition process. The present volume, again, reflects this ambition. Additionally, efforts towards understanding issues for adolescents growing up in a diversity of cultural, ethnic, and social class contexts have also been emerging. A new professional European Society for Research on Adolescence has recently been established and the Society for Research on Adolescence in the United States has recently expanded its international focus. The present volume reflects this growing awareness of the importance of societal contexts and has substantially revised its introductory section to elaborate, more fully, some of the historical and socio-cultural conditions making adolescent identity problematic for young people in societies with particular features in common.

At the same time, *Identity in Adolescence* has retained its developmental focus by examining some of the predictable ways in which young people, across varied social settings, may mature to reinterpret and make new sense of important relationships and their surrounding environments. The chapters of this volume focus on the writings of five major theorists of identity development: Erik Erikson, Peter Blos, Lawrence Kohlberg, Jane Loevinger, and Robert Kegan, who have all grappled with the nature of identity and the special transformations it normatively undergoes during adolescence. While taking different avenues of approach, each theorist maps a model of identity that allows us, in some way, to formulate more facilitative individual and institutional responses to those undergoing transition during the adolescent passage.

The terms 'identity', 'self', 'ego', 'I', and 'me' have all been used as referents to an 'observing center of awareness' described by Erikson (1968). Erikson, himself, chooses 'ego identity' to denote the psychosocial nature of the 'I', formed by a meeting of biological endowment and internal organization with social reality. Peter Blos uses the term 'character' to describe that observing center, more indicative of the intrapsychic nature of reorganizations that must occur during adolescence if development is to proceed unimpeded into adult life. Lawrence Kohlberg prefers to address the 'ego' as the organizer of the 'I', an entity accessible only through its various subdomains of functioning. Moral reasoning is one such subdomain studied extensively by Kohlberg which can offer us insight into structural features of the ego at various life stages; adolescence appears to be a time of heightened activity in the restructuring of moral logic. Jane Loevinger selects the term 'ego' to refer to that master trait of personality, holistic in form, through which we perceive and interpret our worlds; again, Loevinger finds the adolescent years to be a time of great change in the organization of the 'I'. Robert Kegan views the 'I' as an evolutionary process of 'meaning-making' – of rebalancing that which we regard as self and that which we take to be other; such rebalancing results in a new, more differentiated self, with adolescence being a particularly active period in the process of striking new balances. While care is taken to articulate the specific meaning the 'I' holds for each identity theorist reviewed in this volume, 'identity', 'self', 'ego', 'I', and 'me' are also used less formally as referents to that underlying 'observing center of awareness and of volition' in personality – that core which is 'in some sense real and not created by our definition' (Loevinger 1984: 50).

Since this work may be serving as an introduction to the field of adolescent identity formation for many readers, introductory sections to key theoretical concepts of each chapter have been retained from the first edition. Where theoretical modifications have been made, I have made every attempt to draw upon the most recent publications available and have changed summaries accordingly. Sections in each chapter on 'Research findings' now include new studies which have appeared since publication of the first edition, while a new topic, 'Current directions in research', has been added to give the reader a sense of the most recent developments in the field. Sections on 'Implications for social response' for each theoretical model have also been expanded to include results of recent intervention studies as well as more recent theory-based proposals.

This volume has again been sparked by my concern over adults' frequent failure to recognize, meet, and respond optimally to the special needs of adolescents in their various stages of identity development. Although each young person is unique in personal history, talents, and attributes, there do appear to be certain underlying and predictable structural reorganizations that comprise the identity formation process; once recognized and addressed, opportunity exists for alleviating developmental arrest as well as supporting the normative process of change in more facilitative ways. Rather than chance occurrence, effective developmental intervention can be a planned event. It is hoped that an understanding of the developmental approaches to identity presented in this volume might enable us to make more effective social responses to adolescents undergoing the identity formation process.

Acknowledgements

Thoughts and observations presented in the pages ahead are the product of many stimulating discussions with colleagues, students, and friends as well as many solitary ruminations over the past two decades of my life. As a university teacher and researcher in the areas of human development and counseling, I am continually learning by all that my students, research interviewees, and colleagues teach me. Since publication of the first edition of *Identity in Adolescence,* I have been very fortunate in having two periods of sabbatical leave which have enabled me to meet and interact with many of the theorists and researchers covered in the pages ahead. Time in 1988–89 as a visiting research associate at the Erik H. and Joan M. Erikson Center, Cambridge Hospital, Harvard Medical School provided me with opportunities for many engaging conversations with both of the Eriksons as well as others in the Cambridge community. A more recent 1993 semester as a visiting scholar at the Henry A. Murray Research Center for the Study of Lives at Radcliffe College again enabled me to engage in many stimulating interactions. I am especially grateful for the thoughtful feedback of Drs Gil Noam, Gus Blasi, and John Levine as I worked towards integrating theoretical models. Dr Bob Kegan provided many wonderful learning opportunities through his teachings on adult development. Dr Anne Colby, Director of the Murray Research Center, provided me with access to the many rich resources of data archived at the Murray Center. Dr James Marcia and his graduate students were very generous with their time in discussions later in 1993 during my month-long interlude in the Psychology Department at Simon Fraser University, Burnaby, BC, Canada, and to them I express my sincere appreciation.

In particular, I would also again like to thank Dr John Coleman, Director of the Centre for the Study of Adolescence in Brighton, and Routledge for their support in producing this volume. Both the Education Department and the Internal Research Committee of Victoria

University of Wellington have been very generous in providing financial assistance for the acquisition of needed materials as well as leave time for the preparation of this volume. Colleagues Dr Lise Bird and Jim Collinge and students Peter Bergantino, Ellen Duckworth, Jennifer O'Connell, Paula Oude-Alink, Ros Pratt, and Beverly Rhodes provided valuable suggestions in reviewing portions of the first edition; Cathy Diggins has given additional helpful feedback to portions of this volume. Since *Identity in Adolescence* was first produced, I have also had the opportunity to meet and correspond with a number of readers, and many of your very helpful ideas have been incorporated in this volume. Thanks go finally again to those adolescents from educational institutions in the greater Wellington area who have enriched the theoretical discussion of the final chapter with their own realities of the identity formation experience.

Grateful acknowledgement is made for permission to quote from the following source: Edgar Lee Masters, 'Marie Bateson,' in *Spoon River Anthology*. Copyright © 1962 by The Crowell–Collier Publishing Company. By permission of Hilary Masters.

Jane Kroger
Wellington, New Zealand
March 1995

1   Adolescence and the problem of identity
Historical, socio-cultural, and developmental views

'Listen', F. Jasmine said. 'What I've been trying to say is this. Doesn't it strike you as strange that I am I, and you are you? I am F. Jasmine Addams. And you are Berenice Sadie Brown. And we can look at each other, and touch each other, and stay together year in and year out in the same room. Yet always I am I, and you are you. And I can't ever be anything else but me, and you can't ever be anything else but you. Have you ever thought of that? And does it seem to you strange?'
(*F. Jasmine Addams in Carson McCullers'* Member of the Wedding)

When and how does [one] develop a sense of 'I'?
(*Erik Erikson,* Infancy and the Rest of Life)

F. Jasmine (alias Frankie) Addams' ruminations cited above address a question adolescents and social scientists alike have pondered over preceding decades: when and how does one develop a sense of 'I'? Although the foundations of 'I' are formed in infancy through the interactions of care-takers and child, adolescence does seem to be a time, at least in contemporary, technologically advanced western cultures, when one is confronted with the task of self-definition. 'I can't ever be anything else but me' begins Frankie. However, trying to find who 'me' is becomes Frankie's task in Carson McCullers' (1946) novel, *Member of the Wedding*. The process of self-definition is something which scholars have attempted to understand from a variety of perspectives – historical, socio-cultural, and developmental. And while Frankie herself is not concerned with all of these issues, she eloquently gives voice to some of the forces that help shape her 'I', her sense of identity, her self-definition.

Frankie's story is set during World War II in a small, rural southern town in the United States during a seemingly endless summer. Frankie is about to turn 'twelve and five-sixths', feeling very much betwixt and between meaningful social niches (which summer has a way of exacerbating), and wrestling with the matter of belonging. Given an option, Frankie would have been a boy and gone to war as a marine. However, this was not to be her fate, so she decided, instead, to give blood (at least a quart a week), and in this way, a part of her would be in the veins of Allies fighting all over the world (the reddest and strongest blood ever – a true medical wonder). Soldiers would return, saying they owed their lives to 'Addams' (not 'Frankie'). But this scenario was not to be her fate either, for Frankie was too young, and the Red Cross would not take her blood. Thinking about the war for very long made Frankie afraid, not because of the fighting but because the war refused to include her, to give her a place in the world. Actually, thinking for very long, at all, made Frankie afraid as well, for it brought up questions of who she was, of what she would be in the world, of why she was standing where she was at that moment – alone. Through the trials of trying to adopt a new name (F. Jasmine Addams), a new family, a new town, Frankie struggled to explore her sense of 'I', her own identity and place in the world.

Had Frankie been born in an earlier *historical* era, her story would probably not have given rise to a novel, for self-definition would not have been a problem. As Erikson (1975) has noted, the issue of identity holds historical relativity. Erikson suggested that identity only became a matter of concern in the United States late in the nineteenth century because a new generation of immigrants were attempting to define themselves in a land far removed from their ancestral homes. Baumeister (1986, 1987) has provided an excellent, more extensive overview of how the problematic nature of identity for many adolescents has evolved and intensified over the course of history.

Baumeister notes that medieval adolescent and adult identities were defined in a very straightforward manner. The social rank and kinship network into which one was born determined one's place in and for life. While some changes of title or role were inevitable over the course of time, general possibilities were circumscribed by the clan. In the early modern period, the rise of a middle class began a shift in the standard for self-definition when wealth, rather than kinship ties, became the new measure of social status and hence, self-definition. The later Protestant split and subsequent decline of the Christian faith gave rise to an era in which individuals became able at least to accept or reject the religious traditions of their forebears. During the Romantic era, most still espoused Christian beliefs, but these held less influence over their daily lives. Furthermore, society was often perceived to be oppressive and the need to reject some of society's demands was recognized. By the Victorian era, late adolescents and adults increasingly began to reject Christian dogma, and a focal concern was whether or not morality could survive without religion. Thus, Victorian adolescents had to define their adult identities without clear guidelines in the midst of general cultural uncertainty on issues of appropriate values.

Such difficulties for adolescents continued into the twentieth century, as the process of self-definition and identity formation have become normative developmental tasks (Erikson 1968). Cushman (1990) further suggests that at least in the United States at the present time, absence of community, tradition, and shared meaning has created the conditions for an 'empty self', a sense of 'I' which experiences chronic emotional hunger for adolescents and adults alike. Cushman argues that the 'empty self' attempts to be soothed, to be 'filled up' by consumer products; advertizing and psychotherapy are the two professions Cushman cites as being most responsible in an individual's attempts to heal the 'empty self'. Viewed historically, the process of identity formation and the process of self-definition, at least for many youths in western contexts, is a relatively recent phenomenon.

In her efforts toward self-definition, Frankie voices her intense desire to break free – free of her family, town, and many of the *sociocultural* conditions that constrain her. Berenice, Frankie's black housekeeper, attempts to understand:

> 'I think I have a vague idea what you were driving at', [responds Berenice]. 'We all of us somehow caught. We born this way or that way and we don't know why. But we caught anyhow. . . . We each one of us somehow caught all by ourself. Is that what you was trying to say?'
>
> 'I don't know,' F. Jasmine said. 'But I don't want to be caught'.
>
> 'Me neither', said Berenice. 'Don't none of us. I'm caught worse than you is'.
>
> F. Jasmine understood why she had said this, and it was John Henry who asked in his child voice: 'Why?'
>
> 'Because I am black,' said Berenice.
>
> (McCullers 1946: 113)

Frankie is 'caught' by her social class and ethnicity as well as the technological influences, societal norms, and legal requirements for adolescents in her culture; the socio-cultural conditions of her society, some would contend, create her problems of identity and self-definition. Lapsley *et al.* (1985: 441) have argued from a socio-cultural perspective that 'adolescence is best understood as the state-appropriation of youth leisure [and] that the imposition of this status was effected through the enactment of compulsory education legislation'. They believe that adolescence is not a by-product of socio-cultural need to develop a compulsory system for secondary education but rather that adolescence was actually created and maintained by a system of compulsory education that enforced dependency and promoted higher rates of consumer expenditure. In their view, the emergence of child-saving legislation (through compulsory schooling) is the origin of adolescence.

Indeed, Bettelheim, writing some sixteen years earlier, would seem to agree. Bettelheim holds an affluent society responsible for the emergence of this life-cycle phase and the identity problems it creates:

> [I]t was only the affluent society – permitting extension of public schooling till eighteen, plus the vast increase in youth going to college – that created the problem of adolescence [b]ecause it meant the postponement of earning a living and a postponing of adult sexuality until well past the age when sexual maturity is reached. Actually the adolescent's estrangement, the struggle he has in order to find himself and his place in society – these exist because he has only so recently come to be. . . .
>
> (Bettelheim 1969: 55)

The economic conditions of an affluent society in which adolescent labors are unnecessary for societal survival and well-being may, indeed, have contributed to the marginality of adolescents and the problematic conditions for adolescent identity.

Fasick (1994) furthers the socio-cultural argument by attributing the 'invention' of adolescence to additional conditions beyond the role of compulsory secondary education and affluence alone. He argues that adolescence is deeply rooted in industrial urbanism, and that three major societal conditions have given rise to the phenomenon of adolescence: the use of technology to improve productivity, the affluence generated by this process, and concomitant demographic transitions. Conditions of affluence affecting the creation of adolescence include a population increase, the institution of compulsory secondary education, the expectation that adolescents should live with their parents as dependants until completing at least secondary school, the small family system, and the growth of commercial enterprises aimed at adolescents. The diversification of occupations and urbanization (with high population density contributing to increased interactions among teenagers) have been results of technology which have contributed to the creation of adolescence.

A further view finds technologically advanced cultures accountable for the (sometimes prolonged) adolescent period spent in pursuit of full power and status accorded adults within the society: 'We can see adolescence, then, as a cultural phenomenon, and not physiologically necessary to the development of the human being' (Sieg 1971: 346). Cultural variations in the adolescent identity formation process are in ample evidence. For example, adolescents in collectivist societies are not faced with the choices and decisions that youths in contemporary western cultures must make in defining their own identities. Tupuola (1993) interviewed New Zealand and Samoan-born youths living in New Zealand about their experiences of adolescence. One Samoan-born participant summarized the responses of many as follows:

> I feel I still can't answer the adolescent thing. As a Samoan born, I had never heard of it [adolescence] until I came to New Zealand. I don't think it was part of my life because it is a western concept, and from a non-western society all those development stages didn't relate to me. All I know is that my aiga [family] and my community and my culture are important. They determine the way I behave, think, and feel. . . . Sometimes I think that we [in Samoa] are children for most of our lives, and it can take a very long time for us to become adults. It does not matter how old you are, [for] if you are not considered worthy or responsible enough by your elders then you will not be treated as an adult. You really have to earn your place in the Samoan culture. So adolescence as a developmental stage is foreign to our culture.
>
> (Subject no.3 in Tupuola 1993: 308, 311)

Cultural conditions for this young woman made the issue of identity formation and finding her place in the societal milieu a rather straight-forward process. While some of the roles that she was expected to fill were not easy, the actual process of identifying suitable roles for herself within the larger society was not, in itself, a complex problem. Tupuola further reports that a number of participants in her study consulted Samoan dictionaries over the course of their interviews and were unable even to find a Samoan word meaning 'adolescence'.

Social and historical circumstances have undoubtedly left teenagers from technologically advanced cultures with ambiguous role prescriptions to struggle with the problem of self-definition. A number of social scientists, however, have focused more intently on what Frankie describes as a changing sense of 'I' – on an internal (intrapsychic) *developmental* transformation of the sense of self and consequent ways of filtering and making sense of one's life experiences. Intra-psychic restructuring during adolescence brings identity questions to the surface; while socio-cultural factors undoubtedly may accelerate, delay, or even arrest this developmental process, sequential stages in the transformation of the self and its way of understanding remain unaltered, according to this developmental perspective. Transformations in cognitive and affective processes or qualitative change in some self (ego) structure which subtends both of these facets of identity have all been held accountable for alterations to the subjective sense of 'I' frequently experienced during life's second decade – at least in societies where adult identities for young people are not prescribed.

While acknowledging the contributions of society to creating the phenomenon of adolescence with its concomitant questions of identity, this book focuses on five developmental models addressing the intrapsychic potential emergence of the self. All approaches attend carefully to the period of adolescence with the internal reorganization it normatively brings; however, all respect the process of identity formation as a lifelong enterprise and are reviewed in this volume in a manner reflecting this orientation. Just as the significance of a painting cannot be fully grasped without knowledge of its contextual origins and resulting influences on later art, so identity formation during adolescence cannot be fully appreciated without knowledge of its childhood antecedents and consequent adult states.

Until the 1960s, much of the literature on adolescent psychology came from psychoanalytic treatment centers. There was often a stress on the 'universality of "ego weakness" in adolescence' and the depiction of an ego 'besieged by the drives and unable to rely on the now-dangerous parental ego for support' (Josselson 1980: 188); such portrayals lay at the heart of the 'turmoil' theory of adolescent development which presented storm and stress as normative features of the teenage years. It was only when researchers of the 1960s and 1970s (for example Douvan and Adelson 1966; Offer and Offer 1975) began to find little evidence of psychopathology or even much storm and stress among large samples of adolescents in the general population that attention began to shift from clinical to more normative populations for an understanding of developmental processes occurring in adolescence. Literature on various features of adolescent development has mushroomed in the last three decades, with the creation of at least six new North American and European journals and two professional societies in these locales devoted solely to research on this stage of the life-cycle. The issue of identity during adolescence, however, has still been approached by many contemporary psychoanalytic writers through accounts of non-normative developmental phenomena. While Erikson's psychosocial model has sparked an array of studies into identity formation among late adolescents primarily at universities, less is known about the course of intrapsychic restructuring by adolescents in the general population. It is the intention of this book to examine, through critical analysis, the contributions of five identity theories, most having psychodynamic origins, for an understanding of the more normative processes involved in intrapsychic reorganization during adolescence. While some less than optimal identity resolutions will be presented, the focus rests primarily on those normative though 'cataclysmic [adolescent] ego changes that hardly make a sound' (Josselson 1980: 190).

THE DEVELOPMENTAL PERSPECTIVE

As developmental models, the theories of Erik Erikson, Peter Blos, Lawrence Kohlberg, Jane Loevinger, and Robert Kegan presented in the pages ahead all have certain features in common. Rather than depicting change in a linear fashion, *quantitative* in nature, all approaches reviewed focus on change more *qualitative* in kind, developmental in form. The linear or non-stage view of change holds that something which exists early in life becomes merely bigger or more pronounced through time, while the developmental orientation attempts to detail how that which existed at earlier life stages 'becomes transformed into something related to, but also different than, what existed earlier' (Breger 1974: 3). Some approaches to identity are non-developmental in nature. The ancient Greeks defined personality in terms of character type; an individual was merely one of four basic personality types, never undergoing qualitative change. More recent efforts to describe personality in terms of body-build (such as endomorph, mesomorph, ectomorph), character disposition (such as introvert-extrovert), or psychiatric diagnostic classification (such as sociopath, schizophrenic, manic-depressive) are all examples of linear or non-developmental views of identity; these labels assume that 'a person's type resides within and is stimulated to unfold with experience' (Breger 1974: 6). In developmental models of identity, by contrast, it is possible to detect qualitatively different stages of organization, each with its own unique features that will never again exist in the same form; once stage reorganization has occurred, it is simply not possible to go back to view the world through earlier, less complex modes of organization (however much one may wish to do so at times). Developmental stages exist in a hierarchical and invariant sequence, each building on that which has gone before, incorporating yet transcending the last stage to provide a foundation for the next

(Loevinger 1987). Theorists reviewed in this volume all describe identity as a developmental process of qualitative stage reorganization rather than a mere unfolding of static personality characteristics.

When identity is viewed as a developmental phenomenon, some important implications for social response become apparent. Rather than being a collection of static traits, identity is conceptualized by developmental approaches as a structural organization more responsive to opportunities that will obviate developmental arrest as well as promote further movement towards maturity. For example, no longer do we need to consider an individual with the label 'sociopathic personality disorder' as having a static personality trait unamenable to change, but rather as someone with a condition of childhood developmental arrest who, with appropriate intervention, may be helped to embark on a more normative developmental course (Kegan 1986a). A discussion of the implications each model holds for social response in the promotion of optimal identity formation is thus an important feature of each theoretical review presented in this volume.

IDENTITY AS THE BALANCE BETWEEN SELF AND OTHER

The terms 'identity', 'self', 'ego', 'I', and 'me' have all held very specific meanings for various social scientists interested in addressing the issue of self-definition. Each theorist reviewed in the pages ahead attaches a somewhat unique meaning to the nature of the 'I' at particular phases of the life-span; however, despite usage of different concepts, a further basic commonality seems present as we look across these developmental approaches to the essence of identity. In some way, shape, or form, identity invariably gets defined (at various stages of the life-cycle) as a balance between that which is taken to be self and that considered to be other. The means by which we differentiate ourselves from other people in our lives as well as from our own organic functions constitutes the very core of our experiences of personal identity. American novelist Thomas Wolfe struggled through his life to differentiate his own identity from that internalized image of his primary care-taker. This intrapsychic battle was replayed in many of his adolescent and adult relationships: 'His popularity [as a writer] is partially due to his being a chronicler of the human aspirations for individuation, for the establishment of a real self, as well as of the feelings of loss associated with this search' (Masterson 1986: Tape 4). Though using differing terms and concepts, Erikson, Blos, Kohlberg, Loevinger, and Kegan all provide descriptions of how the internal balancing and rebalancing of boundaries between self and other produce more differentiated subjective experiences of identity at various life stages. Adolescence encompasses one phase of heightened activity for most in this intrapsychic juggling act.

From psychodynamic beginnings, Erikson's work was the first to appreciate the psycho*social* nature of identity with the important role played by the community in recognizing, supporting, and thus helping to shape the adolescing ego. A true developmental theorist, he distinguishes the identity solutions of *introjection* during infancy and *identification* in childhood from the process of *identity formation* during adolescence. It is during the adolescent phase of the life-span that Erikson sees opportunities for identity resolution through a synthesis that incorporates yet transcends all previous identifications to produce a new whole, based upon, yet qualitatively different from that which has gone before. 'The final identity, then, as fixed at the end of adolescence, is superordinated to any single identification with individuals of the past: it includes all significant identifications, but it also alters them in order to make a unique and reasonably coherent whole of them' (Erikson 1968: 161).

Here the new balance between self and other involves a reorganization of the means to identity itself. That self of childhood, derived from significant identifications with important others must, during adolescence, give way to a self derived from yet transcending those foundations – to a new whole greater than the sum of its parts. Others now become important not merely as potential sources of identification but rather as independent agents, helping to recognize the 'real me'.

Blos, more strongly than Erikson, has maintained his alliance with classic psychodynamic theory. However, Blos's account of the second individuation process of adolescence has paved the way for a new approach to the study of adolescent individuation and identity. Relying on the ground-breaking work of Margaret Mahler in detailing the infant separation and individuation processes, Blos regards adolescence as a second individuation experience. While the successful establishment of an autonomous self in life's earliest years rests with the toddler's ability to incorporate or internalize an image of its primary care-taker, such intrapsychic organization hinders further development during adolescence. During the second individuation process, it is this very internalized parent which must be relinquished if development is to progress. Blos sees adolescence as a time spent unhinging the old intrapsychic arrangement of that which has been considered self (the parental introjects) and that taken to be other; he finds regressive thoughts and actions, necessary for further development, to be common phenomena accompanying this loss of the childhood 'I'. A sense of heightened distinctiveness from others is the subjective experience following successful adolescent individuation. Now others can be recognized as agents in their own right rather than merely as internalized orchestrators of one's responses to life.

Kohlberg, unlike other theorists in the pages ahead, does not address the formation of identity directly. Rather, he conceptualizes identity (or in his terms, ego) as an entity which can only be approached through specific subdomains of ego functioning. These subdomains (for example, cognition, moral reasoning) develop alongside one another, often exhibiting only conditional links; thus, a certain stage of cognitive development seems to be a necessary but not sufficient condition for reasoning at a more advanced level of moral judgment. Kohlberg has been particularly interested in the evolution of moral reasoning, and an understanding of his developmental model does enable us to view one aspect of identity in formation. Normatively over the course of adolescence, one can see movement from moral reasoning driven by self-interest and later by the need for social approval to moral reasoning motivated by a desire to uphold the law for its own sake; it is only beginning in late adolescence that one can sometimes hear a logic based on internalized ethical principles which may transcend the written law. Through Kohlberg's stage sequence, we can again see an internal developmental reorganization of self and other in the logic of decision-making on matters moral. Where self-interest and then social approval were once necessary cornerstones of the self's architecture, both organizations may give way in late adolescence to a more differentiated and autonomous self, the author of its moral decisions based on a universal respect for human life.

Loevinger views identity in a more holistic manner as that 'master trait of personality'. The ego, to Loevinger, is a screening device which allows us to perceive (or misperceive) reality in such a way as to reduce anxiety. Based on extensive psychometric studies of responses to her projective Sentence Completion Test, she has described a series of developmental stages in the formation of the ego or the experience of self. Taking great care to clarify her concept of the ego as one which is distinct from most earlier psychoanalytic usages of the term, Loevinger proceeds to detail stages through which this master trait of personality comes into being during infancy and develops to (or becomes arrested at) more mature stages of functioning during late adolescence and adulthood. In so doing, she examines common forms of impulse control, interpersonal style, conscious preoccupations, and cognitive style in each stage. Normatively during adolescence, we can view the shift from an impulsive organization, where self-interest is the primary motivator, to one of conformity to dictates of the immediate social group. A more mature state of self-awareness seems to be the modal organization (at least within the United States) of the late adolescent and adult ego; at this level, some degree of self-awareness and appreciation of the multiple possibilities of situations exists. Loevinger's paradigm thus traces stages of self–other differentiation during adolescence from one of self-interest or conformity to others' attitudes and behaviors to the organization of a self more distinct from others, appreciative of individuality, and capable of greater mutuality in relationship.

Lastly, Kegan views the formation of identity as a lifelong evolutionary process of meaning-making. His developmental scheme draws upon Piagetian, Kohlbergian, and object-relations theories to conceptualize identity as a holistic process that subtends both cognition and affect. Identity formation is about how that which is regarded as self (or subject) is structured, lost, and then reformed. At various stages of the life-span, the self is intrapsychically embedded in particular contexts from which it is unable to gain distance. Thus, the young child *is* its impulses, and only later does the self differentiate so as to *have* its impulses and desires. That which is regarded as other (or object) undergoes transformation as development proceeds to a new stage of self–other (subject–object) balance. The young adolescent's self is normatively embedded in its own needs and interests, unable to distance from or gain a perspective on them. Only later is this outworn self 'thrown away' so that that which was once subject (needs and interests) becomes the object in a new subject–object balance. When such change occurs, the mid-adolescent can now reflect upon his or her own interests and coordinate them with those of other people. The limitation of this new normative mid-adolescent balance lies, however, in the self's embeddedness in its own interpersonal context; now one *is*, rather than *has*, his or her relationships. It is only during late adolescence that the self–other balance may tilt once again; if it so moves, the self comes to *have* its friendships (the new object) while becoming embedded in its institutional roles such as work (the new subject). Kegan's construct depicts identity development (or meaning-making) as an ongoing process of finding, losing, and creating new balances between that which is regarded as self and that taken to be other; normative adolescence encompasses a time of increased movement in the balancing and rebalancing of subject and object.

The general aim of this volume is to understand how adolescents navigate through life, more or less successfully, developing a sense of who they are and how they can best find personal satisfaction in the adult worlds of love and work. Five developmental models of the identity formation process are presented, accompanied by critical comment, reviews of related research, and a discussion of the implications each theory holds for social response. Einstein once noted that it is the theory which decides what we can observe. It is hoped that this theoretical overview, however, will in no way set limits to our future ways of understanding and responding to the process of identity formation during adolescence.

2 Adolescence as identity synthesis
Erikson's psychosocial approach

Siddhartha reflected deeply as he went on his way. He realized that he was no longer a youth; he was now a man. He realized that something had left him, like the old skin that a snake sheds. Something was no longer in him, something that had accompanied him right through his youth and was part of him: this was the desire to have teachers and to listen to their teachings. He had left the last teacher he had met, even he, the greatest and wisest teacher, the holiest, the Buddha. He had to leave him; he could not accept his teachings.

(*Hermann Hesse,* Siddhartha)

In his novel, *Siddhartha*, Hermann Hesse movingly recounts the journey of a man in search of his own identity. The story opens in an idyllic communal setting along a sunny and tranquil river bank (complete with fig tree), as Siddhartha senses the first nuances of inner discontent. Family and friends alike love and admire the handsome and supple Siddhartha, and his destiny as a prince among Brahmins is the fate envisaged by all for this great Brahmin's son. For Siddhartha, however, knowledge of such a future brings no satisfaction or peace of mind. After a final meditation, the young man announces his intention of joining the Samanas, a wandering group of ascetics who practice a life-style in all ways contrary to the values held dear by childhood friends and mentors. Through such action, Siddhartha's single goal is to let the self die, to become empty, to become something other than himself. Despite all efforts of self-denial through pain, hunger, thirst, and fatigue, however, Siddhartha cannot escape his own existence. After several unsatisfying years with the Samanas, Siddhartha once more finds new hope for peace by testing the way of the Buddha in conquering the self. After a short time it becomes clear, however, that such efforts will also fail to bring salvation, and it is at this point that we meet Siddhartha ruminating on his new-found learnings as he leaves the grove of the Buddha. It seems that neither complete identification with childhood's teachers nor their complete banishment from his existence help Siddhartha to solve the riddle of the self and so structure an identity that will see him through (or at least into) adult life. Perhaps no piece of literature so adequately and accurately anticipates the themes central to Erikson's writings on identity formation during adolescence, and it is to Siddhartha we shall later return for illumination of Erikson's concepts.

Erik Erikson was the first psychoanalytic writer to enquire seriously into the phenomenon of identity formation during adolescence. His approach was based upon, but diverged in important ways from, Freud's biologically based psychosexual orientation to personality development. Erikson moved beyond classic psychoanalysis with its focus on the id and libidinal drivers of development to emphasize the ego and its adaptive capacities in the environment. Rather than viewing others as objects of cathexis important to intrapsychic functioning as did Freud, Erikson saw others as interacting with and regulating the ego to provide a context in which the self can find meaning and cohere. Moving beyond Freud's goal of raising human misery to mere unhappiness, Erikson painted not only a more optimistic picture of human capabilities but also shifted the emphasis of psychoanalysis from pathology to healthy functioning. Finally, Erikson recognized that personality development did not end in adolescence but rather continued to evolve throughout the life-span.

ERIKSON, THE PERSON

Born in Germany in 1902 to Danish parents who separated before his birth, Erikson was raised by his mother and a German pediatrician stepfather. A sense of being 'different' both as a stepson in a reconstituted family and as a blond, blue-eyed Dane growing up in a German, Jewish community pervaded much of Erikson's childhood and later life. In late adolescence, the young Erikson was drawn to the occupational role of an artist, a 'passing' identity providing some income while still allowing the young man a much needed psychosocial moratorium before choosing his life's work. Additionally, sketching gave training in the recording of impressions, a skill vital to his later profession. (The artist's vocational choice also made a definitive statement to his stepfather about the role in medicine the physician had envisaged for his stepson.)

It was eventually the invitation of childhood friend Peter Blos to join the staff of a small school in Vienna which placed Erikson in a position to meet Freud's inner circle. Again, not quite belonging to

Freud's community of medical rebels, Erikson's stepson relationship to the psychoanalytic profession did not furnish him with a more settled sense of vocational identity until much later, when his own artistic talents could be integrated with his psychoanalytic practice through theoretical writing – the sketching of impressions through linguistic rather than visual form.

Erikson and his wife, Joan, left Vienna with their two young sons as Hitler came to power in Germany and eventually migrated to Boston, where a psychoanalytic association had recently been founded. It was in this social context that Erikson, one of the society's few non-medical members, found a professional niche as one of the area's first practicing child analysts. Throughout his impressive career, Erikson accepted appointments at Yale, the University of California, Berkeley, the Austin Riggs Center, and Harvard, all without accruing a single earned academic degree. It was in 1950 that Erikson's theoretical framework was adopted in total by the White House Conference on Children, which provided a national charter for child and adolescent development in the United States. In 1978, Harvard University awarded Erikson an honorary doctorate and later established the Erik H. and Joan M. Erikson Center to provide a forum for interdisciplinary studies of the life-cycle. Erikson died in 1994 following a brief illness at the age of 91 years.

It is not surprising that the theme of identity so central to Erikson's own life became central in his writings on life-cycle development. Now, with at least ten books and a collection of individual papers dedicated to examining the nature of identity formation during adolescence and the life-cycle, Erikson's contributions seem an appropriate beginning for our enquiries into adolescent identity development.

THE NATURE OF EGO IDENTITY

What, then, is identity and how does it develop during adolescence? Erikson first used the term 'ego identity' to describe a central disturbance among some returning World War II veterans who were experiencing a loss of sameness and continuity in their lives:

> What impressed me most was the loss in these men of a sense of identity. They knew who they were; they had a personal identity. But it was as if subjectively, their lives no longer hung together – and never would again. There was a central disturbance in what I then started to call ego identity.
>
> (Erikson 1963: 42)

He continued by noting that it was often a decisive yet innocent moment in the lives of these soldiers wherein the needs of a man's social group, those of his biological organism, and those idiosyncratic to his own development and family history met in irreconcilable conflict, heralding the breakdown of personal meaning and life continuity.

Several concepts basic to Erikson's later work emerged from the observation of these veterans. Firstly, identity seems to be most easily definable through its absence or loss; it is only when one can no longer take for granted the fabric of one's unique existence that its foundation threads become exposed and more clearly apparent. It is through such loss of ego identity or its developmental failure that opportunity does exist for understanding more normative modes of identity formation and the means by which society can provide for optimal development. Erikson's clinical experience sensitized him to questions of how identity forms and develops for the wider non-patient population.

Furthermore, the soldiers' tales brought the tripartite nature of identity into view. Freud had left psychoanalysis focused on the role played by biology in personality development. However, for a somewhat dissatisfied Erikson, 'traditional psychoanalytic method ... cannot quite grasp identity because it has not developed terms to conceptualize the environment' (Erikson 1968: 24). While biology is important to individual biography, so, too, are an individual's life history and the presiding cultural and historical context, argued the analyst. For one medical officer veteran who came to Erikson's attention, it was the combination of lowered group morale in his unit followed by group panic over loss of leadership (social and historical context), physical fatigue and illness (biological state), and his lifelong denial of anger following a traumatic childhood incident (individual life history) which culminated in his loss of ego identity. Erikson conceptualizes and defines identity in an interdisciplinary way; biological endowment, personal organization of experience, and cultural milieu all conspire to give meaning, form, and continuity to one's unique existence.

Following his initial statement on identity, Erikson was persuaded to expand and elaborate the construct. As a psychosocial phenomenon, he saw identity rooted both within the individual as well as within the communal culture (Erikson 1970). Subjectively, the theorist suggests what it feels like to have a sense of identity by citing a letter from William James to his wife:

A man's character is discernible in the mental or moral attitude in which, when it came upon him, he felt himself most deeply and intensely active and alive. At such moments there is a voice inside which speaks and says: '*This* is the real me!'

(James, cited in Erikson 1968: 199)

One knows when identity is present, in greater or lesser degree. For the individual, identity is partly conscious and partly unconscious; it gives one's life a feeling of sameness and continuity yet also a 'quality of unselfconscious living' and is taken for granted by those in possession. Identity involves conflict and has its own developmental period during adolescence and youth, when biological endowment and intellectual processes must eventually meet societal expectation for a suitable display of adult functioning. Identity depends upon the past and determines the future; rooted in childhood, it serves as a base from which to meet later life tasks (Erikson 1970). Erikson does not elaborate in similar detail on the 'social' side of the psychosocial partnership, though he does stress the importance of the social context in providing 'something to search for and . . . be true to' (Erikson 1968: 235). Erikson also views identity as a generational issue, pointing to the responsibility of the parent generation for providing an ideological framework for its youth (if only for the purpose of giving adolescents a structure against which to rebel and forge their own values).

IDENTITY: DEVELOPMENT AND RESOLUTIONS

Perhaps Erikson's most concise account of how identity develops is to be found in *Toys and Reasons:* '[T]he process of identity formation depends on the interplay of what young persons at the end of childhood have come to mean to themselves and what they now appear to mean to those who become significant to them' (1977: 106). This deceptively simple statement is based upon a number of developmental principles basic to Erikson's concept of identity. The theorist distinguishes identity formation, which generally occurs during adolescence, from the childhood processes of introjection and identification. That first sense of 'I', he suggests, emerges only through the trustful interplay with a parental figure during infancy (Erikson 1968). It is in the experience of a safe relationship that the child comes to know itself as distinct from its beloved developmental partner. At this point, *introjection* or the incorporation of another's image operates and prepares the way for more mature forms of identity resolution. During childhood 'being like' admired others and assuming their roles and values reflects the mechanism of *identification* as the primary means by which the self is structured; it is only when the adolescent is able to select some and discard others of these childhood identifications in accordance with his or her interests, talents, and values that *identity formation* occurs. Identity formation involves a synthesis of these earlier identifications into a new configuration, which is based on but different from the sum of its individual parts. It is a process also dependent on social response; identity formation relies on the way society 'identifies the young individual, recognizing him as somebody who had to become the way he is and who, being the way he is, is taken for granted' (Erikson 1968: 159). Thus, identity does not first emerge during adolescence, but rather evolves through earlier stages of development and continues to be reshaped throughout the life-cycle.

Erikson uses the term *epigenesis* to describe this property of identity development as well as broader aspects of personality change. Meaning literally 'upon' (*epi*) 'emergence' (*genesis*), epigenesis implies that 'one item develops on top of another in space and time' (Evans 1967: 21-2). Suffice it to say at this point that identity formation during adolescence emerges from what youngsters (through their introjections and identifications) at the end of childhood come to know as their selves; yet, it also transcends these earlier forms in the individual's realization and society's recognition of personal interests and talents.

To return now to Siddhartha and his beleaguered quest: in his journey, this Brahmin's son tries many means by which Erikson suggests identity resolution is possible. Through his childhood years, Siddhartha appears successfully to have internalized and identified with his father and the later vocational, ideological, and sexual roles he is expected to play as an up-and-coming Brahmin priest. We are told of his father's happiness in watching the son 'growing up to be a great learned man, a priest, a prince among Brahmins' (Hesse 1980: 339). A psychosocial *foreclosure* appears well on the way, whereby Siddhartha seems prepared to step into predetermined roles in his family and culture. While Erikson does not detail this identity solution, it has been elaborated through empirical research which will be presented in a later section of this chapter.

Soon, however, shadows pass across Siddhartha's eyes and a 'restlessness of the soul' makes its presence known as he begins to 'feel the seeds of discontent within'. The late adolescent's decision to join a group of wandering ascetics whose values present a diametric contrast to all those of his own heritage seems to be a choice of *negative identity;* such a solution for Siddhartha illustrates the ego's attempt to adhere to something distinctly other than its past, to go beyond the bounds of given experience and begin anew. Here, there is no synthesis of previous identifications to give some foundation to later identity but rather an effort to jettison all identifications and start the task of creating a self completely different from its origins. Siddhartha attempts to cancel his previous self through denial of physical needs and the self-destructive infliction of pain. Erikson comments on such a form of negative identity resolution:

> Such vindictive choices of a negative identity represent, of course, a desperate attempt at regaining some mastery in a situation in which the available positive identity elements cancel each other out. The history of such a choice reveals a set of conditions in which it is easier for the patient to derive a sense of identity out of a total identification with that which he is least supposed to be than to struggle for a feeling of reality in acceptable roles which are unattainable with his inner means.
>
> (Erikson 1968: 176)

For some troubled adolescents, it is better to be somebody totally other than what existed during childhood rather than struggle to reintegrate the past into a present and future having some continuity with one's previous existence. There is often much relief following the choice of a negative identity, however destructive that solution may ultimately be.

For Siddhartha, however, that relief did not come. We are told of his realization that complete immersion in the 'contra-culture' of the Samanas' community and later Buddhist collective fail to solve the riddle of his existence. He departs, and it is at this point that we meet the young man continuing his ruminations presented at the beginning of this chapter:

> The reason why I do not know anything about myself, the reason why Siddhartha has remained alien and unknown to myself is due to one thing, to one single thing – I was afraid of myself, I was fleeing from myself. . . . I wished to destroy myself . . . in order to find in the unknown innermost, the nucleus of all things . . . . But by doing so, I lost myself on the way. . . . [Now] I will learn from myself, be my own pupil; I will learn from myself the secret of Siddhartha.
>
> (Hesse 1980: 359)

At this point Siddhartha enters a moratorium that carries him in search of different roles that would seem to allow greater possibilities for synthesizing and integrating all that has gone before. Anxiety, however, soon becomes his companion:

[A]n icy chill stole over him. Previously when in deepest meditation, he was still his father's son, he was still a Brahmin of high standing, a religious man. Now he was only Siddhartha ... he was over-whelmed by a feeling of icy despair, but he was more firmly himself than ever. That was the last shudder of his awakening, the last pains of birth. Immediately he moved on again ... no longer homewards, no longer back to his father, no longer looking backwards.

(Hesse 1980: 360)

Siddhartha's 'awakening' or resolution to one part of his identity riddle brings with it a new challenge for development: to *achieve* an identity, a sense of self that synthesizes earlier identifications into a new whole that is now uniquely his own.

Siddhartha's life is a case study of the evolution of identity from adolescence into old age. After experiencing many roles and building various lifestyles that fit his innermost needs at the time, Siddhartha returns in his old age to the river over which many of his earlier life journeys had crossed and beside which he eventually finds peace. Through many inward and external travels in adult life, Siddhartha demonstrates how the achievement of an identity does not remain fixed, resolved once and for all, but rather is constantly open to change through shifting needs and circumstances:

Such a sense of identity is never gained nor maintained once and for all. Like a good conscience, it is constantly lost and regained, although more lasting and more economical methods of mainten-ance and restoration are evolved and fortified in late adolescence.

(Erikson 1956: 74)

AN OPTIMAL SENSE OF IDENTITY

If soma, ego, and society have done their jobs, what should be present by the end of adolescence and the beginnings of early adulthood? Subjectively, there should be a sense of well-being: 'Its most obvious concomitants are a feeling of being at home in one's body, a sense of "knowing where one is going" and an inner assuredness of anticipated recognition from those who count' (Erikson 1968: 165). With its psycho-social connotation, optimal identity formation should show itself through commitment to those work roles, values, and sexual orienta-tions that best fit one's own unique combination of needs and talents. It is this more directly observable commitment feature of ego identity that has been at the heart of most empirical attempts to address some of its properties.

IDENTITY AS A STAGE IN THE LIFE-CYCLE SCHEME

As hinted previously, identity has a past. Erikson portrays identity as the fifth stage in an eight-act sequence of life conflicts one encounters along the road from birth to death in old age. While the primary focus in this chapter is on identity, it nevertheless is important to appreciate the contribution that both earlier and later acts make to the complete life drama.

Erikson conceptualizes the life-cycle as a series of stages, critical periods of development which involve bipolar conflict that must be addressed and resolved before one can proceed unhindered. According to the epigenetic principle, each stage has 'its time of special ascendancy, until all parts have arisen to form a functional whole' (Erikson 1968: 92). There is a proper rate and sequence of development which underlies all epigenesis; the child must crawl, before she can walk.

The polarity of each stage presents a crisis, a crucial turning point where development must make a move for better or for worse as one orients to the physical environment, and social and historical context. 'Each successive stage and crisis has a special relation to one of the basic elements of society, and this for the simple reason that the human life cycle and man's institutions have evolved together' (Erikson 1963: 250). The developmental possibilities of each stage do not demand 'either-or' resolutions, but rather require some dynamic balance of 'more or less' between the poles; hopefully that balance will favor the positive end. Erikson describes his fifth stage, which comes to the fore during adolescence, as that of *identity* versus *role confusion*. Here, as mentioned earlier, the young person is faced with the psychosocial dilemma of synthesizing yet transcending earlier identifications of childhood to realize aptitudes in social roles, while the community, in turn, provides its recognition and contribution to an individual's sense of self. Ironically, it may be one's willingness to undergo times of temporary uncertainty that gives the achievement resolution its ultimate strength. Stage resolutions should not be regarded as achievement scales based only on the more positive pole; they represent a balance between positive and negative poles that determines an individual's characteristic mode of adapting to the environment. One does not, however, enter the life drama during the fifth identity formation act. Identity versus role confusion has been preceded by four earlier stages, each having a necessary place in the unfolding chain of life-cycle tasks. All of Erikson's eight stages will now be briefly reviewed to illustrate their relationships to the identity crisis of adolescence.

Trust versus mistrust/hope

As the opening scene in the life-cycle production, *trust* versus *mistrust* sets the stage for all that is to follow. It is during infancy that the developmental crisis of trust is met, based in part on Freud's biological concern with early oral experience. Through the mutual regulation and interaction between care-taker and infant, a rudimentary sense of ego identity is born, and the child comes to know itself in relation to another and gains a sense of inner continuity, sameness, and trust in itself and its developmental partner.

In her short story 'The Door of Life', Enid Bagnold recounts the fine-tuning of responses between a mother and her four-day-old infant that reflect the building blocks of basic trust:

> [M]other and child [were] on the rails of development with fine movements, [care-taker] setting order into the baby's life, creating peace, keeping off the world, watching, reflecting, adjusting, jockeying the untidiness of civilization into perfection, teaching even so tiny a baby manners and endurance; to cry at the proper time for exercise, to sleep at the proper hour.
>
> (Bagnold 1972: 7)

This heightened sensitivity of both players to the nuances of the partner's movements illustrate the importance of mutuality to development. The quality of the care-taker's messages gives the infant a sense that it is all right to be, to be oneself, and to become 'what other people trust one will become' (Erikson 1963: 249).

Somewhere in between the polar extremes of trust and mistrust, most of us find an adaptive balance; neither complete trust nor complete mistrust of the world is ultimately beneficial. An optimal resolution to this infant crisis will find scales tipped more firmly towards the trusting pole, leading to *hope*, which, in turn, is the basic ingredient of later survival. It is also through this dynamic balance that a sense of 'I', as one who can hope, emerges to serve as the very rudimentary foundation for identity in adolescence.

Autonomy versus shame and doubt/will

Following the sense of basic trust, life's next developmental hurdle during the second and third years is that of developing autonomy. Again finding a biological base in Freud's anal stage of development, Erikson's sense of autonomy is characterized by the child's increasing awareness of its self through control of bodily functions and expression of other motor and linguistic skills (performing in concert with the expectations of important others in the social milieu).

Holding on or letting go of body wastes is one of the child's earliest opportunities to exercise complete control over the outcome of events, regardless of parental desire. Such auspicious occasions as toilet-training episodes provide toddlers with an experience of *will*, something originating from within in response to social conditions and highlighting the issue that wills of developmental partners can differ. With *trust* in order, it is now possible to risk one's own *will* against the response that such self-expression may bring. This 'counterpointing of identities' again carries the rudiments of later adolescent identity.

New-found linguistic and locomotor skills conspire to aid the development of autonomy during toddlerhood. By the age of 2 ½ years, the child is using the personal pronoun 'I' (as well as the declarative 'No') to give further evidence of will. Now possessing the motoric status of 'one who can walk', one is also in a position to encounter social response, for better or worse. The account of socialization experiences for a young Papago Indian girl cited by Erikson illustrates, again, the role the social environment plays in aiding and abetting this developmental task:

> [T]he man of the house turned to his three-year-old granddaughter and asked her to close the door. The door was heavy and hard to shut. The child tried, but it did not move. Several times the grandfather repeated: 'Yes, close the door.' No one jumped to the child's assistance. No one took the responsibility away from her. On the other hand, there was no impatience, for after all the child was small. They sat gravely waiting until the child succeeded and her grandfather gravely thanked her. It was assumed the task would not be asked of her unless she could perform it, and having been asked, the responsibility was hers alone just as if she were a grown woman.
>
> (Erikson 1963: 236)

Such an experience of personal autonomy in completing a difficult task is met with a social response that can only convey a sense of respect for and recognition of the child's developing 'I'.

Like all of Erikson's stages, an adaptive balance between the two extremes is necessary for optimal development. When the scale is weighted towards shame and doubt, one retains a sense of inferiority, of being 'not good enough' through all life's later stages. As a corollary, however, it is knowledge that one is fallible and capable of evoking a less-than-favorable social response that tempers absolute autonomy and serves to regulate the self in a social order.

Initiative versus guilt/purpose

The third act of Erikson's life drama is met during the preschool years and coincides with Freud's phallic stage of development; pleasure in infantile genitality gives rise to Erikson's social as well as sexual sense of being 'on the make' in the stage of *initiative* versus *guilt*. Now adept at mastering such skills as playing batman on a tricycle and more complicated sex roles, the preschooler possesses the ability to imagine. This capacity, so central to early childhood play, carries with it the seeds for *initiative* in the translating of thoughts to action. Only from an autonomous position is it possible to initiate; in knowing *that* one is, it is then possible to learn *what* one is. Issues such as what kind of person to become and what kind of sex role to adopt now become critical questions. From initiative grows a sense of purpose and ambition vital to tasks of adolescence and adulthood. It is initiative that 'sets the direction towards the possible and the tangible which permits the dreams of early childhood to be attached to the goals of an active adult life' (Erikson 1963: 258).

Locomotor skills and language continue to develop. One is now able to move and expend energy finding out what this status of one who walks means and of how moving can be used for purposes other than pleasure alone to accomplish more far-reaching goals. Language becomes a tool for communication with others in sorting out the often complex and confusing state of world affairs, or a least those of the preschool playground. The following conversation, recorded by Welker (1971), illustrates not only this new linguistic function but also the young child's fascination with sexual differences and roles in later life:

Laura got her hair cut very short. She and Tony were on the swings.
Laura: Tony, do I look like a boy?
Tony: No.
Laura: Look at the back of my head where my hair is so short.
Tony: No, you're a girl.
Laura: You know I'm a girl cause you saw me before I got my hair cut.
Tony: I know you're a girl cause you have curly hair . . .

Laurie, playing with Marian, said: 'When I grow up, I'm going to be a daddy.' Marian replied, 'You can't. Girls grow up into ladies.'

'Yes I can too,' retorted Laurie, 'Look, I've got big hands, and daddies have big hands.'

(Welker 1971: 67–8)

Thus, identity in adolescence has roots in the purposeful activities of early childhood. Out of initiative comes the ability to fantasize about and experiment with social and sexual roles of critical importance to adolescent and young adult life.

At this stage, however, the potential for guilt exists; a tip of the scales towards this negative end may leave the individual immobilized in taking future action through guilt or fear. An optimal balance would see boundless sexual and social initiative tempered by an awareness of the possibilities for social criticism and sanctions. Such a balance can best be obtained by a social environment aware of its role in fostering curiosity within the limits of cultural convention.

Industry versus inferiority/competence

According to Freud, the primary school years are marked by a shift from libidinal energy focused on bodily zones to a time of sexual latency; attention becomes channeled outward towards the world of the school yard and neighborhood. In contrast to Freud's focus on sexual latency, Erikson views the primary school years as ones in which the practicing of skills and the completion of tasks anticipating those of later adult work roles is life's main focus. Industry has been described as an apprenticeship to life; feelings of competence and achievement are the optimal results here. Thus, it is only through the *initiative* of an *autonomous* self which *trusts* the social milieu that the challenge of *industry* versus *inferiority* can be addressed. Social recognition for a job well done is the milieu's contribution to fostering development at this stage.

In her short story 'Prelude', Katherine Mansfield illustrates an optimal response to industry in a brief interchange between young Kezia and her grandmother:

[S]he decided to go up to the house and ask the servant girl for an empty match-box. She wanted to make a surprise for the grandmother. . . . First she would put a leaf inside with a big violet lying on it, then she would put a very small white picotee, perhaps, on each side of the violet, and then would sprinkle some lavender on the top, but not to cover the heads.

> She often made these surprises for the grandmother, and they were always most successful.
> 'Do you want a match, my granny?'
> 'Why, yes, child, I believe a match is just what I'm looking for.'
> The grandmother slowly opened the box and came upon the picture inside.
> 'Good gracious, child! How you astonished me!'
> 'I can make her one every day here,' she thought, scrambling up the grass on her slippery shoes.
>
> (Mansfield 1972: 90)

Such wisdom in social response can only serve to strengthen the sense of accomplishment in making and giving experienced by this young girl.

Crucial to this sense of industry is the 'positive identification with those who know things and know how to do things' (Erikson 1968: 125). One special teacher in the lives of many gifted individuals has often been credited as the spark which ignited outstanding later achievements (Erikson 1968). Finding one's special skills and talents during the phase of industry may have long-range implications for later vocational identity. Wise parents, teachers, or other important identification figures play a critical role in fostering a sense of industry or inferiority.

Erikson (1968: 124) notes the child's possible negative resolution of this stage, 'the development of an estrangement from himself and from his tasks'. A home environment insufficiently preparing the child for life outside its boundaries or failure of the wider cultural milieu to recognize and reward real accomplishments of its younger members may be perpetrators of inferiority. Again, healthy resolution to the industry versus inferiority conflict would see a ratio favoring industry. At the same time, feelings of limitless competence must be checked by an awareness of one's genuine limitations in order for optimal development to occur.

Identity versus role confusion/fidelity

Moving away from Freud's biological orientation to personality development during puberty, Erikson saw physiological change as only one aspect of a more pervasive adolescent dilemma. 'But even where a person can adjust sexually in a technical sense and may at least superficially develop what Freud called genital maturity, he may still be weakened by the identity problems of our era .... fully developed genitality is not a goal to be pursued in isolation' (Erikson, cited in Evans 1967: 29). Identity, to Erikson, incorporates yet transcends the endocrinological revolution of puberty to include psychosocial issues. It is finding a 'feeling of reality' in socially approved roles.

Drawing upon resolutions to earlier stages, one must now approach the task of identity formation. Erikson suggests fidelity is the essence of identity. To become faithful and committed to some ideological world view is the task of this stage; to find a cause worthy of one's vocational energies and reflecting one's basic values is the stuff of which identity crises are made. It is ultimately to affirm and be affirmed by a social order that identity aspires.

We have already seen and described some possible ways of negotiating life's conflicts during the fifth act through Siddhartha's quest. Suffice it to say here that the stage of *identity* versus *role confusion* is one of life's critical crossroads in the transition to adult life; not only must this stage incorporate a *trustworthy* 'I' who has evolved as an *autonomous* individual capable of *initiating* and completing satisfying tasks modeled by significant others, but it must also transcend such identifications to produce an 'I' sensitive to its own needs and talents and capable of chipping its own niche in the surrounding social landscape.

In contrast to Freud, the curtain on development for Erikson does not fall at this point. With a favorable resolution to the identity crisis of adolescence, it is now and only now possible to proceed to the stage of *intimacy* – that meeting of an 'I' with an 'I,' each firm on its own unique identity foundations. The remaining three acts of the life-cycle production, however, involve a shift of developmental focus from 'I' to 'we'.

Intimacy versus isolation/love

For Erikson, intimacy in young adulthood encompasses far more than sexual fulfilment; in fact, sexual activity may be used in the service of identity conflict rather than as a reflection of *love*. 'Intimacy is the ability to fuse your identity with somebody else's without fear that you're going to lose something yourself' (Erikson, cited in Evans 1967: 48). Intimacy involves the desire to commit oneself to a relationship, even when such commitment may call for personal sacrifice or compromise. Intimacy involves communion and can occur in a variety of forms – in same-and opposite-sex friendships, in love, in sexual union, and even in relationship with oneself or one's life commitments (Evans 1967).

To Erikson, genuine intimacy is not possible until issues of identity are reasonably well resolved. Relationships of earlier adolescence often serve only the purpose of self-definition rather than intimacy; another may be used merely as a mirror to reflect a form less visible to its owner. Relationships may also involve attempts to find one's own identity through merger with another – efforts which similarly preclude intimacy. Indeed some marriages serve such a function for those in whom identity issues remain unresolved: 'Many young people marry in order to find their identity in and through another person, but this is difficult where the very choice of partner was made to resolve severe unconscious conflict' (Erikson, cited in Evans 1967: 49). Ultimately, there is only enough identity for one.

Drawing upon Martin Buber's concepts of 'I' and 'Thou', Moustakas captures the character of genuine intimacy in the following passage:

> Growth of the self requires meetings between I and Thou, in which each person recognizes the other as he is; each says what he means and means what he says; each values and contributes to the unfolding of the other without imposing or manipulating. And this always means some degree of distance and independence. It does not depend on one revealing to another everything that exists within, but requires only that the person be who he is, genuinely present.
>
> (Moustakas 1974: 92)

Here the identities of 'I' and 'Thou' must be assured in order for such a relationship of mature, unselfish love to occur.

Isolation is the psychosocial alternative creating conflict at this stage. If true 'engagement' with another is elusive, one may 'isolate himself and enter, at best, only stereotyped and formalized interpersonal relations; or one may, in repeated hectic attempts and dismal failures, seek intimacy with the most improbable partners' (Erikson 1968: 167). Isolation can occur in the context of relationship just as intimacy can exist in the physical absence of a partner. '[T]here are partnerships which amount to an isolation *à deux,* protecting both partners from the necessity to face the next critical development – that of generativity' (Erikson 1963: 266). An ideal balance between intimacy and isolation results through a relationship which allows time for both withdrawal and communion between partners. It is the recognition of one's ultimate aloneness which gives intimacy its base, and it is one's capacity for security in that aloneness which makes genuine intimacy possible.

Generativity versus stagnation/care

The next task for that 'we' to meet during adulthood is taking a place in society at large and *caring* – for one's offspring, productions, social contributions, and future generations. Erikson again notes the limitations of Freud's psychosexual scheme with its emphasis on genital maturity as the epitome of development:

> I would go even further than that and say that Freud, by paying so much attention to the prepubertal impediments of the genital encounter itself, underemphasized the procreative drive as also important to man. I think this is a significant omission, because it can lead to the assumption that a person graduates from psychoanalytic treatment when he has been restored to full genitality. As in many movies, where the story ends when lovers finally find one another, our therapies often end when the person can consummate sexuality in a satisfactory, mutually enriching way. This is an essential stage but I would consider generativity a further psychosexual stage, and would postulate that its frustration results in symptoms of self-absorption.
>
> (Erikson, cited in Evans 1967: 52)

Erikson's concept here does not imply that generativity can be met only in parenting; it resides also in the desire of an *autonomous* 'I' as part of an *intimate* 'we' to contribute to the present and future well-being of other life-cycles. Such generative individuals provide the models needed for introjection and identification by younger members of the society.

The counterpart of generativity is stagnation or self-absorption, whereby personal comfort becomes the primary motivator for action. When this resolution occurs, individuals 'often begin to indulge themselves as if they were their own – or one another's – one and only child; and where conditions favor it, early invalidism, physical or psychological, becomes the vehicle of self-concern' (Erikson 1963: 267). Alternatively, procreation or other forms of production are not necessarily the expression of generativity; true care must take root for generativity to flourish.

Again, an optimal balance between generativity and self-absorption is necessary. One must be selective of those people and projects to nurture in the interests of self-preservation; unlimited energy and resources are not available to one through life's passages and some attention to self-interest is crucial in perpetuating a generative life attitude.

As in all previous life stages, the ratio needs to favor the more positive pole for healthy development to proceed, however.

Integrity versus despair/wisdom

The final act of the life drama requires facing the developmental task of balancing *integrity* with *despair*. More difficult to define than preceding stages, integrity 'is the acceptance of one's one and only life-cycle as something that had to be and that, by necessity, permitted of no substitutions .... In such final consolidation, death loses its sting' (Erikson 1963: 268). One gauge of integrity is the ability to accept one's own mortality. A life lived in contributing one's guidance, gifts, and talents to future generations is not regretted, and death is not feared as time shortens before the last curtain call. An old age favoring integrity is characterized by the *wisdom* of mature judgment and a reflective understanding of one's own 'accidental' place in the historical scheme of things.

On the other hand, the potential for despair in old age exists to counterpoint integrity. A life culminating in despair finds remaining time too short to locate a different path towards a more comfortable and satisfying conclusion. In his 'Reflections on Dr Borg's life cycle', Erikson (1976) illustrates the conflict of the final stage of development through a character study of Dr Borg, the leading figure in Ingmar Bergman's film *Wild Strawberries*. In a car journey to Lund to receive the highest honor of his medical profession, an aged and retired Dr Borg also departs on a psychological journey back in time through his own development. Borg's precarious psychosocial balance as the scene opens is tipped towards despair:

> At the age of seventy-six, I feel that I'm much too old to lie to myself. But of course I can't be too sure. My complacent attitude towards my own truthfulness could be dishonesty in disguise, although I don't quite know what I might want to hide .... I have of my own free will withdrawn almost completely from society .... I have found myself rather alone in my old age.
>
> (Bergman, cited in Erikson 1976: 2)

One of the car's passengers, Borg's daughter-in-law Marianne, takes it upon herself to drive the old man's despair to the surface. Through her doings, Borg is offered some opportunity for salvation through the journey by rebalancing solutions to earlier psychosocial stages that enable him to find a more fulfilling old age. Identity themes are carried forward for Borg as he reworks his sense of self to become more intimate with and caring about that which he will soon leave behind.

And so identity themes are met again in old age, where the sense of the 'I' that has developed and established itself in social contexts through earlier stages of development must rest content (or not) on what it *is;* unlike Dr Borg in Bergman's film fantasy, such opportunities for change are limited for most.

> [A] sense of 'I' becomes a most sensitive matter again in old age, as an individual's uniqueness gradually and often suddenly seems to have lost any leeway for further variations such as those which seemed to open themselves with each previous stage. Now, non-Being must be faced 'as is'.
>
> (Erikson 1984: 102)

The favorable balance of integrity with despair again gives wisdom its ultimate strength. Remaining open to existential issues of being and non-being as well as Kierkegaard's sense of dread present very real opportunities for despair. Willingness to address sobering questions such as the meaning of one's existence makes deeper the tranquility that integrity brings.

Identity is thus an ingredient of all stages of the human life-cycle. Having roots in infant trust, identity is also present in the *integrity* versus *despair* conflict of old age. Identity formation during adolescence reflects developmental resolutions to all preceding stages and serves as a base for personality developments that lie ahead. In adolescence, however, identity assumes a change in form; through a process different from the internalizations and identifications of earlier psychosocial stages, its configuration now evolves into a new structure, different from (but related to) the sum of its parts. Through the synthesis and resynthesis of all earlier childhood identifications, the 'I', like Siddhartha's sense of self, is now ready to move forward, 'no longer homewards . . . no longer looking backwards'.

CRITICISM OF ERIKSON'S IDENTITY CONCEPT

Erikson's definition of identity has been criticized on a number of grounds. Unclear or imprecise formulations of identity have been the source of numerous difficulties for many readers of Erikson. The analyst himself suggests that the concept should be defined 'from different angles', and proceeds to use the term for emphasizing different issues at different points. At times, identity refers to a structure or a configuration; at other points, it refers to a process. Still on other occasions, identity is viewed as both a conscious, subjective experience as well as an unconscious entity. In a rather candid comment given during a radio interview, Erikson stated, 'I think one could be more precise than I am, or than I am able to be. I very much feel that scientific training and logic would have helped a lot' (Erikson, cited in Stevens 1983: 112). Yet it is this very breadth of phenomena captured through Erikson's formulation of identity that other social scientists have argued make the construct more amenable to research than much of psychodynamic theory.

Empirical validation of the psychosocial issues addressed at different stages that were described by Erikson have come to be questioned by some critics. Ciaccio (1971) was one of the first investigators to test whether or not conflicts purported by Erikson to be inherent in some of the early developmental stages were actually at issue for groups of boys aged 5, 8, and 11 years. Although psychosocial strengths or attitudes did seem to progress with age in the sequence described by Erikson, the negative aspects (or crises) of the stages did not find such confirmation. Additional research using Constantinople's (1969) Inventory of Psychosocial Development has raised questions regarding Erikson's proposed timing of development; issues of focal concern at given ages have varied across samples, possibly reflecting the influence of different cultural and/or historical factors (Waterman and Whitbourne 1981). While finding empirical support for central propositions of Erikson's theory, Côté and Levine (1989) have argued that longitudinal studies are necessary that address problems of causation from a wider, social psychological perspective.

Erikson's views on womanhood and the inner space have drawn equally sharp responses from critics. To Erikson, anatomy is destiny and initially determines the style of engagement with the social milieu; reflecting sexual morphology, boys emphasize outer space in their predominantly aggressive and intrusive play, while girls focus on the inner space in their more peaceful, passive activities. The scientific validity of this observation has been called into question by Caplan (1979), who failed to replicate results from Erikson's single experiment in any findings from a series of studies; Caplan further notes that the statistical grounds of Erikson's claim to significant sex differences in play configurations accounted for less than 2 per cent of the total variance in the analyst's results. Furthermore, many have attacked Erikson's statement that the problem of identity definition for women must wait until a suitable partner is found and 'welcomed to the inner space'. Not only does this notion contradict the theorist's earlier proposal that identity issues must be resolved before genuine intimacy can be experienced, but it also has been regarded as inappropriate to many contemporary social contexts in which women are more frequently delaying marriage and procreation in pursuit of careers important to their self-definitions. Still others have argued that stages of identity and intimacy in Erikson's scheme may be reversed or at least coexist for women (Gilligan 1982a). Additional critics have indicated that Erikson needs either to add new stages or substantially modify existing ones to portray accurately both male and female development (Logan 1986; Vaillant and Milofsky 1980; Franz and White 1985).

Finally, Erikson's epigenetic scheme of identity formation may reflect cultural bias. It would seem that only in cultural contexts which allow choice as to social, ideological, and vocational roles are conditions for identity crises ripe. While Marcia (1983) argues that such social conditions of choice promote ego development at puberty, they may not reflect the cultural norm for the majority of the world's teenage population. Furthermore, Bettelheim (1969) argues that Erikson's model of psychosocial development needs modification when applied to development of children growing up in extended family circumstances. The continuity and sameness important to basic trust between mother and child takes on a different slant in the communal childrearing experiences for the kibbutz infant. Despite such criticism, however, Erikson's model continues to offer important insights and has sparked an array of empirical enquiries into identity formation during adolescence.

RESEARCH FINDINGS ON ADOLESCENT IDENTITY FORMATION

Erikson's vivid descriptions of the adolescent identity formation process have presented a challenge to researchers attempting to examine and understand the phenomenon empirically. In a frequently cited definition of ego identity, Erikson (1959: 116) describes many different dimensions of identity's structure and functions: '[Ego identity is] an evolving configuration of constitutional givens, idiosyncratic libidinal needs, favored capacities, significant identifications, effective defenses, successful sublimations, and consistent roles.' It is not surprising, then, that different research traditions have emerged to examine different dimensions of the identity formation experience.

Three general approaches have arisen to study the identity formation process (see Kroger 1993a for a more complete review of these traditions). One stream has focused on the place that 'identity versus role confusion' holds in Erikson's larger, eight-stage epigenetic scheme.

Investigators working within this framework have argued that by focusing on only one psychosocial stage, identity research fails to do full justice to Erikson's model of life-cycle development (Constantinople 1967, 1969; Hamachek 1988, 1989; Markstrom-Adams *et al.* 1994; Rosenthal *et al.* 1981). A second orientation has focused on the 'identity versus role confusion' task alone. From this perspective, identity is defined as a resolution that lies somewhere on a continuum between identity and role confusion, and measurement scales developed within this tradition have explored identity scores in relation to other personality variables (for example, Simmons 1983; Tan *et al.* 1977). A third general approach has focused on one of the specific dimensions of identity described by Erikson. Hauser (1972), for example, has studied issues of structural integration and stability of self-image during adolescence, while Blasi and his colleagues (Blasi 1988; Blasi and Glodis in press; Blasi and Milton 1991) have investigated some of the more subjective aspects of identity. However, it is the element of fidelity which has attracted greatest research attention, and it has been through studies initiated by James Marcia (1966, 1967) that the process of identity exploration and commitment have been most fully examined. Marcia's elaboration of Erikson's fifth psychosocial stage has now generated over 300 studies of the identity formation process, and this approach will be the focus for the remainder of this section. (See Bosma *et al.* (1994) for an excellent overview of interdisciplinary perspectives and studies of identity.)

Fidelity or commitment to a vocation, a set of meaningful values, and a sexual identity are the observable cues indicative of a more or less successful identity resolution during late adolescence. From Marcia's observations, commitment or fidelity comes in several forms. While Erikson saw identity as some balance between commitment and confusion about one's roles in society, Marcia identified two distinct types of commitment and two of non-commitment. Individuals adopting an achievement or foreclosure orientation have both made commitments to social roles; however, achievements have done so following a crisis or decision-making period, while foreclosures have bypassed the identity formation process and merely adopted roles and values of childhood identification figures. For the identity achieved individual, commitment has resulted from a process of ego synthesis, whereby earlier identifications are 'subordinated to a new, unique Gestalt which is more than the sum of its parts' (Erikson 1968: 158). For the foreclosure, however, the identity formation process has not yet begun and identification remains the mode of identity resolution. Similarly, moratoriums and diffusions both are lacking commitment to a place in the social order; however, moratoriums are undergoing an evaluative process (ego synthesis) in search of suitable social roles, while diffusions are not. These commitment types or identity statuses have been empirically validated as four distinct modes of dealing with identity-defining issues of late adolescence.

Based on Marcia's semi-structured 'ego identity status interview' which taps vocational, ideological, and sexual expression and/or sex role commitments, each identity status has been associated with distinct personality characteristics, family antecedents, and developmental patterns of change over time. (More recently, Adams and his colleagues have also developed a paper and pencil measure to assess identity status – Adams 1994, Adams *et al.* 1989; identity statuses identified via their measure have shown similar relationships with associated variables.) Extensive reviews of the identity status literature can be found in Bourne (1978a, 1978b), Kroger (1993a), Marcia (1980), Marcia *et al.* (1993), and Waterman (1982, 1984). Here, important characteristics associated with each identity status will be briefly reviewed.

Identity achievement

Marcia (1979, 1994) has suggested what it might be like to sit down with a young person in each of the identity statuses through brief character sketches based on his own observations of university students. For the identity achieved, flexible strength describes their manner of relating to the world. Thoughtful and introspective, they do not become immobilized by their reflections and function cognitively very well under stress. They may or may not be aware that their identity-defining commitments may very likely undergo future change. A sense of humor as well as openness to new experiences accompany a willingness to listen and judge according to their own inner standards.

From empirical studies, identity achieved youths have scored consistently higher on measures of autonomy and are less reliant on the opinions of others to make their decisions; in terms of cognitive capacities, the identity achieved function well under stress, are more creative, and use more planful, rational and logical decision-making strategies than other identity statuses (Blustein and Philips 1990; Boyes and Chandler 1992; Marcia 1966, 1967; Waterman and Archer 1979). No significant differences in intelligence have appeared across the identity statuses as assessed in various studies by at least six different measures (Marcia *et al.* 1993). Achievers engage in intimate relationships and are androgynous in sex role attitudes (Fitch and Adams 1983; Hodgson and Fischer 1979; Kacerguis and Adams 1980). While mixed results have appeared for the sexes on measures of self-esteem (Marcia 1966; Marcia and Friedman 1970; Orlofsky 1978; Prager 1982; Schenkel and Marcia 1972), sex differences have appeared on fear of success measures. Male achievements have demonstrated low success fear and females have evidenced high anxiety in anticipation of success (Orlofsky 1978). Identity achievements function most frequently at the highest level of post-conventional moral reasoning (Hult 1979; Rowe and Marcia 1980; Skoe and Marcia 1991). Furthermore, these individuals are intrapsychically more differentiated from others and more secure in their attachment patterns (Ginsburg and Orlofsky 1981; Josselson 1987; Kroger and Haslett 1988; Papini *et al.* 1989). The identity achieved are able to perceive parental strengths and weaknesses and have come from families which have parents supporting adolescent autonomy (Grotevant and Cooper 1985; Jordan 1971; Willemsen and Waterman 1991).

Moratorium

From Marcia's (1979, 1994) character portraits, some moratoriums may be animated and anxious in their identity struggles, while others are more quietly thoughtful. Moratoriums do not yield easily to demands for conformity, and they have a stable sense of self-esteem. Although able to describe what intimacy must be like, moratoriums are not as a rule *in* such a relationship. Intrapsychically, they have difficulties detaching themselves from parents, particularly the parent of the opposite sex; this difficulty may underlie reluctance for relationship commitment. Moratoriums may use the identity status interview as a kind of therapy in an effort to disentangle their conflicting identity elements. 'Ambivalent struggle characterizes the moratorium' (Marcia 1979: 8).

Empirical studies have found moratoriums to be consistently more anxious than achievement or foreclosure individuals (Marcia 1967; Podd *et al.* 1970; Sterling and Van Horn 1989). Moratoriums may be volatile and intense in their interpersonal relationships; while possessing the capacity for intimacy, they shy away from the commitment demanded by such a relationship (Donovan 1975; Dyk and Adams 1990; Josselson 1987; Orlofsky *et al.* 1973). In many ways, however, moratoriums resemble achievements in their cognitive complexity, higher levels of moral reasoning, and failure to conform or rely on judgments of others for making decisions (Bourne 1978b; Skoe and Marcia 1991; Slugoski *et al.* 1984). Moratoriums have demonstrated greater degrees of scepticism than other identity statuses (Boyes and Chandler 1992), as well as greater openness to experience and experiential orientation (Stephen *et al.* 1992; Tesch and Cameron 1987). Intrapsychically, moratoriums are in the process of disengaging from parental introjects and have more mixed attachment profiles (Kroger and Haslett 1988). Again, however, parents of moratorium youths tend to emphasize independence in their child-rearing practices (Frank *et al.* 1990; Grotevant and Cooper 1985).

Foreclosure

According to Marcia's (1979, 1994) profiles, foreclosures may appear very similar to the identity achieved in their initial interview impressions; however, their inflexibility and defensiveness soon become apparent. Foreclosures are happy and may be smugly self-satisfied; they are very authoritarian and unbending in their opinions of 'the right way'. Conventional in their moral reasoning and very committed to vocational and ideological values, foreclosures are particularly drawn to the values of a parent or strong leader who can show them this 'right way'. 'The strength of the foreclosure is a rigid and brittle strength, rather like glass; if you push at it in one way, it is very strong; if you push at it in a different way, it shatters' (Marcia 1979: 9). In some contexts where communal values are stressed as necessary for group survival, however, foreclosure is the most adaptive identity status (Marcia 1993).

Empirical studies have consistently found foreclosures of both sexes to be the identity status most authoritarian in attitude (Côté and Levine 1983; Marcia 1966, 1967; Marcia and Friedman 1970; Schenkel and Marcia 1972). Such individuals tend to be very approval-seeking and base actions on the opinions of others; measures of foreclosures' autonomy have consistently produced low scores (Marcia 1966, 1967, 1993). Perhaps as a result of their rigid adherence to authoritarian values, foreclosures are also the least anxious of the identity groups (Marcia 1966; Marcia and Friedman 1970; Schenkel and Marcia 1972) and least open to new experiences (Stephen *et al.* 1992; Tesch and Cameron 1987); if there is no openness or willingness to question life commitments, there is little room for anxiety to enter. Foreclosures also use less integratively complex cognitive styles and are pre-conventional or conventional in their levels of moral judgment (Hult 1979; Rowe and Marcia 1980; Skoe and Marcia 1991; Slugoski *et al.* 1984). Furthermore, along with diffusions, foreclosures show greater realist and defended-realist epistemic stances in comparison with moratorium and achievement statuses (Boyes and Chandler 1992). In interpersonal relationships, foreclosures are 'well-behaved', placid individuals engaged in stereotypic or merger styles of interaction (Dyk and Adams 1990; Josselson 1987; Levitz-Jones and Orlofsky 1985; Orlofsky *et al.* 1973). Still undifferentiated intrapsychically from parental introjects, youths who remain foreclosed during late adolescence are more nonsecure (anxious or detached) in attachment profiles than youths of any other identity group (Kroger 1985b; Kroger and Haslett 1988; Papini *et al.* 1989). They report very close relationships with parents, while parents, in turn, encourage conformity and adherence to family values (Frank *et al.* 1990; Grotevant and Cooper 1985; Jordan 1971; Willemsen and Waterman 1991).

Sex differences for foreclosures have appeared on some self-esteem and fear of success measures in early identity status research. Generally mixed results for women on measures of self-esteem have appeared over the past two decades and may reflect differential social support for the foreclosure status in different social contexts and historical eras (Marcia 1980; Marcia *et al.* 1993). Foreclosure women have shown little fear of success in contrast to high fear by male counterparts (Orlofsky 1978). Again, there may be differential social support of identity achievement for the sexes, at least in some locales and periods of recent history (Kroger 1993b).

Diffusion

From Marcia's (1979, 1994) character sketches, diffusions are less homogeneous as a group than individuals of other identity statuses. Encompassing a range of individuals unable to make identity commitments, the diffusion status may result from cultural conditions (producing few viable identity options) as well as developmental deficits. Diffusion males tend to be either 'superficial or unhappy' (Marcia 1979: 9). Some diffusions may drift through life in a carefree, uninvolved way, while others may evidence severe psychopathology with great loneliness. Diffusions are not involved in intimate relationships and seem to lack any real sense of self to contribute to a dyad or group. Generally, diffusions give the sense of lacking any central core.

From empirical studies, diffusions evidence low self-esteem and autonomy (Marcia *et al.* 1993). They function at pre-conventional or conventional levels of moral reasoning and use less complex cognitive styles than moratoriums and achievements (Hult 1979; Podd 1972; Skoe and Marcia 1991; Slugoski *et al.* 1984). They have scored highest of all identity statuses on hopelessness (Selles *et al.* 1994). In terms of interpersonal relationships, diffusions tend to be distant and withdrawn, most likely to be stereotyped or isolated in their dealings with others (Donovan 1975; Orlofsky *et al.* 1973). Their reports of parents' child-rearing practices indicate care-takers who were distant and rejecting (Jordan 1971; Josselson 1987); such individuals are likely to have had great difficulty internalizing a parental introject during early child-hood. Sex differences on measures of fear of success resemble foreclosure patterns; male diffusions exhibit high fear, while females have shown low fear of success (Orlofsky 1978).

Developmental change in identity status

Waterman (1982) has proposed a descriptive model of identity development which depicts possible avenues of change. Transition to a different identity status may be progressive or regressive. Identity status trajectory patterns have begun to be examined over the course of adolescence in at least two longitudinal studies (Adams *et al.* 1992; Goossens 1992). Factors responsible for differential patterns of identity status movement remain largely unresearched issues. However, there is some evidence from Goossens (in press) that negative views of the environment and readiness for change may be predictive of progressive development and from Kroger (1995) that high nurturance-seeking needs among late adolescent foreclosures is predictive of identity status stability, at least over two years of university study. Additionally, moratorium individuals have shown greater disposition towards adaptive regression than other identity statuses (Bilsker and Marcia 1991); adaptive regression may play an important role in the identity formation process.

A number of longitudinal investigations during the years of adolescence have indicated clear patterns of progressive movement from foreclosure and diffusion positions to moratorium and achievement stances (Costa and Campos 1989; Fitch and Adams 1983; Goossens 1992; Kroger 1995, 1985b; Marcia 1976a; Meeus and Dekovic 1994; Phinney and Chavira 1992; Streitmatter 1993; Waterman *et al.* 1974; Waterman and Goldman 1976; Wires *et al.* 1994). The moratorium status has generally been the least stable of the identity groups, indicative, perhaps, of the discomfort in prolonging identity conflict. From a moratorium position in late adolescence, movement to the achievement status appears most likely from those longitudinal studies cited above in which it is possible to trace individual change. Among achievement, foreclosure, and diffusion groups there is some indication that the young adult choice of life-style is related to the stability of each of these statuses; women opting for full-time homemaking responsibilities after receiving a BA or professional vocational qualification have been found to be more likely to remain foreclosed throughout adulthood than women with the same level of professional qualification who have pursued other employment/family combinations of vocational commitment (Kroger and Haslett 1987).

Current directions in identity status research

The identity status approach has continued to generate new directions in efforts to understand more fully the adolescent identity formation process. Attention over the past five years has turned to issues as diverse as the process of ethnic identity formation (Phinney 1989; Phinney and Rosenthal 1992), identity styles and defensive strategies (Berzonsky 1994), the role of relationships in the identity formation process (Archer 1993), the integration of identity components (Grotevant 1993; Goossens and Schillebeeks 1994; van Hoof 1994), the evolutive style of identity formation (Flum 1994), the role of optimal experience in the identity formation process (Waterman 1993), a dynamic systems perspective to the process of adopting commitments (Bosma 1994), and the process of identity development for adopted adolescents (Grotevant 1994). Different 'types' of foreclosures and diffusions have been proposed (Archer and Waterman 1990; Marcia 1989), and the role of historical epoch and social context in the identity formation process has begun to be examined (Côté 1993; Côté and Levine 1988; Kroger 1993b; Kraus and Mitzscherlich 1994; Roker and Banks 1993). Additionally, new measures which adopt a status approach are being developed to assess resolutions to other Eriksonian stage tasks – 'industry versus inferiority' (Kowaz and Marcia 1991); 'generativity versus stagnation' (Bradley and Marcia 1993); 'integrity versus despair' (Hearn and Marcia 1994).

IMPLICATIONS FOR SOCIAL RESPONSE

Social response is intimately linked to identity development through all eight of Erikson's life-cycle stages. From the mutual recognition and regulation between infant and care-taker to the definition of self through social role in adolescence to reflection over social participation in the integrity of old age, recognition from both a developmental partner and a larger social group is critical to resolving the conflict of each stage in the favorable direction. Without retracing society's role in identity development through all life-cycle stages at this point, it is important to highlight conditions for healthy resolution to the identity versus role confusion conflict of adolescence.

Assuming more or less favorable solutions have been found to the conflicts of preceding eras, parents, close associates, and the educational, employment, recreational, religious, health, political, and legal systems of one's cultural context have a vital role to play in the formation of identity during adolescence. All such orders regulate attitudes and behavior of their younger members, and all are capable of becoming too cooperative in the provision of labels that may not ultimately serve the best interests of youths seeking self-definition. It is through social willingness *not* to predetermine roles and to allow youth a moratorium that identity formation can best be facilitated; it is social tolerance for role experimentation without labeling that eventually benefits all concerned.

Erikson himself cites numerous examples of ways in which the psychiatric profession and legal system can provide youths with labels that offer a ready identity to troubled adolescents but do not allow optimal resolution to the conflict of this stage. In two cases of negative identity, Erikson illustrates the critical nature of social response to eventual identity resolution:

> The daughter of a man of brilliant showmanship ran away from college and was arrested as a prostitute in the Negro quarter of a southern city, while the daughter of an influential southern Negro preacher was found among narcotic addicts in Chicago. In such cases it is of utmost importance to recognize the mockery and vindictive pretense in such role playing, for the white girl had not really prostituted herself, and the colored girl had not really become an addict – yet. Needless to say, however, each of them had put herself into a marginal social area, leaving it to law enforcement officers and psychiatric agencies to decide what stamp to put on such behavior.
>
> (Erikson 1968: 175)

Just as an adolescent psychiatric patient may 'choose the very role of patient as the most meaningful basis for an identity formation' (Erikson 1968: 179), the two adolescent girls noted above might gratefully adopt the 'criminal' or 'delinquent' roles that courts and psychiatric agencies could so easily and cooperatively confer. Society's *refusal* to provide ready role definitions for such adolescents and *not* to treat their experimentations as the final identity are in the best interests of the entire community.

In social response to the formation of identity, the importance of the community's recognition has been emphasized. Such recognition, however, must extend beyond a mere response to achievement alone. Social lip-service to adolescent achievement cannot replace genuine opportunities provided by society for individual talents to be both realized and recognized. Elder's (1974) research on those 'adolescing' during the Great Depression vividly demonstrates the psychological and social results when adolescent work has some genuine meaning and input towards family survival. Furthermore, response must be genuine in its appreciation of the skills and talents being offered by the young.

It is beyond the scope of this chapter to examine the means by which a variety of different social institutions might facilitate the identity formation process for its youth (see Archer (1994) for an excellent comprehensive examination of such issues). However, comment will be made on how educational and therapeutic intervention might best serve adolescents in each of Marcia's four identity statuses; each identity status reflects a time of special need requiring differential social response.

Resolution of identity issues for the identity achieved makes need for psychotherapeutic intervention unlikely. Self-definition has been constructed through the identity formation process and resolution to the conflicts of preceding stages has been successful in order for identity achievement to have occurred. The need for counseling might arise for such an individual only in situations of crisis and would involve short-term intervention techniques (Marcia 1986, 1993). Educational settings must continue to provide new opportunities for insight and exploration, meet genuine needs, and allow opportunity for individual talent to be expressed and channeled into real social roles. Experimental schools such as those described in Rogers' (1983) *Freedom to Learn for the 80's* and Neill's (1972) *Summerhill* would initially appear to offer the ideal in educational opportunity for identity achievements. In such settings, encouragement is given students to pursue curricula of relevance to their own interests and talents. However, Erikson would seek a less radical solution to the curriculum dilemma, at least during the stage of industry:

'Teacher, *must* we do today what we *want* to do?' Nothing could better express the fact that children at this age [industry] do like to be mildly but firmly coerced into the adventure of finding out that one can learn to accomplish things which one would never have thought of by oneself, things which owe their attractiveness to the very fact that they are not the product of play and fantasy but the product of reality, practicality, and logic; things which thus provide a token sense of participation in the real world of adults.

(Erikson 1968: 127)

Schools with flexible curricula designed both to address changing student and social need and also to provide challenge and conflict situations are best suited to enhancing later identity development, according to Erikson.

Recent research has supported his claim. Markstrom-Adams *et al.* (1993) have produced some evidence which suggests that short-term intervention training strategies in social perspective-taking may facilitate ideological identity achievement, while Dreyer (1994) offers a comprehensive review of identity-enhancing curricula which promote responsible, self-determined choice. It is the job of the school and other social institutions to provide avenues for enhancing the achievement's way of 'having an effect on the world and on others'.

Moratoriums, very much in the throes of the identity formation process, often appear in psychotherapeutic or counseling settings; ironically, they probably need direct intervention less than foreclosure or diffusion youths, who are less likely to request assistance (Marcia 1986). A sympathetic 'other' who does not become aligned with various aspects of the moratorium's struggle but rather acts in a Rogerian way to reflect prospective identity elements in the interests of identity synthesis would seem the best form of assistance here. It is important that therapist or counselor not be allied with one side of the moratorium's conflict; such a therapeutic attitude merely 'externalizes the conflict into the therapeutic relationship and delays its resolution' (Marcia 1979: 16). It is also important to remember Erikson's warnings about labeling and not provide the moratorium youth with a 'disturbed adolescent' identity. Like identity achievement, it is unlikely that the moratorium's conflicts during adolescence have resulted from less-than-satisfactory resolutions to early psychosocial stages; identity formation occurs when preceding stages have found a favorable balance between polarities, and social conditions exist that encourage exploration rather than adherence to prescribed adult roles. Educational environments similar to those proposed for the identity-achieved individual would best help the moratorium to explore vocational, ideological, and sexual roles available in his or her society and find a social niche that matches individual interests and endowments. A curriculum relevant to the genuine needs of adolescents (for example, human sexuality, peace education, education for parenting, vocational skills, international relations) have been the focus for many programs of psychological education

(Blustein *et al.* 1989; Ivey 1976). Opportunities for adolescents to become exposed to and 'try out' a variety of work roles through work-study programs at high school or college as well as having interested and sympathetic adults available for listening also facilitate resolution to a psychosocial moratorium period. Raskin (1994) provides further discussion of interventions that may promote career exploration in secondary and tertiary educational contexts.

For the foreclosed individual, identity has been reached through mechanisms of introjection and identification rather than ego synthesis; much has been vested in 'being loved and cared for' by childhood identification figures at the expense of self-definition and ego development. Appearing to proceed smoothly along the track towards occupational goals and steadfast in their ideological beliefs, these youths have avoided any form of serious exploration. As a consequence, rigid identity structures are formed which are impervious to challenge from new life situations. Confidence and security have been the foreclosure's reward for adhering to prescribed role expectations. These youths rarely come for counseling or psychotherapy except when such beliefs have been threatened; foreclosures would seem to be the most neglected status for psychotherapeutic, counseling, or educational intervention in cultural contexts where *identity formation* is adaptive (Kroger 1985a).

Indeed, many social institutions even in western, technologically advanced societies would seem to promote a foreclosure status. One might argue against the necessity for intervention with these adolescents, who are generally staying out of trouble and meeting social expectation. However, considerable potential for the actualization of unique talents and social contributions may be lost in retaining this identity structure. Additionally, the adolescent foreclosure is extremely vulnerable to shifting environmental circumstances demanding new adjustments; ultimately, decisions which were avoided by many foreclosed adolescents may press for attention further down the road in adult life.

Counseling or psychotherapy with such adolescents must recognize the rigidity of this identity structure and the security it provides, while striving slowly to provide new models for identification and introducing greater alternatives for choice. It should be noted that direct challenge to foreclosure commitments are likely to result in a further solidifying of defenses and closure to new possibilities (Marcia 1986). Vocational or personal counseling should proceed very slowly, with gradual encouragement to consider new options and identify with potentially new role models. Marcia (1993) points out that people cannot be 'taught' to explore alternatives; the process of considering alternatives for many foreclosures becomes laden with fears of rejection from significant others. 'What the adult intervener can do is to provide, first of all, safety then structure, facilitation, and some direction' (Marcia 1993: 406). An educational environment which supports open exploration of occupational and ideological alternatives rather than rewarding premature commitment could do much to foster identity development among the adolescent foreclosed; however, it must be recognized that a secure context is essential for those who might begin to question internalized roles and standards and move towards self-determined choice.

The diffusion status captures the greatest range of individuals having difficulty in finding a social niche. Here, failure to resolve favorably conflicts of preceding psychosocial stages may be primarily responsible for adolescent identity difficulties. For some diffusions, early massive ego failure makes 'being something' beyond the realm of the possible; just being, and developing some feeling of coherence, represents their main developmental task. Intervention efforts with such individuals would occur primarily in a psychiatric setting; difficult though it may be, therapeutic aims within Erikson's scheme would address issues of basic trust in relationship and ultimately in oneself (Erikson 1968). It is only through a return to this basic developmental conflict that any possibility exists for the emergence of an autonomous sense of self. If a diffusion's difficulties begin no earlier than the stage of industry, a facilitative psychotherapeutic or educational response might assist the individual in finding or reconnecting with interests and talents that have lain dormant through childhood (Brenman-Gibson 1986; Marcia 1986). Efforts should be made to help the diffusion become aware of his or her own unique attributes and experiences; some forms of structured choice in the therapeutic or educational arenas might eventually be presented to diffusions in the interests of providing an experience of self through choosing an alternative best suited to personal preferences and competencies (Kroger 1985a). Jones (1994) has noted that most, if not all school-based prevention and intervention efforts for adolescents have focused on specific, isolated problem behaviors (such as substance abuse). (Drug abuse problems are furthermore experienced more frequently among the identity-diffuse.) Jones points out that if intervention programs were designed to address specific underlying developmental deficits at an individual level, then reduction of problem behaviors would be a side effect of a generally more effective developmental intervention.

SUMMARY

Ego identity as conceptualized by Erik Erikson is a psychosocial construct which can be understood only through the interaction of biological need, ego organization, and social context. During adolescence, features of identity which have formed through more or less favorable resolutions to earlier stages of developmental conflict must now evolve into a new configuration, different from yet based upon the earlier introjections and identifications of childhood. Furthermore, the balance achieved during the identity conflict of adolescence will affect all developmental stages encountered during adult life. James Marcia has empirically elaborated Erikson's identity versus role confusion conflict and describes four identity resolutions based on attitudes of crisis and commitment towards social roles. These identity statuses are characterized by different styles of personality organization which must be appreciated for effective educational, counseling, or psychotherapeutic intervention.

3 Adolescence as a second individuation process

Blos's psychoanalytic perspective and an object relations view

My mother packed a little bundle of clothes . . . . At last came the afternoon when I was to leave . . . . she put her arms round my neck, weeping and unable to utter a word . . . and so we parted . . . . It was a lovely sunny afternoon, and soon my fickle childish mind forgot its sadness. I rejoiced in all the new things I was seeing . . . however, [before long] I realized how alone and left to my own resources I was, and how I had no other than God in heaven . . . . It was all so strange, that I seemed to be far out in the wide world.

(*Hans Christian Andersen, in da Ponte's* Memoirs)

A mother's job is to be there to be left.

(*Anna Freud, in Furman*, Mothers have to be There to be Left)

Another sunny afternoon setting of mixed emotion marked not only home-leaving for Hans Christian Andersen but also a milestone in his personal identity development. That Andersen persisted towards his own dream of a career in Copenhagen theaters with much joy and determination despite contrary pressure and the awesome reality of a big wide world beyond Odense attests to the young man's healthy individuation process. Anna Freud's whispered aside quoted above captures the essence of optimal conditions for the development of identity, according to both psychoanalytic and object relations traditions – a parent–child partnership that enables not only an adolescent's confident, guiltless physical departure from the home of childhood both to love and to work in the wide world beyond, but also an intrapsychic departure from an internalized parental image that has to this point been their source of guidance, support, and self-esteem. Hans Christian Andersen's actions are possible through both reduction of his need for an intrapsychic parental representation as well as the gradually unfolding individuation process, concepts elaborated by Peter Blos in his psychoanalytic account of identity development (or in his terms, character formation) during adolescence.

Through a complex labyrinth of psychoanalytic routes, Blos's work emerges and marks an interesting crossroads in the evolution of psychodynamic theory itself. While retaining many contours of classic psychoanalytic maps which stress the resolution of Oedipal conflict for healthy personality development, Blos also appreciates the significance of pre-Oedipal experience in determining modes of later interpersonal relatedness. An awareness of the potentially productive rather than unconditionally maladaptive role played by regression in adolescent character formation is also critical to Blos's modification of orthodox psychoanalytic theory. Although retaining an appreciation of the place of adolescence on the road to genital maturity, Blos is one of the few psychodynamic theorists to focus almost exclusively on developments taking place during this youthful transition.

In line with most psychodynamic contributions, Blos's notions come to us via the experiences of troubled individuals seeking relief from distress. While developmental difficulty is of enormous value in highlighting normative psychodynamic processes, the deviant foundations of Blos's theoretical architecture must be remembered. In this chapter, particular effort will be made to select and describe psychodynamic processes central to Blos's conceptualization of *normative* character formation during adolescence; later in the chapter, Blos's contributions will be elaborated with recent insights from object relations theory and research on the second individuation process of adolescence derived from non-clinical populations.

BLOS, THE PERSON

Peter Blos, Erikson's childhood friend and later teaching colleague, has retained and elaborated much of Freud's psychodynamic groundwork that Erikson had found wanting. Blos was born in Germany in 1904, and his initial training was in biology – a field in which he was awarded a PhD from the University of Vienna in 1934. Greatly stimulated by his associations with Anna Freud and August Aichhorn at the Vienna Psychoanalytic Institute, Blos (like Erikson) migrated to the United States with Hitler's rise to power. In a career spanning six decades, Blos has devoted his professional energy primarily to the study of adolescence and its place in the human life-cycle. Blos has held several faculty and supervisory positions, most recently at the New York Psychoanalytic Institute and the Columbia University Center for Psychoanalytic Training and Research. Among his most recent professional honors has been receipt of the Heinz Hartmann Award from the New York Psychoanalytic Institute. Blos's lifelong interests in the psychodynamic processes of adolescence are reflected in some of his many book titles: *On Adolescence* (1962); *The Young Adolescent: Clinical Studies* (1970); and *The Adolescent Passage* (1979). His most recent volume, *Son and Father: Before and Beyond the Oedipus Complex* (1985), traces the reciprocity of the son–father relationship over the course of the generations, as son becomes a father in turn. Blos is currently in private practice in New York.

THE NATURE OF CHARACTER FORMATION

Where Erikson uses the term 'ego identity', Blos prefers the use of 'character' to denote that entity which restructures and consolidates during adolescence. However, the nature of that entity, which both gives and takes form at the end of adolescence, differs for the two psychoanalysts. Character, to Blos, is that aspect of personality which patterns one's responses to stimuli originating both within the environment as well as within the self. Blos does not focus primarily on ego processes in the formation of character but rather on the dynamic balance between id, ego, and superego structures.

Blos (1968) posits four challenges which are related to the formation of character; without addressing and favorably resolving each of these issues, adolescents retain a character deficient in the structure necessary to healthy functioning during adult life.

> The credentials of character are to be found in the postadolescent level which, if attained, renders character formation possible. . . . The extent to which the four preconditions have been fulfilled. . . will determine the autonomous or defensive nature of the character that ensues.
>
> (Blos 1968: 259)

Failure to resolve adolescent challenges may or may not be based on earlier developmental arrest.

Blos's four character challenges of adolescence, detailed in the next section, are those of (1) the second individuation process (2) reworking and mastering childhood trauma (3) ego continuity, and (4) sexual identity. The second individuation process of adolescence involves the relinquishing of those very intrapsychic parental representations which were internalized during toddlerhood and have formed the structure of childhood identity; Blos finds regression to be a normative feature among adolescents as they disengage from early object ties. In reworking childhood trauma, adolescents must return to, rather than avoid, the scene of early organismic insult and re-experience the injury so that it may be mastered rather than defended against through adult life. Similar to Erikson's suggestion of the need for a sense of inner continuity and sameness to healthy identity formation, Blos's notion of ego continuity refers to the need for a sense of personal history; one cannot have a future without a past. In line with orthodox psychoanalytic theory, Blos sees the reactivation of childhood Oedipal issues and the formation of a sexual identity as the final critical challenge to adolescent character formation; it is the young person's ability to seek romantic relationships outside the original family constellation that indicates successful resolution to this challenge.

These four challenges, central to adolescent character formation, rest on a history of individual antecedents – from constitutional givens to infant interpersonal experience to resolution of early childhood Oedipal conflict. Like ego identity, character can be conceptualized only in developmental terms; its origins begin in infancy and its stabilization appears at the end of adolescence. Blos does not trace its development through adulthood, however. Character formation involves progressively higher levels of differentiation and independence from the environment. Subjectively, one's character is one's sense of self. 'Psychic life cannot be conceived without it [character], just as physical life is inconceivable without one's body. One feels at home in one's character. . . . If must be, one dies for it before letting it die' (Blos 1968: 260). The four character formation challenges should be regarded as components of a total process; their integrated resolution marks the end of adolescence (Blos 1976). Blos's four cornerstones of character formation will now be detailed.

THE CHALLENGES DETAILED

Crucial to the psychoanalyst's portrayal of adolescent character is a basic understanding of object relations theory. This approach, broadly defined, rests on the assumption that in our relationships we react according to the internal representations we hold of people important to us in the past as well as to the person actually before us now. Greenberg and Mitchell put it succinctly:

> People react to and interact with not only an actual other but also an internal other, a psychic representation of a person which in itself has the power to influence both the individual's affective states and his overt behavioral reactions.
>
> (Greenberg and Mitchell 1983: 10)

Thus, our responses to those before us now may have only the vaguest of associations with present-tense external reality. Rather, interactions may be governed equally by internal representations of past important others who, in turn, define the present limits of our autonomous functioning.

Within psychoanalysis, a number of object relations theorists have made their contributions by exploring the implications of this last statement (for example, Fairburn, Guntrip, Jacobson, Kernberg, Klein, Kohut, and Mahler). Blos's writings on the restructuring of internal representations during adolescence draw particularly upon the work of Margaret Mahler. Though Mahler's work is based on development in early life, Blos finds great parallels in the processes by which adolescents must deal with issues of self differentiation. Blos's second individuation process will be discussed more fully than remaining challenges, for it is this issue which has stimulated the greatest theoretical and empirical interest among those attempting to understand the normative adolescent experience. The past ten years, in particular, have seen a burgeoning of both theoretical and empirical efforts to elucidate intrapsychic and interpersonal ramifications of this differentiation process.

The second individuation process

In ground-breaking work of the 1960s, Margaret Mahler conducted extensive observations of healthy mother–infant and mother–toddler dyads in a naturalistic setting to delineate the process by which the child differentiates itself from its primary care-taker and becomes an autonomous person. Separation and individuation refer to two tracks in the sequence by which the infant moves from an undifferentiated experience of self to a toddler with a sense of separateness from yet relatedness to the physical world of reality. By separation, Mahler *et al.* (1975: 4) allude to the child's 'emergence from a symbiotic fusion with the mother', while individuation denotes 'those achievements marking the child's assumption of his own individual characteristics'. In short, Mahler and her colleagues have attempted to chart 'the psychological birth of the human infant'.

Mahler follows these developmental tracks through a sequence of specific stages; one's resolution to these phases determines the health or pathology of character during the course of later life. Successful navigation of these stages is to Mahler what resolution of the Oedipal crisis was to Freud in setting the foundation for adult character structure. The hyphenated term 'separation-individuation' refers specifically to four subphases of development experienced during infancy and toddlerhood; separation-individuation subphases follow neonatal stages of autism and symbiosis.

At the beginning of life, according to Mahler, the newborn is unable to differentiate itself from its surroundings. There are not internal representations of the external world, for there is little awareness of external objects. Maintaining physiological homoeostasis is the main task for the infant in this *autistic* phase of life, and it is only the gradual awareness of a care-taker (the mother, in Mahler's observations) which propels the child into the next stage of *symbiosis* at about three to four weeks of age. Now there is dim recognition of mother, but she is perceived only as an extension of the infant's self. In the observations of Mahler *et al.*, 'the infant behaves and functions as though he and his mother were an omnipotent system – a dual unity within one common boundary' (1975: 44). It is from this base that the four subphases of separation-individuation proceed, encompassing a growing intrapsychic differentiation between self and other.

Recent research on infant development has challenged Mahler's descriptions of autistic and symbiotic stage capacities by demonstrating that infants are born with perceptual and cognitive capacities too sophisticated to suggest their inability to differentiate self from other (Stern 1985; Horner 1985). This research casts doubt on the whole existence of a symbiotic phase and the *raison d' être* for the stages of separation-individuation that lie ahead. Pine (1990, 1992), however, has responded with the proposition that infants experience *moments* of merger or non-differentiation which have an affective significance sufficiently strong to account for the merger wishes observed in later life. While young infants may not spend all of their time in states of merger, such experiences, along with care-taker response, will affect the subsequent course of separation-individuation subphases that lie ahead.

Beginning awareness of mother's existence as a separate person heralds the first subphase of the separation-individuation process, according to Mahler. She uses the term *hatching* to capture development during this time of *differentiation,* when the 5–10-month-old infant achieves the physical and intrapsychic capacities to check out holdings of the external world. Tentative explorations begin as infant slides from lap to floor and becomes a veteran of the not-too-far-from-mother's-feet environment. With increased locomotion, a new subphase ensues; *practicing* makes its developmental entrance between about 10–15 months and marks an interval of increased exploration, escalating into an exhilarating 'love affair with the world'. As long as mother remains available, a 'home base' for emotional 'refueling' through the day's new ventures, all is well. It is not until about 15–22 months in the *rapprochement* subphase that mother is experienced as a separate person, a self in her own right. Such recognition brings a sense of great loss to the toddler and calls for new strategies (seemingly regressive) in response. Attempts at 'wooing' mother, at re-engaging her in external activity as a hoped-for-filler to an intrapsychic vacuum, lie at the heart of the *rapprochement crisis;* the realization ultimately dawns, however, that there is no return to the self–object fusion of earlier times. The toddler's conflict between the need for maternal incorporation on the one hand and separation and individuation on the other is at its height; father plays a vital role here in supporting the child against the backward symbiotic pull. It is not until the final, open-ended subphase of *libidinal object constancy* during the third year that life becomes less painful. Two accomplishments occur at this time: '(1) the achievement of a definite, in certain aspects lifelong, individuality, and (2) the attainment of a certain degree of object constancy' (Mahler *et al.* 1975: 109). Object constancy implies the child's intrapsychic incorporation of both the 'good and bad' parts of the maternal image to allow it some physical distance from the mother of reality; such accomplishment sets the foundation for an intrapsychic structure that will be the basis of identity, at least until adolescence. While Mahler notes that clinical outcome to the infant *rapprochement* crisis will be mediated by developmental crises of adolescence, she does not comment specifically on the implications of optimal infant separation-individuation subphase resolutions for adolescents (Mahler *et al.* 1975).

Blos was quick to appreciate the applications of Mahler's work to the intrapsychic restructuring occurring during adolescence:

> I propose to view adolescence in its totality as the second individuation process, the first one having been completed toward the end of the third year of life with the attainment of object constancy. Both periods have in common a heightened vulnerability of personality organization. Both periods have in common the urgency for changes in psychic structure in consonance with the maturational forward surge. Last but not least, both periods – should they miscarry – are followed by a specific deviant development (psychopathology) that embodies the respective failures of individuation.
>
> (Blos 1967: 163)

He likens the infant's 'hatching from the symbiotic membrane' described by Mahler to the adolescent process of 'shedding family dependencies', that loosening of ties with the internalized parent which has sustained the child though phallic and latency periods. Adolescent disengagement from this internalized parental representation allows the establishment of new, extra-familial romantic attachments. Where such adolescent intrapsychic restructuring does not occur, the young person, at best, may merely substitute the original infantile attachment with a new love object, leaving the *quality* of the attachment unaltered.

Blos (1967) notes further accomplishments contingent upon successful resolution to the second individuation process: (1) the acquisition of stable and firm self and object boundaries, (2) the loss of some rigidity and power by the Oedipal superego, (3) greater constancy of mood and self-esteem, resulting from less dependence on external sources of support. Up until adolescence, the child has been able to make legitimate demands upon the parental ego, which has often served as an extension of its own, less developed structure. Maturation of the child's own ego goes hand in hand with disengagement from the internal representations of care-takers; 'disengagement from the infantile object is always paralleled by ego maturation' (Blos 1967: 165). It is through ego maturation that a firm sense of self, different from that of parents, not overwhelmed by internalized superego demands, and more capable of self-support, emerges to mark the end of the second individuation process:

> Individuation implies that the growing person takes increasing responsibility for what he does and what he is, rather than depositing this responsibility onto the shoulders of those under whose influence and tutelage he has grown up.
>
> (Blos 1967: 168)

As Anna Freud has indicated, a mother's (or primary care-taker's) job is to be there to be left; only in this way are adolescents able to disengage from parental internalizations and seek their own vocational and romantic fortunes in the world beyond the family doorstep.

Central to successful resolution of adolescent individuation is regression. It is only through the young person's ability to renew contact with infantile drives that the psychic restructuring of adolescence can occur.

> Just as Hamlet who longs for the comforts of sleep but fears the dreams that sleep might bring, so the adolescent longs for the comforts of drive gratification but fears the reinvolvements in infantile object relations. Paradoxically, only through regression, drive and ego regression, can the adolescent task be fulfilled.
>
> (Blos 1967: 171)

In the words of one wall poster I observed recently in a university bookshop, 'The best way out is always through'. Though not drawing any direct comparisons with the intrapsychic conflicts and regressive behavior of Mahler's *rapprochement* toddlers, Blos finds parallels between adolescent and toddler regressive functions to be striking. In Blos's view of the years of post-infancy, it is only during adolescence that regression can serve a normative developmental function.

Common adolescent regressive behaviors are phenomena such as a return to 'action' rather than 'verbal' language (for example, passivity in response to situations best addressed by verbal expression of need), idolization of pop stars and famous characters (reminiscent of the young child's idealization of parents), emotional states similar to merger (such as with abstractions like Theodore Dreiser's Right, Justice, Truth, Mercy, or with religious and political groups), and constant, frenetic activity to fill the sense of internal object loss. Blos hastens to add that it takes a relatively intact ego to survive the test of non-defensive regression during adolescence. Where ego organization has been deficient through infant separation-individuation subphases, such deficiencies are laid bare with the removal of parental props during adolescence. 'The degree of early ego inadequacy often does not become apparent until adolescence, when regression fails to serve progressive development, precludes individuation, and closes the door to drive and ego maturation' (Blos 1967: 175). It is the peer group which, under optimal conditions, supplies support during the loss of childhood psychic structure. Just as the *rapprochement* child tries to re-engage mother or care-taker in its activities to cope with the pain of object loss, so, too, the adolescent seeks solace from peers while relinquishing intrapsychic object ties. Mourning accompanies the loss of childhood's self.

Blos illustrates, with clinical examples, the second individuation process in need of outside assistance for resolution. Let us, however, move from the clinical to the commonplace and view, by way of example, a more normative adolescent experience in terms of Blos's first character challenge:

> To pass from the romantic to the commonplace, imagine if you will the father of an adolescent boy settling into his chair in front of the television set after a grueling day with the conviction that he has earned his preprandial drink and a half hour's peace. His son, with whom he has been on surprisingly good terms for several days, slouches into the room and in response to his father's greeting mutters something that might equally well be understood as either

'Hello' or 'Hell, no!' Ten minutes or so go by in silence, until, in response to the news commentator's remarks on the energy crisis, the son begins to mutter angrily. The father, thinking the boy's vocalizations are an invitation to conversation, says something viciously provocative such as, 'It looks as if we'll be facing some pretty tough problems in the next few years.' In response the boy launches into a condemnation of his father's entire generation. As he warms to the task, he becomes more pointed and specific, reminding his father that if he were only willing to walk or bicycle the seven or eight miles to work instead of driving that gas-guzzling Volkswagen, the energy shortage would soon be resolved. But no! The hedonistic, materialistic, and self-indulgent orientation displayed by his father and all his contemporaries is robbing the boy's generation of any hope of physical warmth, mobility, and perhaps even survival.

To emphasize his disgust with the situation, the boy announces he is going to find his mother. If dinner isn't ready, he plans to raise hell. If it is ready, he won't eat. His father once more is left feeling that whenever he interacts with his son, he misses some crucial point that would explain the whole interchange.

(Coppolillo 1984: 125–6)

The saga continues as the son returns within several hours to greet his father cheerfully and request use of the family car to drive his girl across town for pizza. To the father's suggestion of a stroll to the nearby pizza parlor to save gas for posterity, he receives an emphatic, 'No! That just won't do! The pizza across town is just what he has a taste for at the moment. All other considerations are unimportant' (Coppolillo 1984: 126). The father concludes that adolescence is indeed a period of 'normal psychosis' (and the son, that his father merely wishes to deprive him of use of the family car).

In considering the above scenario, the young man's argumentative efforts with his father over the energy crisis appear as possible intrapsychic distancing techniques designed to combat fears of infantile re-engulfment. In attacking that life-style of the parental generation, the youth presses an ideological stand of 'his own' – a stand that is quickly abandoned, however, when inconvenient. The queen's well-known line to Hamlet, 'The lady doth protest too much, methinks', illustrates how forceful opposition to an innocuous reality may be fighting an other-than-external battle. Additionally, regression to infantile demands for immediate drive satisfaction (in both the Freudian and auto-motive senses here), coupled with rapid mood swings, are common to adolescence, indicating the fluidity of self and object representations. 'The unavailability of the accustomed and dependable internal stabilizers of childhood seems to be responsible for many of the typical and transient personality characteristics of this age' (Blos 1983: 582). Only when this labile young man is firm in his own sense of self will such fluidity disappear, along with the need to push anything other than his own genuinely felt (ego-syntonic) ideological concerns.

Before leaving Blos's second individuation challenge, brief mention must be made of resolutions which are less than optimal. Certainly, the tragic lives of many great artists and writers have been traced to both severe infant and adolescent separation and individuation difficulties. In chilling visual form, Norwegian painter Edvard Munch has dramatically communicated the separation anxiety plaguing his own existence in his well-known painting, 'The Scream'. Terrified, despairing eyes and an open mouth forming an unbridled scream are primitive features of the artist's central character, who appears against the background of a sky ablaze. Munch's multiple and severe early losses resulted in his own incomplete adolescent separation and individuation processes; this theme of profound separation anxiety is reflected in many of his works (Masterson 1986). The life of Jean-Paul Sartre was also dulled by separation and individuation arrest (Masterson 1986). In his autobiography, *Words,* Sartre says of his own life, 'I had no true self' (1964: 75). 'My mother and I were the same age and we never left each other's side. She used to call me her attendant knight and her little man; I told her everything' (1964: 148). Indeed the theme of his play, *No Exit,* depicts the existential dilemma of three adult characters, who do not appear to have resolved adolescence's second individuation demands. Already set in hell after death, the play offers no escape for the enmeshed three, each dependent on another for ego functions the self cannot provide and each tortured beyond endurance when a needed response is not forthcoming. Garcin's famous concluding line, 'There's no need for red-hot pokers. Hell is – other people!', attests to the pain of individuation uncompleted (Sartre 1976: 47).

Among means of avoiding the adolescent individuation challenge are efforts at distancing from parents in ways other than through intrapsychic separation. Blos (1967) notes that attempts by adolescents to create physical or ideological space from their families do little to address the underlying intrapsychic task; such abortive resolutions are reminiscent of Erikson's negative identity.

> By forcing a physical, geographical, moral, and ideational distance
> from the family or locale of childhood, this type of adolescent

renders an internal separation dispensable . . . . The incapacity to
separate from internal objects except by detachment, rejection, and
debasement is subjectively experienced as a sense of alienation.

(Blos 1967: 167–8)

It is noteworthy that Blos here also makes use of the term
separation in association with the second individuation process,
though he does not detail either the separation or individuation
tracks outlined by Mahler.

Reworking and mastering childhood trauma

Blos suggests that even those exposed to the kindest of childhood fates
have innumerable opportunities for emotional injury. Furthermore,
childhood trauma is a relative term; its impact depends both on the
magnitude of the danger itself as well as the child's own vulnerability
to such assault (Blos 1962). Mastering childhood trauma is a lifelong
task; one often sets up life situations which, in effect, recreate the
original injury and thereby provide opportunities for mastery and resolution. Adolescence, because of its role in the consolidation of character,
is a time when 'a considerable portion of this task is being accomplished' (Blos 1962: 132). At the close of adolescence, infantile trau-
mas are not removed but rather (optimally) integrated into the ego and
experienced as life tasks. In cases of optimal character formation the
individual is able to find satisfying ways to cope with what was originally an unmanageable childhood ordeal. Each effort at mastery of
residual trauma results in heightened self-esteem. Reworking childhood's Oedipus complex is one specific example of this more generic
adolescent task.

Blos (1968) draws upon Freud's writings to conclude that childhood
trauma can have both positive and negative effects on character formation. Individuals may attempt to reactivate trauma, remembering and
reliving it for integration into character as described above, or they
may avoid the entire process, 'a reaction that leads to the reactive
character formation via avoidances, phobias, compulsions, and inhibi-
tions' (Blos 1968: 255). Adolescents who choose this latter option do
not allow themselves the opportunity to come to terms with trauma,
but rather remain under its directive in defensive maneuvers during
the years that follow.

Because of the anxiety generated by residual trauma, there is often
an urgency, a strong push towards expression in character. 'Due to its
origin character always contains a compulsive quality; it lies beyond

choice and contemplation, is self-evident and compelling: "Here I stand, I cannot do otherwise" (Luther)' (Blos 1968: 255). The lives of many highly creative individuals such as Martin Luther have been presented as psychoanalytic evidence of attempts to remold child-hood trauma into a mature ego organization at the close of adolescence.

Ego continuity

The third precondition for optimal character formation is that of ego continuity. Blos regards this phenomenon as critical to character forma-tion: '[A]dolescent development can be carried forward only if the adolescent ego succeeds in establishing a historical continuity in its realm. If this is prevented, a partial restructuring of adolescence re-mains incomplete' (Blos 1968: 256–7). Particularly apparent in situa-tions where a child must accept a distorted reality to survive, lack of ego continuity results from a denial of one's own experience.

Ego continuity during adolescence serves a purpose beyond that of conflict resolution; rather, it has an integrative and growth-stimulating function as the internalized parental representation is no longer needed and is cast by the wayside. Ego maturation gives rise to a 'sense of wholeness and inviolability' during adolescence; it is only during late adolescence that the capacity to form one's own view of the past, present, and future emerges (Blos 1976). Character formation at the close of adolescence is dependent upon the framework provided by ego continuity.

Sexual identity

The formation of character also involves establishment of a sexual identity, a sense of masculinity or femininity with irreversible bounda-ries; sexual identity differs from gender identity, which is formed in early life. In traditional psychoanalytic form, Blos views adolescence as a necessary regressive return for completion of phallic stage Oedipal issues in order to establish, ultimately, a sexual identity. Just as Blos stressed the necessity of an adolescent return to pre-Oedipal periods for restructuring intrapsychic parental bonds, he indicates that mature heterosexual interest can emerge only upon a return and final resolu-tion to conflicts of childhood's Oedipal years:

> I venture to say that not until adolescence has the developmental moment arrived for the oedipal drama to be completed and the

realization of mature object relations to be initiated. This step must be taken in adolescence or it never will, certainly not without circumstantial good fortunes and therapeutic intervention – in any case, not without much suffering which not every human adult is capable to endure.

(Blos 1989: 17)

With ego consolidation through the time of latency, however, the adolescent experiences such renewed Oedipal strivings at a different level; the Oedipus complex revived during adolescence is not identical to the childhood conflict.

From my work with adolescents – male and female – I have gained the impression that the decline of the Oedipus complex at the end of the phallic phase represents a suspension of a conflictual constellation rather than a definitive resolution, because we can ascertain its continuation on the adolescent level. In other words, the resolution of the Oedipus complex is completed – not just repeated – during adolescence.

(Blos 1979: 476–7)

Resolution during adolescence involves addressing both positive and negative Oedipal components (sexual love for both the opposite- and same-sex parent, respectively).

Blos believes it is the positive Oedipal complex that finds some resolution through identification with the same-sex parent during childhood, while children are left to resolve their sexual love for the same-sex parent during adolescence.

It might now be stated: since the resolution of the negative Oedipus complex is the task of adolescence, the coming to terms with the homosexual component of pubertal sexuality is an implicit developmental task of adolescence. In fact, we might say that sexual identity formation is predicated on the completion of this process.

(Blos 1979: 479)

An adolescent who frenetically pushes heterosexual behavior to the forefront of existence may, in a defensive way, be avoiding the threat of dealing with sexual feelings towards the same-sex parent. Blos finds such response common among young, sexually acting-out teenagers.

A fourteen-year-old girl when asked why she needed ten boy friends at once, answered with righteous indignation: 'I have to do this; if I didn't have so many boy friends they would say I am a lesbian.'

(Blos 1962: 68)

Alternatively, if one acknowledges yet prolongs the wish for love from the parent of like sex, such action ultimately arrests the development of heterosexual interest, Blos argues.

As resolution to the negative Oedipus complex proceeds, the ego ideal, or that which one hopes to be and to achieve, forms into a mature structure. Blos uses the term 'ego ideal' to refer to an 'abstracted, goal-intentional, and action-motivating force'.

> [T]he ego ideal, as it emerges at the termination of adolescence, is the heir to the negative Oedipus complex . . . . By inference, I assume that adolescent psychic restructuring which progresses unaided by therapeutic help follows a similar course.
>
> (Blos 1979: 322)

One's capacity to set and pursue realistic goals reflects a mature ego ideal. As long as one's energy is engaged in Oedipal struggles, it remains impossible to experience the sense of well-being that accompanies the achievement of such goals. As resolution of the negative Oedipus complex proceeds, the adolescent moves from a passive striving for love from the same-sex parent (often evidenced by failure to achieve in the vocational or academic sphere, at least for boys) to a more action-orientated life-style.

Blos notes sex differences in the means by which the positive and negative Oedipus complexes are resolved. For all children, the first object of infantile love is the mother. Since the female always remains the ultimate love object for the boy, his Oedipal dealings and psychosexual development are less complicated as a result. The girl, by contrast, must abandon the first object of her sexual affection at a very early age and shift to the father for a sense of fulfilment of her femininity. As a result, the girl's Oedipal relationship is never brought to as distinct a completion as that of her male counterpart, according to Blos. This situation has lifelong repercussions in the dynamics of sexual identity formation.

> One difference has always struck me, namely, the requisite of a radical extinction of the positive and negative Oedipus complex in the adolescent boy before his progressive development towards adulthood moves vigorously ahead. In contrast, the adolescent girl tolerates – within limits, to be sure – a far greater fluidity between the infantile attachments to both parents and her adult personality consolidation, without being necessarily encumbered in her advance toward emotional maturity.
>
> (Blos 1980: 16)

Space limitations prohibit elaboration of Blos's account of sex differences here, and you are referred to Blos (1979: chaps 11 and 15; 1985) for more complete descriptions of resolutions to both positive and negative Oedipal strivings.

CHARACTER FORMATION THROUGH ADOLESCENCE

Whereas Freud saw adolescence as one general stage of psychosexual development, Blos felt the need for further detail here also. In tracing the formation of character through the adolescent passage, Blos (1962; 1971) describes four phases of development during which the challenges are addressed. Each phase forms part of an orderly sequence which has its own time and place of ascendance; phases are not linked to specific chronological ages but rather to the intrapsychic issues they address. Although Blos does not attend to all life-cycle phases in charting the evolution of identity, he does detail phases preceding and following adolescence; they, too, encapsulate important times in the building and consolidation of character.

The period of *latency,* which precedes adolescence, provides a time in which the ego and superego gain growing control over the instincts. While the early Freudians saw latency as a time of sexual quiescence, Blos acknowledges that sexual interests and activities remain alive and well during this phase (as do many neo-Freudian psychoanalysts). In sum, the key function of latency is to provide a time for consolidation after the upheaval of the Oedipus complex.

Pre-adolescence heralds an increase in both sexual and aggressive drives with a concomitant decrease in ego control; stimuli which trigger impulse arousal often seem to have little direct relationship to the drive itself. Those working with young adolescents are aware how quickly any experience can become the source of sexual excitement:

> There are 'certain' words and conversations unhappily impossible to eradicate in schools. Boys pure in mind and heart, almost children, are fond of talking in school among themselves of things, pictures, and images of which even soldiers would sometimes hesitate to speak.
>
> (Dostoevsky, cited in Blos 1962: 61–2)

Direct gratification of instinctual impulse ordinarily meets strong superego resistance. Solution, for the mediating ego, rests with defenses such as repression, reaction formation, and displacement. Compulsive interests and activities also function to contain pre-adolescent anxiety within manageable limits.

Early adolescence is distinguished by pubertal maturation alongside the young person's genuine beginnings of separation from early object ties. Additionally, sexual energy previously attached to the Oedipal triangle now begins to seek extrafamilial outlet. Superego codes are diminished as the old internalized ties with parents loosen, and the ego is left to fumble in its regulatory function. Same-sex friendships of early adolescence are idealized; that is, young people search for friends who possess qualities that they do not have. In this way desired characteristics can be obtained vicariously. One's ego ideal is often represented by such a friend. Not surprisingly, these early adolescent relationships are generally doomed to sudden demise. Not only are the demands placed on such friendships too burdensome to bear for long, but homosexual fears may also arise and bring abrupt closure.

It is only during the emergence of *adolescence proper* that one's interests turn to the heterosexual arena. Now there is no return to old Oedipal and pre-Oedipal object ties, and such finality shakes intrapsychic organization to the core. Life, according to Blos, is generally in turmoil; yet at the same time new doors to development begin to open. The consolidation of heterosexual love involves the ability to shift from the early adolescent overvaluation of the self (as evidenced by the self-serving function of the same-sex chum) to a genuine interest in the identity of an other. Before this can happen, however, one must experience the intrapsychic vacuum between 'old' and 'new' loves, the time of transitory nothingness. Coping mechanisms often involve states of heightened affect or frenzied activity, ways to 'feel alive' and thus fill the intrapsychic void with an overdose of reality. In this way, boundaries of the self are protected from feared dissolution, accompanied frequently by poor judgment. Resolutions to both positive and negative Oedipal strivings are gradual and extend into adolescence's final phase.

Late adolescence sees a continued interest in the search for heterosexual love. Additionally, 'the individual registers gains in purposeful action, social integration, predictability, constancy of emotions, and stability of self-esteem' (Blos 1962: 128). Late adolescence is primarily a time of consolidation – a stabilizing of sexual identity into an irreversible pattern, establishing firm representations of self and others, and developing a greater sense of autonomy. Character has thus been formed.

Blos terms the final transition phase from adolescence to adulthood *postadolescence*. It is marked by further structural integration:

In terms of ego development and drive organization, the psychic structure has acquired by the end of late adolescence a fixity which allows the postadolescent to turn to the problem of harmonizing the component parts of the personality.

(Blos 1962: 149)

The work of postadolescence is to find outlets in a social reality through which sexual drive and 'life tasks' (those resolutions to early trauma) can be expressed. With the decline of instinctual conflict, the ego is free to attend to this job.

Blos's general developmental progression of adolescent sexual interest is nicely reflected in responses of teenagers to the projective sentence completion items presented below:

Eleven-year-old girl:	FOR A GIRL, BOYS are a sort of disease.
Eleven-year-old boy:	FOR A BOY, GIRLS are a pin prick in the side.
Thirteen-year-old girl:	FOR A GIRL, BOYS although stupid are important to us.
Thirteen-year-old boy:	FOR A BOY, GIRLS are great enemies.
Fifteen-year-old girl:	FOR A GIRL, BOYS are strange – they hate you if you're ugly and brainy but love you if you're pretty but dumb.
Fifteen-year-old boy:	FOR A BOY, GIRLS are the main objective.
Seventeen-year-old girl:	FOR A GIRL, BOYS are a pleasant change from girls.
Sixteen-year-old boy:	FOR A BOY, GIRLS have their good and bad points. Fortunately the good outnumber the bad.

(Kroger 1983: 3)

A HEALTHY CHARACTER STRUCTURE

What, then, is optimal psychic functioning at the close of adolescence? Blos (1983) has suggested that it involves the capacity to tolerate some degree of anxiety and depression, inevitable concomitants of the human condition. While the beginnings of adolescence go hand in hand with pubertal change, no such physiological delimiters mark its end.

In summary fashion, I might say that puberty is an act of nature and adolescence is an act of man. This statement emphasizes the fact that neither the completion of physical growth, nor the attainment of sexual functioning, nor the social role of economic self-support are, by and in themselves, reliable indices for the termination of the adolescent process.

(Blos 1979: 405–6)

What *is* a reliable index of character formation is the degree of coordination and integration among ego functions; adolescent closure occurs when character challenges become integrated and function in unison to mark an ensuing phase of greater autonomy and stability. Blos (1979: 410) notes this arrival 'when ego autonomy, in alliance with the ego ideal, challenges partially but effectively the dominance of the superego'. There is also a gradual change in the nature of relationships, both public and private, which are chosen with more discrimination and as a reflection of the individual's own needs and desires. Thus, if all goes well for our erstwhile pizza-driven, conservation-minded citizen of an earlier section, we might look several years hence to find a young man, very much in love with his marital and business partner, seated at Sunday dinner with his parents and engaged in a lively exchange of ideas on how the young couple's established fast-food packaging business might make use of recycled paper. Blos does conclude with a final warning, however, that '[e]ven if the consolidation of late adolescence has done its work in good faith, the framework of any personality structure can only stand up well over time if relatively benign circumstances continue to prevail' (1979: 411).

ELABORATIONS ON THE SECOND INDIVIDUATION PROCESS OF ADOLESCENCE

There has been no single effort paralleling that of Mahler to delineate phases and subphases of the adolescent separation and individuation processes. While Blos has drawn general attention to parallels between the infant task of self–object differentiation and the differentiation between self and internalized object representations by adolescents, later writers have attempted to delineate some aspects of the adolescent process more fully. While similarities between the *processes* of infant and adolescent differentiation may exist, it must be remembered that the intrapsychic *organizations* during these two phases of the life span are quite different.

In extending Blos's conceptualization of adolescence as a second individuation process, several recent contributions from object relations theory have provided guides as to how Mahler's phases and subphases of infant differentiation might be applied to the adolescent experience (for example, Brandt 1977; Esman 1980; Isay 1980; Josselson 1980, 1988). These speculations have generally rested on theoretical and clinical observation, however, rather than empirically based data. Through several recent longitudinal investigations with late adolescents functioning in a university context, colleagues and I have been attempting to shed some light on subphases of adolescent intrapsychic reorganization which may parallel subphases of self–object differentiation during infancy (Kroger 1985b, in press; Kroger and Haslett 1988). Comments will be drawn from this work to propose mechanisms by which late adolescents undergo the second individuation challenge. It is recognized that such efforts provide only a start to understanding the normative differentiation experience and that frequent and intensive interviews with diverse groups of adolescents over time are necessary to delineate the course of life's second individuation process.

It is proposed that parallels to Mahler's stage of normal symbiosis and separation-individuation subphases (differentiation, practicing, *rapprochement*, and libidinal object constancy) occur in normative adolescent development; similarities to infantile autism can be found among those adolescents who have failed, by varying degrees, to internalize a parental representation from earlier years. Empirical indicators for these suggestions have come via studies of ego identity status – a psychosocial measure providing clues as to underlying intrapsychic organization.

Marcia's psychosocial identity statuses (described in the previous chapter) may reflect various stages in the underlying differentiation between self and object representations. Identity achievements are characterized by an intrapsychic organization in which self and object representations are clearly distinct. Support for this proposal has come from various studies indicating an association of greater individuation (in terms of ego development, locus of control, field independence, object representation, and relationships with others) with the identity achievement position (Brickfield 1989; Chapman and Nicholls 1976; Currie 1983; Ginsburg and Orlofsky 1981; Josselson 1982, 1987; Kroger 1990; Orlofsky *et al.* 1973; Papini *et al.* 1989; Shulkin 1990). Moratoriums, differentiating from internalized parental representations, have shown parallels to infants in subphases of differentiation, practicing, and *rapprochement*. In work by Josselson (1982), Orlofsky and Frank (1986), and Kroger (1990), early memories of moratorium subjects found them wishing to explore the world, with or without others (reminiscent of infant differentiation and practicing); observations of moratoriums vying for power but ambivalent once it was held are reminiscent of behaviors during the infant *rapprochement* crisis (Donovan, cited in Marcia 1976b; Podd *et al.* 1970).

The foreclosure status would seem to reflect an intrapsychic organization having parallels with the symbiotic phase of infancy; research with foreclosure adolescents has shown little differentiation between their self and internalized parental representations (Jordan 1970, 1971; Josselson 1973, 1982, 1987; Kroger 1985b, in press; Kroger and Haslett 1988; Papini *et al.* 1989; Shulkin 1990). Diffusions have, on the whole, had little opportunity for internalizing parents with concomitant difficulty in developing a cohesive sense of self (Jordan 1970, 1971; Josselson 1987). From Kroger and Haslett (1988), those late adolescents remaining foreclosed over a two-year interval were very likely to evidence a separation disorder as reflected in a non-secure attachment profile; moratoriums at the conclusion of the study were about equally divided between secure and non-secure attachment styles, while achievements at that time were highly likely to be secure in their attachment style, evidencing greater intrapsychic self–other differentiation. Furthermore, those adolescents who remained identity-achieved over the two-year time span were very likely to be secure in attachment style through the duration of the study. More recent longitudinal work by Kroger (1995) has differentiated between 'firm' and 'developmental' foreclosures. Late adolescents who remained foreclosed over the course of their university study evidenced significantly higher nurturance-seeking needs at the outset (and conclusion) of the study than those initial foreclosures who later proceeded to moratorium and achievement positions.

Lapsley and his colleagues have also been examining the adolescent separation-individuation process and exploring functions that the imaginary audience and personal fable phenomena may serve during this transition time (Lapsley 1992; Lapsley and Rice 1988). Lapsley's research suggests that adolescents' use of imaginary audiences and personal fables are best conceptualized as defensive and restitutive mechanisms and facilitate resilience and coping during the second individuation process. Although Lapsley's initial research on these mechanisms has not been able to be replicated (Goossens 1994), a greater understanding of adolescent coping mechanisms for weathering the second separation-individuation process promises to be a productive line of future research activity.

There has been a growing body of theoretical literature related to the use of transitional objects which facilitate the infant separation-individuation process. *Transitional object* is a term originally devised by Winnicott to refer to the first 'not me' possession – an object such as a blanket or cuddly toy different from the infant's own body yet 'not fully recognized as belonging to external reality' (1953: 90). Such an object functions as a representation of the attachment figure; a child knows its blanket or toy is not mother; yet comfort is derived from the transitional object in a way similar to the soothing derived from mother (or care-taker) herself. Tolpin (1971) has argued that such objects function as an 'auxiliary soother', symbolically re-creating union with the mother, to aid in the process of infant differentiation from its care-taker. Adolescents may use transitional objects or phenomena such as diaries, all-consuming hobbies, or idolized others to facilitate their differentiation from internalized object representations. Few empirical studies of normative adolescent development, however, have attempted to document this phenomenon. Transitional object use would appear to be a fruitful area for further enquiry into mechanisms involved in the second individuation process.

A pictorial scheme for adolescents, in the process of differentiating themselves from the internalized parent, appears in Figure 3.1.

In this scheme, the diffusion position has not been described, for diffusion (in the Eriksonian sense of having no central 'core') would not reflect a normative resolution to the second individuation process. Subphase representations should serve as a useful base for describing societal reaction to best facilitate the adolescent individuation process. Just as the care-taker must adjust his or her response to infant action through each developmental subphase for optimal ego structuralization, so, too, must social reaction resonate with adolescent need in each second individuation subphase to provide a context for optimal development.

CRITICISM OF BLOS'S IDENTITY CONSTRUCT

In a critical general analysis of psychodynamic literature on adolescent development, Adelson and Doehrman have noted the enormous gap between psychodynamic potential and its present contribution to an understanding of this age period:

> It is hard to imagine a satisfying theory of adolescence without the strongest contribution from psychodynamic theory. No other approach can offer, potentially, a comparable depth and range of observation; no other approach is as well suited – again, potentially – to pull together evidence drawn from other sources. Yet it is even harder to imagine that happening today, given the sad state of the

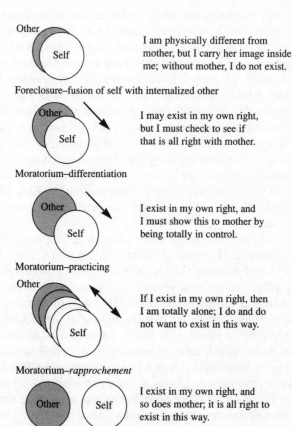

Other

Self

I am physically different from mother, but I carry her image inside me; without mother, I do not exist.

Foreclosure–fusion of self with internalized other

Other

Self

I may exist in my own right, but I must check to see if that is all right with mother.

Moratorium–differentiation

Other

Self

I exist in my own right, and I must show this to mother by being totally in control.

Moratorium–practicing

Other

Self

If I exist in my own right, then I am totally alone; I do and do not want to exist in this way.

Moratorium–*rapprochement*

Other

Self

I exist in my own right, and so does mother; it is all right to exist in this way.

Achievement–self–other constancy

Figure 3.1 Subphases of adolescent separation-individuation

art. It is at the moment a fossilized doctrine, resisting innovation in method, unshakably parochial in outlook.

(Adelson and Doehrman 1980: 115)

In the years since this statement was made some theoretical progress has occurred, particularly in ego psychoanalytic psychology and object relations arenas, but many phenomena remain unexamined.

Resting on limited clinical recordings, Blos's construct evokes criticism applicable to much of the psychodynamically orientated literature; not only are empirical foundations shaky, but normative developmental principles are inferred from observations of those appearing in clinical settings. Furthermore, Blos fails to deliver. In his discussion of regression, many specific questions regarding systems affected by and circumstances associated with a return to earlier stages remain unanswered (Adelson and Doehrman 1980). Such lack of attention to detail also appears in Blos's discussion of the second individuation process. While we are certainly 'now eager to trace the steps of individuation during adolescence', such steps are not subsequently delineated (Blos 1967: 166). A further instance of Blos's lack of precision has been raised by Richmond and Sklansky (1984) in pointing out his different usages of the term *character*; at times, Blos views character as that which regulates the adolescent process, while at others, character refers to the period's end product. These writers feel that Blos has been unable to find an organizing principle to account for development during adolescence.

An additional problem arises when we turn to empirical literature related to adolescent character challenges in the next section. Studies support another of Adelson and Doehrman's (1980: 112) general observations regarding psychodynamic theory: 'The realm of theory and the realm of empirical inquiry exist separately and fail to recognize or support each other'. There is frequent failure of empirically based research to support a number of Blos's theoretical postulates. While adolescence does, indeed, seem to encompass a second individuation process, research suggests that it is a phenomenon generally addressed in later, rather than middle, phases as indicated by the psychoanalyst. Rather than being a state of siege when Oedipal anxieties come to the fore, normative adolescence seems, rather, a time of steady, non-tumultuous maturation. 'Researchers who investigate normal adolescents continue to find evidence that development during adolescence is slow, gradual, and unremarkable' (Josselson 1980: 189). Indeed, results of Masterson and Costello (1980) and Offer (1991) show adolescent turmoil to be an indicator of psychopathology rather than normality. Many gaps between Blosian theory and research on the normative adolescent experience need filling.

Criticism has been also been leveled at Blos's utilization of the infant individuation concept itself. Both Pine (1985) and Schafer (1973) caution against the application of separation-individuation subphases to times of the life-span other than infancy. During adolescence, for example, there is no primitive merging of self and object as in infancy, and these analysts find it misleading to refer to later developmental processes with identical terms. Schafer (1973: 43) has criticized what he sees as Blos's confusion between 'individuation' and 'giving up infantile objects'; '*psychologically,* only an already highly individuated person is capable of giving up his infantile relations to others'. Caution is clearly necessary in defining the meaning of separation and individuation processes, particularly when referring to different stages of the life-cycle.

A final voice of protest has come from feminist writers – such as Gilligan (1982a) and Kaplan and Klein (1985) – who argue against conceptualization of women's development as that of 'shedding of family dependencies, the loosening of infantile object ties in order to become a member of society at large' (Blos 1967: 163). However, Blos does not equate adolescent individuation with severing emotional bonds with parents. Rather, he describes a separation from infantile objects that in fact allows for a more mature form of relationship with parents as well as significant others. It is change in the quality of *how* one is both related and autonomous as a result of differentiation from internalized object ties that is the hallmark of the separation-individuation process of adolescence (Kroger 1992; Marcia 1993). Despite such criticism, infant developmental processes of separation and individuation continue to generate theoretical and research interest in their modified application to intrapsychic restructuring during adolescence.

RESEARCH FINDINGS ON ADOLESCENT CHARACTER FORMATION

Of Blos's four character challenges, it is the second individuation process which has drawn the most extensive attention in a growing body of psychodynamically orientated empirical research. The issue of assessment has been problematic. As Bourne (1978b) has noted, intrapsychic restructuring does not lend itself easily to measurement. Time since the 1980s, however, has seen several innovations in instruments designed to explore issues of separation and individuation during adolescence (Separation-Individuation Theme Scale: Coonerty 1989; Separation-Individuation Process Inventory: Christenson and Wilson 1985; Adolescent Separation Anxiety Test: Hansburg 1980a,b; Psychological Separation Inventory: Hoffman 1984; Separation-Individuation Test of Adolescence: Levine *et al.* 1986; The Individuation Scale: Maslach *et al.* 1985; Adolescent Individuation Measure: Sabatelli and Williams 1993). The 1990s have seen continued refinement of some of these measures: see, for example, McClanahan and Holmbeck (1992), Levine and Saintonge (1993), Kroger and Green (1994), Levine (1994), and Holmbeck and McClanahan (1994) for refinements to Levine's Separation-Individuation Test of Adolescence, and Dolan *et al.* (1992) for refinements to the Separation-Individuation Inventory.

The second individuation challenge entails both intrapsychic and interpersonal change. Among attempts to integrate these two dimensions have been studies of intrapsychic issues in relation to external relationships and/or social adjustment. Mazor *et al.* (1993) have explored intrapsychic and interpersonal aspects of adolescent separation-individuation in a cross-sectional study of kibbutz children and adolescents in Israel. They found that their older subjects construed self and self–other relationships from a more differentiated perspective than younger ones and that the fear of engulfment anxiety was higher in early adolescence and subsequent age groups than in late childhood. Furthermore, in mid and late adolescence, there appeared ambivalence between fears of merging and separateness in relationships with others. Quintana and Kerr (1993) found that participation in relationships which supported autonomy, mirroring, and nurturance needs was associated with freedom from depression among college students and that, conversely, engulfment anxiety, separation anxiety, and denial of dependency were associated with depressive complaints. Rice *et al.* (1990) investigated the relationship between adolescent separation-individuation, family cohesion, and college adjustment, and found that the affective response to separation-individuation is strongly related to college adjustment; students who reported positive separation feelings (non-anxious and unresentful reactions to a variety of separation experiences) also reported being well adjusted to university life, while those with negative, angry, or resentful responses to separation had more difficulty managing adjustment to college. An insightful narrative account of intrapsychic and interpersonal issues in the separation-individuation process of adjustment for late adolescent immigrant students in Israel has been documented by Mirsky and Kaushinsky (1989).

Studies of adolescent intimacy, ego identity status, and early memories have found reasonably consistent results across several methods of assessing separation-individuation resolution. High intimacy has been associated with a firm sense of identity and intrapsychic separateness from early object ties; additionally, those adolescents forming either enmeshed or superficial (stereotypic) relationships have not differed in type of disorder rating for separation-individuation capacity (Levitz-Jones and Orlofsky 1985; Millis 1984). Similar results have also come from a study of intimacy among young adult women (Bellew-Smith and Korn 1986). Studies of ego identity status have been presented in the section elaborating Blos's second individuation concept. Generally, those findings link well with results from research on adolescent and young adult intimacy; achievement and moratorium identity statuses have been associated with high intimacy and a highly differentiated intrapsychic structure, while the foreclosed identity status has been linked with low intimacy and an undifferentiated intrapsychic structure (Marcia *et al.* 1993). Early memories used as an index of underlying character structure have also pointed to more infantile intrapsychic organization among foreclosure and diffusion subjects (Josselson 1982; Orlofsky and Frank 1986; Kroger 1990). Furthermore, early memories considered as expressions of relationship paradigms have also been linked more directly with dimensions of the adolescent separation-individuation process (Acklin *et al.* 1991).

A growing body of work has been exploring the relationship between separation-individuation difficulties and eating disorders among late adolescent women (Armstrong and Roth 1989; Friedlander and Siegel 1990; Rhodes and Kroger 1992; Smolak and Levine 1993). This body of work points to similar intrapsychic and familial factors that contribute to the etiology and maintenance of eating disorders for women and the serious consequences for those who may fail to attain a sense of psychological separateness.

Research which has less directly tapped intrapsychic adolescent separation-individuation issues include studies of ability to tolerate aloneness, home-leaving strategies, and relationships with peers and parents. Home-leaving strategies have been an additional area of research providing clues to the development of intrapsychic separation and individuation processes. Secure emotional attachment (reflecting engagement in the second individuation challenge) has been associated with an easier leave-taking during late adolescence, while conflicted attachment has been linked with problematic departure (Henton *et al.* 1980; Kraemer 1982; Sullivan and Sullivan 1980). Moore and Hotch (1981, 1982, 1983) have found that the best indicators of successful intrapsychic separation from parents are economic independence, personal control, and separate residence; emotional dissociation has been the most negative indicator of successful intrapsychic separation. Anderson and Fleming have suggested the following:

> [W]hile it is important, as others have found, . . . for adolescents to maintain a positive, supportive relationship with parents, their own identity and psychosocial adjustment needs require that this be outweighed by feelings of physical separateness and personal control over their own lives.
>
> (Anderson and Fleming 1986: 457)

Adjustment to demands of the world-at-large appears intricately interwoven with resolution to the second individuation challenge.

The peer group, used by teenagers in different ways through the adolescent years, provides support in meeting the individuation challenge as well as giving an index of adolescent separation-individuation status. A developmental approach to teenagers' perceptions of their peers has been used by Coleman (1974, 1978) and Brown *et al.* (1986) to tap changing demands adolescents place on their friends; such studies also provide an indirect measure of the intrapsychic reorganization taking place. Indeed, research reveals that peers generally do provide a 'way station' along separation and individuation tracks. The ability to tolerate aloneness also allows insight into intrapsychic development during adolescence. Part of Coleman's (1974) work focused on feelings associated with solitude. The following sentence-completion responses extracted from that research indicate increasing tolerance of solitude with age:

Eleven-year-old girl:	WHEN THERE IS NO ONE ELSE AROUND you are lonely as if the world was empty.
Eleven-year-old boy:	IF A PERSON IS ALONE he gets nervous.
Eighteen-year-old girl:	IF A PERSON IS ALONE they have time to think about life.
Seventeen-year-old boy:	IF A PERSON IS ALONE he chooses his own path.

(Coleman 1974: 37–8)

Responses of the younger subjects may be interpreted as reflecting separation anxiety when external objects are not available to support an intrapsychic structure as yet undifferentiated from early object ties; older adolescents appear more comfortable with using aloneness in the service of their own individuation efforts.

The entire field of adolescent/parental attachment research is a burgeoning one, complementing research on adolescent intrapsychic restructuralization. Ultimately, it is relationships with parents themselves that provide a crucial gauge of success in the intrapsychic restructuring of early object ties. The GAP Report (Group for the Advancement of Psychiatry 1968) has indicated that, among other accomplishments, it is when one can return to parents in a new and equal relationship that adolescent individuation is complete. Studies of adolescent differentiation from and attachment to parents have produced consistent results. Quintana and Lapsley (1990) have found a positive relationship between attachment to parents and differentiation from them, while Rice (1991) found continuity in attachment to parents over time coupled with increases in independence from them for a sample of late adolescent college students. Benson *et al.* (1992: 189) report that 'the secure base provided by attachments to mothers and fathers acts as a protective factor against a floundering inability to make commitments', while results from Blustein *et al.* (1991) have shown that attachment to and independence from at least the same-sex parent is predictive of progress in career commitment. Generally, results of optimal character formation indicate the coexistence of individuality and connectedness in adolescent relationships with their families; the quality of such relationships provides some measure of intrapsychic developmental progress.

Valuable developmental insights have also come through research on adolescents' changing perceptions of relationships with parents; extremely positive attitudes towards parents have emerged in late adolescence in contrast to all earlier life stages (Pipp *et al.* 1985). Researchers interpret this strengthened bond as a defense against fears of separation and autonomy. Weinmann and Newcombe (1990) also investigated changing adolescent perceptions of parental relations, finding identity commitment among adolescents to be directly related to their perceptions of the amount of love they felt for and experienced from their mothers over time. In a meta-analysis of adolescent attachment relations with parents, Rice (1990) calls for further longitudinal studies to examine the importance of attachment relations for adolescent ego development. Individuation appears most likely within the context of a family structure capable of supporting and encouraging such maturation (Adams and Jones 1983; Enright *et al.* 1980; Grotevant and Cooper 1986; Silverberg and Steinberg 1987).

Reworking and mastering childhood trauma has received scant research attention. However, Blos's proposal that adolescent regression is both normative and necessary to later healthy adult functioning has obtained some backing from several longitudinal studies. Psychologically healthy adults in two different samples showed the greatest trends towards intensified emotionality (regression) existing alongside enhanced coping abilities during adolescence; those least healthy during adulthood maintained or increased control between pre-adolescence and adolescence, rather than abandoning themselves to unrest (Peskin 1972; Haan 1974). From this work, the ability to regress in adolescence does seem to be associated with healthier adult functioning. However, much remains to be done for a more complete understanding of these phenomena and their role in normative adolescent development.

The challenge of ego continuity has been addressed indirectly through much of the identity status research cited in the previous chapter. One study particularly relevant to this task has been that by

Rappaport *et al.* (1985) in their investigation of the relation between adolescent identity and temporal perspective. Exploring two temporal dimensions relevant to ego continuity, the study found identity achievements and foreclosures to be orientated towards the distant future, while moratoriums and diffusions were orientated particularly towards the recent past. Diffusions de-emphasized the future, in line with prediction that a future is difficult to anticipate if one is unable to commit to the present; in order to have a sense of future, one must feel a continuity between past and present.

The development of sexual identity during adolescence has been the focus of a multitude of investigations. However, efforts directly empirically examining Blos's proposal that adolescence involves revival of and final resolution to the negative Oedipal crisis are not readily available in published accounts of the process. Support has been provided, anecdotally, through clinical records (Blos 1985); however, the psychodynamic postulation of adolescence as a time of turmoil, regression in drive and ego functions, and a phase when Oedipal anxieties are central has generally not been supported by studies of normative adolescent development (Douvan and Adelson 1966; Offer 1969, 1991; Offer and Offer 1975).

Currently, a major attempt has been to elucidate general dimensions of human relationships (Josselson 1992). As measures of these dimensions (such as holding, attachment, eye-to-eye validation, idealization and identification) become available, future research on the adolescent separation-individuation process might well address the changing meanings of these dimensions over the course of intrapsychic restructuring.

IMPLICATIONS FOR SOCIAL RESPONSE

Though Blos does not discuss, in depth, the role of the social context in facilitating adolescent resolution to the four character challenges, parents, teachers, counselors, psychotherapists, and others working closely with young people may all play critical parts in facilitating movement through the second individuation process. Other adolescent character challenges are also affected by reactions from these socialization agents as well as from the general structure of society itself. In passing from the family to a place in the larger social order, that order must be ready to receive:

[N]o adolescent, at any station of his journey, can develop optimally without societal structures standing ready to receive him, offering him that authentic credibility with which he can identify or polarize

.... the psychic structure of the individual is critically affected, for better or worse, by the structure of society . . . . what I try to emphasize here is the fact that the successful course of adolescence depends intrinsically on the degree of intactness and cohesion which societal institutions obtain.

(Blos 1971: 975)

Blos continues by noting that character formation may, at times, be helped not by efforts at individual remediation but rather by the rehabilitation of those very social institutions in which the adolescent is expected to find some suitable niche. Disaffected youth, though often instigators of social revolution, are seldom its cause; a society, through its institutions, must remain sensitive and responsive to youth's insights (often deadly accurate) into problems of the social structure (Blos 1979).

In comments on the earlier onset of puberty, Blos cautions against the simplistic conclusion that family and school must respond to the earlier arousal of sexual drive. 'We have ample evidence to demonstrate that an acceptance of the young adolescent as a self-directing, sexually active "young person" interferes severely with the preparatory functions of this stage' (Blos 1971: 970). He continues to argue that it is critical to prolong rather than abbreviate childhood in order to allow time for intrapsychic restructuring to occur. A young person pressing towards earlier sexual activity may do so at the expense of a firmly established sexual identity in adult life.

Blos's general comments on the role of parents through developmental phases of adolescence caution against ignoring personal inclination in favor of 'expert' advice.

Tradition has become replaced by the expert who offers answers to all of life's problems. . . . Parents who reluctantly or eagerly put the bewildering jumble of advice into practice soon abdicate their personal responsibility in favor of the expert; thus, they are surrendering their own convictions rather than passing judgment on what has been offered them. This submission to the expert has drained parental actions or attitudes of consistency, integration, and integrity.

(Blos 1971: 972)

The net result of such action is parental self-doubt and confusion at the very point when confidence in their own values is most necessary. Parents, authoritative in child-rearing style, offer their adolescent children the most optimal conditions for finding and consolidating identity; where such style wavers, adolescent character challenges may be aborted (Blos 1971).

Blos cautions that parents and social institutions must also recognize the role they may play in adolescents' struggles for freedom from infantile dependencies. Where intrapsychic change is difficult, declarations of independence are often projected outward, in exaggerated form, onto institutions (for example, universities) which have provided youth with temporary accommodation through the adolescent passage. It is important for adults to recognize their potential for association with an internalized parental image rather than their existence merely as external agents of reality in evoking adolescent response.

In terms of the second individuation challenge, it is informative to move beyond Blos to recent efforts at subphase delineation, for each stage presents a time of special need which must be recognized and addressed in order to provide optimal conditions for development. Mahler's observations of what constitutes 'ordinary devoted mothering' through each subphase of infancy is helpful in understanding ways to facilitate the second individuation process. Assuming the adolescent has enjoyed the security provided by significant overlap between self and parental representation since the end of pre-Oedipal stages, the removal of that overlap is now possible; as Mahler has observed for infants, a stage of normal symbiosis is absolutely critical for separation-individuation subphases to proceed.

In normative adolescent development, the differentiation process begins of its own accord. It can be facilitated by adults who, despite youths' withdrawal from the closeness of earlier latency relationships, do not react in retaliation but rather with understanding of new needs for distance and independent action. Respect for adolescents as individuals in their own right rather than as extensions of one's self are crucial adult attitudes to aiding the second individuation process. As in all adolescent separation-individuation subphases, use of transitional objects may also assist adolescents' efforts in relinquishing infantile object ties. In recent interviews with late adolescents, I was intrigued to learn how frequently even the burliest of rugby players often resurrected the 'teddy' (or similar artefact) of childhood as a companion on the intrapsychic and external journeys in the transition from home to university life. Photographs of old, familiar figures often served similar purposes.

Counseling or psychotherapeutic intervention may be necessary when delayed or premature differentiation from the internalized parental representation takes place. Inhibited differentiation is likely to be responsible for what Erikson and Marcia describe as a foreclosed identity. Here, many of the adolescent's actions will be aimed at receiving parental approval, thereby gaining narcissistic gratification and self-esteem. With such youths it is the therapeutic aim to promote differentiation in a manner age-appropriate yet paralleling the way in which a 'good enough' mother assists her infant through the differentiation process. Following establishment of a caring relationship, therapeutic response might take the form of gentle, developmental 'nudges' coupled with explorations of the youth's guilt and fear over abandoning the internalized parent (Feldberg 1983). Additionally over time, therapeutic work must involve the adolescent's de-idealization of the internalized love object as well as working through the mourning process (Blos 1979). It is beyond the scope of this discussion to indicate appropriate forms of therapeutic assistance for arrest stemming from unresolved separation-individuation issues of infancy, but reviews of possible interventions based on Mahler's work can be found in Edward *et al.* (1992) and Pine (1990).

Premature differentiation in adolescence is characterized by separation which cannot keep pace with individuation; such misalignment may stem from fear of engulfment by the internalized parent. As a result, there is insufficient ego strength to support the push towards expression of autonomous action; poor decisions, which may result in serious injury or situations having long-term consequences, are often the result. Here, it is the therapeutic aim to harness differentiation by setting firm limits and assisting the family to do likewise. Interpretation and confrontation may also be used to work through anxieties and so bring adolescent separation and individuation tracks into closer alignment (Feldberg 1983).

Adolescent parallels to the practicing subphase of infancy bring continued efforts to test an intrapsychic structure permitting more autonomous functioning. As the practicing toddler is assisted in further exploration by new locomotor abilities, so, too, may adolescents acquire the skill (and driver's license) necessary for motorized movement further into the world beyond where buses and family outings go. It is still vital, however, that significant others offer the adolescent a solid 'refueling' base from which new explorations can be launched. Parental support and encouragement for such exploratory effort during adolescence parallels the importance Mahler *et al.* (1975) place on maternal reaction to the infant in all separation-individuation subphases. A balance between support and limit setting would seem to provide the optimal conditions for resolution to demands of this practicing subphase of adolescence.

Adolescent *rapprochement* is marked by swings between efforts at distancing and renewed efforts for closeness, as youths seek to return internalized self and object overlap to earlier levels of organization. The ability of adults to maintain their own ground in the face of adolescent regressive and progressive development is a difficult but necessary stance; a caregiver's vulnerability to adolescent assault (in defense against the latter's infantile regressive pulls) does not enable one to remain emotionally available as youths' intrapsychic moorings become unfastened.

Libidinal object constancy represents the infant resolution to separation-individuation subphases; for the adolescent, this stage involves a consolidation of structural reorganization. Brandt nicely states features of this final phase:

> The identity crisis of adolescence is thus caused not only because it is hard for the adolescent to find himself, but because in the process he must find himself alone. Kramer (1958) . . . sees the 'experience of identity as finding oneself painfully separated from one's accustomed environment, alone, and forced to rely on one's own resources. The experience of separation from the first love object, mother, and the sensation of aloneness is one of the factors in the creation of a sense of identity.' Without this separation no true autonomy or independence of the ego or superego is possible, and hence no real sense of identity can be achieved.
>
> (Brandt 1977: 517–18)

This final phase, the aim of normative parenting, counseling, and psychotherapeutic effort, would see adolescents able to meet in a relationship of 'I' and 'Thou', alone and separate but able to hold genuine interest in the identity of an other.

SUMMARY

Character formation as outlined by Blos involves the resolution of at least four challenges in order for identity to develop and stabilize at the close of adolescence. Challenges addressed through a sequence of phases are the second individuation process, reworking and mastering childhood trauma, developing a sense of ego continuity, and forming a sexual identity. Object relations theorists have proposed more detailed accounts of mechanisms which may operate during the second individuation process, and a growing body of research is exploring this phenomenon. It is vital that individuals and social institutions involved with youth appreciate their potential associations with adolescents' internalized representations of infantile love objects which must be relinquished by adolescents if optimal resolution to character formation is to occur.

4 Identity through a cognitive-developmental lens
Kohlberg's contributions

All this simply bewilders me, mother. People may differ about matters
of opinion, or even about religion; but how can they differ about right
and wrong? Right is right; and wrong is wrong; and if a man cannot
distinguish them properly, he is either a fool or a rascal: that's all.
(*Stephen, in George Bernard Shaw's* Major Barbara)

Young Stephen's bewilderment in response to varying opinions of the
'one true morality' reflects not only his conception of matters moral
but also the very structure of his identity itself. Set in an upper-class
drawing room at the turn of the century, *Major Barbara* opens as late
adolescent Stephen discusses with his mother, Lady Britomart, the
financial futures of her three children. It seems that the siblings' only
assurance of future monetary security rests in financial support from
the estranged husband and father, Undershaft, a manufacturer of muni-
tions which destroy human life. Elder daughter Barbara, a major in the
Salvation Army, is at this point in her career 'saving' starving souls in
the exchange of bread for salvation. Upon reunion with her father at
the close of Act I, Barbara and Undershaft agree to sample the other's
understanding of morality (each with hope of converting the other).
Through Acts II and III, assorted lovers and Salvation Army shelter
'converts' all add their own constructs of morality to the family
debate, as Barbara undergoes transition to a new level of moral reasoning. The dialogue and interpretations of justice by each of the play's
central characters reflect their markedly different constructions of
morality which, in turn, point to underlying differences in the very
structure of their own identities. Characters from *Major Barbara*
neatly exemplify stages in the evolution of moral understanding within
Kohlberg's cognitive-developmental framework and will later be
revisited to introduce the theorist's stage sequence.

Questions about universal justice and the development of one's sense of ethics led Lawrence Kohlberg into a career devoted to the study of moral reasoning. Drawing upon Piaget's investigations of children's moral philosophies, Kohlberg not only helped legitimate moral enquiry as a field of scientific study but also extended the observation of moral development from childhood into the adolescent and adult years of life. Unlike many other cognitive theorists addressing the growth of knowledge, Kohlberg was not content merely to chart developmental change but continued to explore, in very practical terms, the implications his views held for social response, particularly in the field of education. 'Educating for a just society' has been the focus of several recent attempts by Kohlberg to work with adolescents in communities aimed at enhancing participants' levels of moral decision-making.

Unlike other theorists discussed in this volume, Kohlberg does not address, directly, the question of identity. Rather, he views the development of moral reasoning as one subdomain of ego functioning, which in turn is an aspect of identity. A study of Kohlberg's work does allow us to make inferences about identity, however, as we tap moral reasoning processes. It also allows us to appreciate the views of another identity theorist, Kegan (reviewed in Chapter 6), who has used Kohlberg's construct to delineate the structural evolution of the self through the course of the life-span.

KOHLBERG, THE PERSON

Born in 1927 in New York, Kohlberg spent his late adolescent years in various laboring jobs. He traced his future career path to a decision he made after high school to help smuggle Jewish refugees through the British blockade into Palestine. Kohlberg then spent three years in the merchant marines, followed by time as an engineer on a Navy iceboat purchased by the Jewish defense force. This boat, full of refugees, was captured on its way to Palestine, and Kohlberg, along with the rest of the crew and passengers, was held in a camp in Cyprus. Eventually Kohlberg and several others escaped and lived on a kibbutz in Palestine until it was safe to return to the United States (Power 1991).

Plagued with moral questions about violence from these experiences, Kohlberg decided to enroll at the University of Chicago and take time for serious ethical reflection through the study of philosophy; at the same time, he completed his BA in a record two years. As an undergraduate, he was torn between a career in law, with the opportunity it provided to work towards social justice, and one in clinical psychology, where help could be offered at a more individual level of intervention. After summer work as an attendant in a psychiatric hospital, Kohlberg decided to embark on graduate studies in clinical psychology through the University of Chicago. A further crucial career turning point came one day during his internship. A paranoid patient in his office was agitated, shouting that the chief psychiatrist of the institution was persecuting her. At this point the chief psychiatrist entered, having overheard the cries, and prescribed electric shock treatment. Kohlberg protested that this action would only confirm the woman's sense of injustice. While his protests were to no avail, they did provide the impetus for a redirection of his studies to research on social justice and the development of moral reasoning.

Kohlberg's PhD revolutionized theories of moral development. In a climate fixated on the role of the Freudian superego for determining concepts of justice, the young researcher's proposal of evolutionary stages in development offered a creative alternative avenue of enquiry into this dimension of human behavior. In contrast to his BA, Kohlberg's PhD was awarded after nine long years of research. His only comment was that it is not always possible to predict human behavior. Appointments at Yale, the Institute for Advanced Study, the University of Chicago, and Harvard University followed. It was at the latter institution that Kohlberg spent most of his academic career, establishing the Center for Moral Education. There he attracted a number of scholars interested in his theory and undertook longitudinal studies of the development of moral reasoning alongside the evaluation of educational programs designed to enhance moral understanding. Kohlberg died in 1987, leaving a legacy of over 100 publications to future generations of researchers for continued exploration of the work he began.

KOHLBERG'S VIEW OF IDENTITY

In contrast to more underlying or holistic notions of identity described by Loevinger and Kegan in the next two chapters, Kohlberg conceptualizes moral reasoning as only one subdomain of ego functioning evolving alongside others (for example, cognition) in the course of identity development. If one examines relationships between such subdomains of ego development, there often appears a 'necessary but not sufficient' conditional link between them. Thus, a certain stage of cognition appears to be a necessary but not sufficient condition for a certain stage of moral reasoning. Additionally, in Kohlberg's view, subdomains of ego functioning develop in relation to different types of environments. Thus, Piaget addresses the development of cognition in relation to the natural or physical world, while Selman explores the impact of cognitive change on the meaning of social relationships; Kohlberg examines the development of moral reasoning in relation to the social world, while Snarey explores the development of moral reasoning in relation to the natural or physical environment (Snarey *et al.* 1983). Though Kohlberg is not a theorist of ego development, many of his notions do allow inferences about identity and provide the foundations for a structural view of the self quite different from those of Erikson or Blos, described in preceding chapters.

Kohlberg proposes that the development of moral reasoning evolves through a series of stages, each capturing a mode of reasoning about justice *qualitatively* different from preceding and succeeding stages. No longer was it necessary to think about people having *quantitatively* different superego controls; rather, Kohlberg pointed the way towards an understanding of morality based on differing constructions or meanings of justice by individuals. Furthermore, each stage appears to occur in a universal, hierarchical, and invariant sequence; progressively more complex and comprehensive structures of moral reasoning emerge through the course of development.

> [My view] implies that moral development may be defined in terms of the qualitative reorganization of the individual's pattern of thought rather than the learning of new content. Each new reorganization integrates within a broader perspective the insights that were achieved at lower stages.
>
> (Colby *et al.* 1983: 1)

In contrast to views of development which stress age-related tasks (for example, Erikson), Kohlberg's theory implies that age may be a less accurate indicator of one's ethical reasoning stage (at least during the adolescent and adult years). Some age-related trends in Kohlberg's scheme do appear, however.

Some twenty-six years before Kohlberg completed his dissertation, Piaget (1932) had suggested that there were just two moralities of justice. Through extensive observations and interviews with children of 'what's fair', Piaget had suggested that shifts in the quality of moral reasoning accompany changes in the stages of cognitive development. A child functioning at the pre-operational level of thought before about 7 years of age evidences a logic of *moral realism*, whereby the rightness of an act is judged in terms of its consequences rather than the intentions of the actor. Piaget often asked questions such as, 'Who is naughtier: John who opens a door and accidentally breaks fifteen cups that were behind the door and that he did not see, or Henry, who tries to sneak some jam out of the cupboard while his mother is out, climbs on a chair, and, in the process, breaks one cup?' A child in the stage of moral realism will reply, 'John, because he broke more cups.' The intentions of the actors are not considered here; only the results of actions matter. At this stage of moral realism rules are also immutable and God-given, or at least handed down by some all-knowing authority. Witness the consternation of any 6-year-old moving to a new school, where the rules of a game may be at considerable variance from those in the preceding locale. The principle of imminent justice haunts the moral realist, as punishment is believed to be forthcoming immediately upon transgression.

Through a transition phase accompanying the shift to concrete operational thought, the young adolescent begins to shift to a stage of *moral relativism*. Appearing more consistently with the acquisition of formal thought during adolescence, the reasoning of the moral relativist not only considers the intentions of the actor but also appreciates that rules are more arbitrary and subject to change upon group consensus. At this stage, Henry becomes the culprit of the earlier dilemma, for his 'less-than-honorable' intentions are weighed against the unintentioned results of John's door-opening behavior. Rules and authority now are also subject to question. The cynical irony of Murphy's law that 'no good deed goes unpunished' can now be appreciated, with the moral relativist's growing awareness that punishment is not inevitable and often escapable.

Upon this Piagetian base, Kohlberg proceeded to develop his evolutionary and revolutionary ideas. He describes the emergence of his research interests as follows:

> As a graduate student planning a study of moral development, [I] knew superego formation was pretty well completed by age 6. As an enthusiastic reader of Piaget, however, [I] knew that the development of autonomous morality was not completed until the advanced age of 12 or 13. To allow for the laggards, [I] decided to include children as old as 16 in a study of the development of moral autonomy. When [I] actually looked at [my] interviews, it dawned on [me] that children had a long way to go beyond Piaget's autonomous stage to reach moral maturity. Accordingly, [I] constructed a six-stage scheme of moral development, a schema in which superego morality was only stage 1 and what Piaget termed autonomous morality was only stage 2.
>
> (Kohlberg and Kramer 1969: 93)

Before detailing Kohlberg's developmental scheme, it must be noted that it is to moral reasoning rather than moral behavior or moral feeling that his research efforts have been addressed. 'I have always tried to be clear that my stages are stages of justice reasoning, not of emotion, aspirations, or actions' (Kohlberg 1984: 224). The complex relationships among these different aspects of morality have been the focus of a host of studies to be discussed in a later section. At this point, we turn to a cognitive-developmental framework for describing moral reasoning, a structural indicator of identity.

MORAL REASONING: ASSESSMENT AND DEVELOPMENT

It is through the reasoning underlying responses to moral dilemmas that Kohlberg has charted the changing bases of moral decision-making. Several problems of justice are addressed by his nine story dilemmas, such as the way in which a community distributes its desirable assets, enters into contracts or agreements, or deals with its offenders. Individuals' reasons behind responses to such dilemmas have been the grist for Kohlberg's theoretical mill, working to process the developmental patterns for this subdomain of ego functioning.

Kohlberg's moral dilemmas all involve conflict – between preserving life or upholding the law, between consideration of extenuating circumstances or punishment, between adhering to authority or upholding a contract. Rather than accepting an individual's 'yes' or 'no' response to the rightness or wrongness of a hypothetical action, he probed extensively the rationale behind responses in order to gauge the structure underlying a subject's moral reasoning. Human life is valued at each stage; however, the way in which it is valued differs. Examples of two of Kohlberg's dilemmas follow:

> In a country in Europe, a poor man named Valjean could find no work, nor could his sister and brother. Without money, he stole food and medicine that they needed. He was captured and sentenced to prison for six years. After a couple of years, he escaped from the prison and went to live in another part of the country under a new name. He saved money and slowly built up a big factory. He gave his workers the highest wages and used most of his profits to build a hospital for people who couldn't afford good medical care. Twenty years had passed when a tailor recognized the factory owner as being Valjean, the escaped convict whom the police had been looking for back in his hometown. Should the tailor report Valjean to the police? Why or why not?

> (Kohlberg 1984: 649)

In this dilemma, the question arises of how a community should deal with its offenders, particularly given the circumstances of Valjean's initial reasons for incarceration as well as his later social contributions.

> Joe is a fourteen-year-old boy who wanted to go to camp very much. His father promised him he could go if he saved up the money for it himself. So Joe worked hard at his paper route and saved up the forty dollars it cost to go to camp, and a little more besides. But just before camp was going to start, his father changed his mind. Some of his friends decided to go on a special fishing trip, and Joe's father was short of the money it would cost. So he told Joe to give him the money he had saved from the paper route. Joe didn't want to give up going to camp, so he thinks of refusing to give his father the money. Should Joe refuse to give his father the money? Why or why not?
>
> (Kohlberg 1984: 643)

In this dilemma, the value of a social contract (a promise) is in conflict with the value of obeying an authority figure. In all dilemmas, additional probing questions – for example, does a good citizen or son have certain duties to perform? Should a lawbreaker be punished if acting out of conscience? Should a promise be kept? – are asked to clarify the logic behind each response.

By extensively questioning an initial sample of eighty-four boys aged 10, 13, and 16 years of age over nine hypothetical dilemmas including those of Valjean and Joe, Kohlberg (1958) attempted to identify the type of reasoning used most frequently by each individual. In so doing, he proposed six hierarchical stages in the development of moral reasoning and continued, with colleagues, to reassess his initial subjects at three-to four-year intervals over the course of twenty years. Results from this longitudinal research have supported the general idea of a developmental hierarchy indicated by his initial scheme (Colby *et al.* 1983).

Kohlberg's hierarchical and invariant stage sequence is comprised of six stages falling into three levels of judgment which reflect the increasing internalization of rules and principles (Kohlberg 1958). Remnants of Piaget's moral realism to moral relativism transition can be seen in the progression from the first to second stages of judgment in Kohlberg's scheme. It is not until the final level of post-conventional moral reasoning that individuals become capable of making moral decisions that are truly their own, unconstrained by self-interest, fear of punishment, the need for another's approval, or the letter of the law. From

Kohlberg's recent longitudinal work, it is sobering that only about 15 per cent of adults at 36 years of age appear to be functioning predominantly at this highest level of reasoning (Colby *et al.* 1983). Indeed, the highest stage (stage 6) within this post-conventional level was dropped from analysis in the twenty-year follow-up, as none of the interviewees were using this mode of reasoning. Let us now return to Shaw's *Major Barbara* to detail Kohlberg's six stages and the types of reasoning used within each.

Level 1: pre-conventional

At this general level, one responds to cultural labels of good or bad, right or wrong, but interprets such labels in the interests of the self. The physical or hedonistic consequences of an action for the self are the prime considerations in moral decision-making, alongside rigid adherence to authority. This level is comprised of two stages.

Stage 1   Heteronomous morality

At this lowest stage of moral reasoning, that which is right or just is that which is in one's own self-interest. Obedience to authority is valued to avoid punishment and achieve self-gratification; the physical consequences of an action to one's own interests determine its 'rightness' or 'wrongness'. This stage is characteristic of reasoning used by children between about 4 and 10 years of age. None of Shaw's late adolescent or adult characters appear to be functioning at this stage.

Stage 2   Individualism, instrumental purpose, and exchange

Here, the respondent holds a one-way concern about another person; another's value is determined by the way in which she can meet the respondent's needs. Still reasoning from a perspective of self-interest, an individual at this stage acknowledges the value of others but does so in a hedonistic way. The needs of another are considered only in so far as they will benefit the stage 2 respondent. 'You scratch my back and I'll scratch yours' rather than a desire for loyalty is the prime motivator here.

At the West Ham shelter of the Salvation Army, a recent 'convert' down on her luck named Rummy Mitchens enters into conversation with a fellow compatriot, Price. Shaw captures the rationale of Rummy's self-interest, characteristic of the stage 2 reasoner, as she offers the Army her soul for salvation in exchange for the bread of survival. Price chides Rummy for her ethical stance:

> *Price:* Oh Rummy, Rummy! Respectable married woman, Rummy, gittin' rescued by the Salvation Army by pretendin' to be a bad un. Same old game!
>
> *Rummy:* What am I to do? I can't starve. Them Salvation Army lasses is dear good girls; but the better you are, the worse they likes to think you were before they rescued you. . . . And where would they get the money to rescue us if we was to let on we're no worse than other people? You know what ladies and gentlemen are.
>
> (Shaw 1966: 30)

Rummy considers another primarily as an agent for meeting her own needs, indicative of stage 2 reasoning.

Level 2: conventional

At this general level, maintaining the expectations of family, social group, or nation as valuable for their own sake, regardless of consequences, is perceived as the 'true morality'. There is a desire here to avoid any disruption to the smooth functioning of social norms, either in the small group or larger legal system. There appears also a need to support and justify these social orders for their own sake. This level usually dominates pre-adolescent, adolescent, and adult thought. Two stages are again present within this general level of moral reasoning.

Stage 3   Mutual interpersonal expectations, relationships, and interpersonal conformity

A concern about conformity to opinions of others and group norms are the motives which drive this stage of moral judgment; the desire to be a 'good boy' or 'nice girl' and to please others characterizes this mode of thought. There is conformity to stereotyped notions of what is 'natural'.

The stage 3 orientation of Shaw's Lady Britomart in an exchange of moral views with husband, Undershaft, is the source of much comedy in Act III. Bound by conformity to social convention and family tradition, Lady Britomart appeals to her husband's sense of familial obligation to make son Stephen his heir:

Lady Britomart: Andrew: this is not a question of our likings and dislikings: it is a question of duty. It is your duty to make Stephen your successor.

Undershaft: Just as much as it is your duty to submit to your husband. Come, Biddy! these tricks of the governing class are of no use with me. I am one of the governing class myself . . . I have the power in this matter; and I am not to be humbugged into using it for your purposes.

(Shaw 1966: 64)

Indeed, Undershaft's power lies in his disembeddedness from the group-orientated, duty-bound, other-pleasing moral logic of his wife.

Stage 4 Social system and conscience

This 'law and order orientation' views right behavior as that which upholds a social system's laws or rules, which are viewed as fixed. Doing one's duty to maintain the social order for its own sake and avoiding a breakdown in the system regardless of consequences is the motivating force behind this stage of reasoning. Here, one often hears cries of 'What would happen if everyone did it?' as a rationale for moral response.

Son Stephen in Shaw's *Major Barbara* is an exemplar of stage 4 morality. His thoughts, cited at the beginning of this chapter, portray a view of morality as black and white, just and unjust. Why 'right is right and wrong is wrong' is the issue which must be addressed to pinpoint Stephen's stage of moral understanding, however. Hints are provided in a statement the young man makes to his father:

Stephen (springing up again): I am sorry, sir, that you force me to forget the respect due to you as my father. I am an Englishman and I will not hear the Government of my country insulted.

(Shaw 1966: 67)

In Stephen, his mother's stage 3 familial duty logic is transcended by a stage 4 need to uphold the government of his nation. Stephen's desire to defend and uphold national rules and values for their own sake arises on several occasions and evidences his law-and-order orientation.

Level 3: post-conventional or principled

At this level, the reasoner is able to define moral values in a manner quite apart from social group conventions or the prevailing legal system. While one may still identify with such systems, they are now considered relative to other possible orders. Morality here is internalized; at this level, one may still be concerned with relationship to the community or one's views of morality may be more individualistic in nature. Two stages are also present within this level.

During the course of *Major Barbara,* Barbara herself undergoes transition from a conventional to a post-conventional level of moral reasoning. Her previous commitment to uphold the heavenly order becomes subsumed under her new commitment to a self-determined code of ethics:

> *Barbara*: I have got rid of the bribe of bread. I have got rid of the bribe of heaven . . . When I die, let him [God] be in my debt, not I in his; and let me forgive him as becomes a woman of my rank.
>
> (Shaw 1966: 89)

Barbara's new-found sense of moral identity comes through her disembeddedness from a context governed by others' rules to a recognition that she now can make them.

Stage 5 Social contract or utility and individual rights

At this stage, one is aware that group values are relative; community norms are now viewed as potentially changeable if warranted. There is a desire to adhere to community rules, but such rules have been critically evaluated by its members prior to commitment. There appears at this stage an emphasis on social order, but on a legal system which is maintained not for its own sake (as in stage 4) but rather in relation to the changing needs of the community. Rules governing the social order are modifiable by mutual consensus. This orientation was present among writers of the United States constitution.

Stage 6 Universal ethical principles

At this stage, that which is right is determined by one's own conscience in accordance with self-chosen ethical principles. Such principles involve an abstract notion of justice and may transcend the written law, if that law is in violation of ethical codes which uphold equality in human rights and a respect for human dignity. At stage 6, a concern for the equality and dignity of each human being is the primary motivating force in the conceptualization of what is just.

In relation to the moral issue of obedience to authority and punishment, these six stages might be summarized with logics as follows:

(i) Obey rules to avoid punishment.
(ii) Conform to obtain rewards, have favors returned, and so on.
(iii) Conform to avoid disapproval, dislike by others.
(iv) Conform to avoid censure by legitimate authorities and resultant gain.
(v) Conform to maintain the respect of the impartial spectator judging in terms of community welfare.
(vi) Conform to avoid self-condemnation.

(Adapted from Kohlberg and Gilligan 1971)

It is important to note here, however, that whether or not one conforms to authority is not that which determines stage placement; only a probing of the logic giving rise to the initial response can illuminate the underlying structure of moral reasoning. Individuals might equally indicate lack of obedience to authority yet present rationales revealing vast differences in underlying stages of moral reasoning.

From Kohlberg's twenty-year longitudinal assessment of moral reasoning development, the great majority of respondents scored at only one stage or at most two adjacent stages over the nine moral dilemmas; only 9 per cent of subjects evidenced a third stage of reasoning in their responses (Colby *et al.* 1983). Furthermore, about 67 per cent of all responses fell within the subject's modal stage, and 32 per cent (almost all) of the remaining responses fell within an adjacent stage. Subjects neither skipped stages nor reverted to the use of a previous stage. These findings are generally consistent with results from earlier administrations and point to a notion of 'structured wholeness' or an underlying logic of moral response to each stage of reasoning. Such findings also support the notion of an invariant stage sequence in the evolution of ideological structure.

Change in one's stage of moral reasoning has been strongly linked to the Piagetian processes of assimilation, accommodation, and equilibrium; furthermore, an individual's mixture of stage responses appears to be a necessary forerunner of change (Turiel 1969, 1974). Kohlberg (1973) and Turiel (1969) have construed moral reasoning development as failure in the process of assimilation. An individual will initially attempt to incorporate a new logic of morality into an existing schema or cognitive structure; when such efforts fail, it becomes necessary to accommodate, to change existing cognitive structures so that a new level of understanding can emerge. When children have been exposed to reasoning one stage beyond their current level of functioning, they often appear capable of perceiving the contrast between the two stages; this awareness, in turn, leads to a state of disequilibrium in cognitive functioning (Turiel 1969). The development of moral reasoning is an ongoing process of re-establishing cognitive equilibrium; such development seems possible only when an individual has already begun to evidence the reasoning of two adjacent stages. Transition to a new stage is not abrupt, but, rather, a slow, gradual process indicated by the increasing frequency of responses at the higher of two adjacent stages. There are, however, vast individual differences in the rate of change and the highest stage an individual reaches during the years after childhood.

Listen now to Major Barbara describe this state of disequilibrium in her transition to a new stage of moral reasoning and its impact on her sense of personal identity:

> *Barbara:* Today I feel – oh! how can I put it into words? . . . I stood on the rock I thought eternal; and without a word of warning it reeled and crumbled under me. I was safe with an infinite wisdom watching me, an army marching to Salvation with me; and in a moment, at a stroke of your pen in a cheque book, I stood alone; and the heavens were empty. . . .
>
> *Undershaft:* Well, you have made for yourself something that you call a morality or a religion or what not. It doesn't fit the facts. Well, scrap it. Scrap it and get one that does fit . . . . Don't persist in that [old] folly. If your old religion broke down yesterday, get a newer and better one for tomorrow.
>
> (Shaw 1966: 80)

For Barbara, the transition phase was not quite as rapid as her extracted statement might indicate, but her words, nevertheless, do portray the experience of transition as she seeks (and eventually finds) a new equilibrium.

Continuing to refine moral reasoning's six stages until the time of his death, Kohlberg has at times suggested the occurrence of additional stages. Kohlberg and Turiel (1971) have suggested the possibility of a 'premoral' stage 0, which precedes stage 1 and is indicated by responses in which the individual neither understands rules or judges good or bad in terms of some higher authority. Additionally, Kohlberg (1973) proposed stage 4½ in an attempt to account for the pattern in early longitudinal data whereby one-fifth of subjects who obtained a stage 4 or 5 modal score during high school seemingly regressed to stage 2 by the second year of university study. Most subjects had returned to stage 4 or 5 by the age of 25. Stage 4½ was intended to reflect a transitional state in the movement from conventional to principled moral reasoning, rather than a 'real' structural regression in level of response. Kohlberg (1973, 1984) has also postulated a seventh stage of reasoning, in which the question, 'Why be moral in a universe filled with injustice and suffering?' is addressed; transition to stage 7 involves a shift from the universal humanistic orientation of stage 6 to a cosmic perspective. Kohlberg continued speculation on the metaphysical features that might characterize a seventh stage throughout his career. Efforts to rescore Kohlberg's longitudinal data with a new Standard Issue Scoring manual have been made; this scoring system allows the assignment of a more exact dilemma score tapping qualitatively different structures rather than more superficial content differences. This new system has continued to identify the original six stages of moral reasoning, though a downward revision of initial principled reasoning scores has occurred. Furthermore, virtually all regression anomalies in earlier data accompanying the transition from stage 4 to stage 5 have disappeared with the more refined scoring system along with responses characterizing stage 6 (Colby *et al.* 1987).

During the early, middle, and late adolescent years, in which stage of moral development might we expect to find most youths reasoning and responding? From Kohlberg's Standard Issues Scoring system used in his twenty-year longitudinal research, stage 5 scores did not rise beyond 15 per cent of total sample scores even as late as age 36; the percentage of those reaching at least the 4/5 transition during mid-adulthood was only 16 per cent. Even under the original scoring system only about 30 per cent of subjects used stage 5 reasoning at the age of 16 (Kohlberg and Kramer 1969). It appears from the recent work of Kohlberg and his associates that conventional reasoning is the predominant mode of adolescent thought on issues of justice; this level also predominates during the young adult years that follow (Colby *et al.* 1983).

AN OPTIMAL LEVEL OF MORAL REASONING

In preceding chapters it has been possible to address the question of what constitutes a healthy identity. For structural theorists such as Kohlberg, however, this question is inappropriate. A focus on the health or pathology of identity must give way here to the concept of development, the stage at which an individual is currently functioning in his or her own evolution. Although Kohlberg believes it is possible and justifiably good to advance one's stage of moral reasoning to a more mature form, the question of health versus illness is not an issue.

Research by Turiel (1966) has indicated that it appears possible to advance one's moral reasoning one stage beyond the present stage of functioning. It has also become apparent that children and adolescents actually prefer a more advanced over a less advanced stage of reasoning (Rest *et al.* 1969). Given that stage advancement is possible, what might Kohlberg regard as the goal for adolescent development within this moral subdomain of ego functioning? Time has brought changes to his views on this issue.

Kohlberg (1980b) traced the development of his own thinking on the aim of educating adolescents for a just society. His first public lecture on the topic was given in 1968 (shortly after the death of Martin Luther King) and called for the promotion of a stage 6 level of morality in which education should aim to cultivate respect for human dignity and universal principles of justice and equity. However, the 1960s, it seemed, 'were no more safe for stage 6 exemplars than was Socrates' Athens' (Kohlberg 1980b: 456). A 1976 bicentennial lecture brought revision to Kohlberg's vision, in which he now called for schools to make the world safe for stage 5 morality (that social contract orientation which still purports the rights of individuals).

> Empirical research between 1968 and 1976 did not confirm my theoretical statements about a sixth and highest stage. . . . My longitudinal subjects, still adolescents in 1968, had come to adulthood by 1976, but none had reached the sixth stage. Perhaps all the sixth stage persons of the 1960s had been wiped out, perhaps they had regressed, or maybe it was all my imagination in the first place.
>
> (Kohlberg 1980b: 457)

However, at that time he recognized stage 5 morality to be in some danger also, possessed by only a minority. (Indeed, a United States majority votes down the Bill of Rights presented each year as an unlabeled proposition in the Gallup poll.) Principled moral reasoners seemed to be falling by the wayside. By 1980, Kohlberg was advocating a further retrenchment to a view that stage 4 was the most appropriate goal of civic education. With the 'me generation' of the late 1970s' United States and its stage 2 narcissistic morality, Kohlberg's hope was that adolescents might come at least to function in a rule-governed school environment which would prepare the way for their participation as future citizens in upholding a larger social order. His hope also was an exposure to and eventual appreciation of fifth stage principles of constitutional democracy. Thus, Kohlberg's initial vision of a population's moral logic based on principles of universal justice and equality at the close of adolescence has been replaced by the hope that most adolescents can at least become capable of adhering to legal norms which govern their societies, with a possible glimpse of the social democratic mode of thought.

CRITICISM OF KOHLBERG'S CONSTRUCT

Two general streams of criticism have been directed at Kohlberg's work. One has raised questions of methodology and the second, conceptual problems and use of the theory. Often described as intuitive rather than empirical, Kohlberg's original scoring system has come under much criticism (Rubin and Trotter 1977; Kurtines and Greif 1974). Imprecise instructions coupled with non-standard administration procedures and lack of reliability (consistency over time) were all problems raised with Kohlberg's early work. This outcry from critics has been responsible for the more clearly defined Standard Issue Scoring procedure mentioned in the preceding section. Rest (1979b) has developed another widely used assessment alternative called the Defining Issues Test (DIT); based on Kohlberg's scheme, the DIT uses a multiple-choice format that can be objectively scored. Further methodological criticisms (which the new scoring procedures do not rectify) have questioned the validity of moral stages based on dilemmas far removed from the 'real life' experiences of most individuals, the use of male characters as central agents of dilemmas for testing female subjects, and cultural bias in the value conflicts addressed by dilemmas, particularly in those societies where human life is not sacrosanct (Kurtines and Greif 1974; Gilligan 1982a; Simpson 1974).

Among conceptual critics have been Gilligan (1982a), Sullivan (1977), Simpson (1974), Kegan (1986b), and more recently Haaré (1987) and Keller et al. (1989); each has addressed different aspects of the assumptions underlying Kohlberg's scheme. Perhaps one of the more popularized critics has been Carol Gilligan, with her plea that women's voices need to be heard in the creation of theories addressing personality development. Gilligan has suggested that morality really involves two different types of orientations: one, a justice and equality perspective (addressed by Piaget and Kohlberg), and the second, an ethic of care and responsibility towards others. Both perspectives are used in the moral decision-making process by both men and women; however, men are far more likely to give responses based on the justice perspective that emphasizes separation and autonomy, while women's responses are more characterized by care and concern for others.

Women not only define themselves in a context of human relationships, but judge themselves in terms of their ability to care. . . . When [moral] maturity is . . . equated with personal autonomy, concern with relationships appears as a weakness of women rather than a human strength. I first became aware of this bias while teaching with Kohlberg in an undergraduate course at Harvard on moral and political choice. Observing that more women than men were dropping Kohlberg's course, I suggested interviewing several of the female dropouts in depth. When I read the transcripts, I was puzzled by what I found. These women were experiencing moral conflicts that simply could not be understood within Kohlberg's framework.

(Gilligan 1982b: 68)

Gilligan's work has sparked studies into the different types of responses most characteristic of each of the two sexes (see recent reviews by Walker 1989, 1991). Lyons (1983) has found that there are two distinct modes of describing the self in relation to others – a separate/objective mode as well as one of connectedness; considerations of justice and care were used by both self–other relationship modes to make moral decisions. Both sexes defined themselves in relation to others with equal frequency; however, men used the separate/objective mode more often, while women made greater use of the connectedness style.

Gilligan, herself, has proposed a three-level alternative to Kohlberg's scheme in which emphasis on the needs of the self (level 1) gives way to a focus on the needs of others (level 2), finally to be balanced at level 3 with a concern for the needs of both self and others (Gilligan 1982a). These levels were based on a study of women in the actual process of making an abortion decision, rather than on responses to hypothetical story dilemmas. At level 1, women in Gilligan's sample considered the possibility of abortion in terms of self-interest alone. Factors such as not having to be lonely and the excitement and novelty of having a baby were weighed against giving up personal freedoms and enduring possible financial hardship; whatever issues were considered, self-interest was the prime motivator. At level 2, issues were reconsidered solely in terms of one's responsibility to others. The ramifications of an abortion to the unborn child, partner, other relations and friends were considered at the exclusion of one's own needs and interests. At level 3, these two earlier ways of reasoning were brought into balance, and the abortion decision was based on consideration of one's own circumstances as well as the impact of the abortion on others. As for Kohlberg's moral dilemmas, it was the reasoning process rather than the decision itself which gave evidence to an underlying stage of development.

In additional work, Pollack and Gilligan (1982, 1983, 1985) have found sex differences in the incidence and distribution of violence on Thematic Apperception Test (TAT) stories written by university students. They conclude that men tend to associate danger with intimacy while women associate danger with isolation, further supporting Gilligan's claim to sex differences in orientation to social relations and the need to hear women's voices in theories of personality. A review by Walker (1984), addressing the question of possible male sex bias in Kohlberg's original theory, has found, however, only eight of 108 studies supporting such a claim. More recent work (see Walker 1989, 1991) has similarly failed to demonstrate sex differences in moral orientations. Gilligan (1985) argues that her thesis does not suggest sex differences in the ways men and women will respond in Kohlberg's stage scheme but rather stresses the need to *hear* another moral orientation (care) in understanding the development of moral logic. In reply, Kohlberg (1984) does not feel that Gilligan's own data adequately support her claim for a different voice. Most recently, Gilligan has indicated that she believes that her sequence complements that of Kohlberg's rather than that it should be considered an alternative model (Gilligan and Attanucci 1988). Although Kohlberg and Gilligan have plotted developmental sequences that parallel each other in many ways, Gilligan does not share Kohlberg's view that development is driven primarily by cognitive and biological maturation for both sexes. Rather, Gilligan (1989) believes that the development of moral reasoning for girls lies in response to a social crisis – that of finding their own voices in contexts which will hear them. Brown and Gilligan (1992) argue that in order to live in contemporary culture, girls at the precipice of adolescence often lose their vitality, their resilience, their sense of themselves and their character to enter adolescence and meet the social expectations for women in their contexts. Gilligan and her colleagues have advocated greater use of a relational model for identifying self and the moral voices of care and justice, particularly for girls on the verge of adolescence (Brown *et al.* 1991).

Sullivan (1977) has argued that Kohlberg's theory is a style of thinking rooted in socio-historical circumstance and not capable of portraying a universal and timeless experience, while Simpson (1974) argues that Kohlberg's stages are not culturally universal. Sullivan has been particularly critical of Kohlberg's conception of stage 6 reasoning as a parochial rather than universally accurate model of a moral being; the stage is abstract and formal and ignores the moral significance of one's ties to the community. Taking a different tack on a similar theme, Simpson has argued that an insufficiently large number of cultures have been studied for the claim of universality to be made. Furthermore, the lack of post-conventional reasoning found in all the cultures Kohlberg has studied also undermines such claims. Kohlberg (1984) disputes the latter argument with recent supportive evidence from a variety of cultural settings. In numerous samples from both western and non-western cultures, stage 5 reasoning has been reasonably well represented. In a recent major review of the issue of cultural diversity on claims of universality, Boyes and Walker (1988) have found that Kohlberg's developmental stage model does hold universally and that the theory does reflect much of what is morally relevant in different cultural settings; however, evidence also indicates that the theory misses or misconstrues some important moral concepts from several different cultures (for example, the concept of harmony in Confucian morality).

Haaré (1987: 220) indicates that a culture may contain a 'multiplicity of interacting, overlapping and complementary moral orders', and that different social contexts hold different systems for defining appropriate moral response. He believes Kohlberg's stage structures simply define different moral orders, none any better or more complex than any other. Thus, to Haaré, the audience to whom moral judgments are directed define the moral order; there is no developmental stage sequence which defines moral response.

Keller *et al.* (1989) have argued that early (pre-conventional) stages of moral reasoning need rethinking. From major reviews of research on children's empathy and pro-social moral reasoning, Eisenberg and Strayer (1987) and Eisenberg and Mussen (1989) have noted that young children's reasoning about their own pro-social behavior contains a good deal of empathic references to other's needs. Keller *et al.* have also completed a review finding interpersonal concerns of young children to be very much in evidence and not based exclusively on punishment and obedience (stage 1) and instrumental orientations (stage 2). Furthermore, qualitative analyses of children's responses in one study undertaken by Keller *et al.* could not be matched to criterion judgments in the Standard Issue Scoring manual.

Kegan (1986b) believes that Kohlberg does not fully recognize the implications of his own work for an understanding of the structure and nature of identity. In fact, Kegan suggests that the development of knowing in the realm of moral reasoning is not the *consequence* of development, but rather is itself the very *process* of psychobiological development.

Although Kohlberg's stages can be easily (and completely misguidedly) caricatured into Sunday-supplement, pop-psychology personality types, the 'stuff' of a given stage is actually no particular content, experience, motive, style, or attitude at all, but something quite abstract, a structure or underlying logic giving form to a person's experiences, motives, attitudes.

(Kegan 1986: 167)

Remarks of Snarey *et al.* (1983) on the relationship between moral development and other developmental substrands of ego functioning are less insightful, in Kegan's view, than that which can be inferred from Kohlberg's research efforts. Kohlberg, he believes, has uncovered a way to tap personality organization at the very root of moral meaning-making. That organization constitutes the very form (rather than content) of one's existence, the form of one's evolving self. The implications of this criticism will be discussed in detail in Chapter 6.

RESEARCH FINDINGS ON THE DEVELOPMENT OF MORAL REASONING

Kohlberg's enormous contributions to our understanding of the development of moral reasoning have generated myriads of studies addressing various aspects of the process. For the purposes of this chapter, the focus will be on the following issues as they affect adolescents in the process of identity formation: the universal and invariant sequence of moral reasoning stages including age and sex related trends, personality variables associated with moral development stages, and the relationship between moral reasoning and moral behavior. You are referred to the three-volume series edited by Kurtines and Gewirtz (1991a,b, and c) for a more thorough review of issues springing from Kohlberg's moral development scheme.

Kohlberg (1969) has claimed his stages to be culturally universal and added further fuel to the fire from critics by advocating that lack of exposure to role-taking opportunities stifles moral development for those growing up in pre-literate and semi-literate cultures. Even with more recent cross-cultural studies which have overcome some methodological problems inherent in his early work, Kohlberg's highest stages have been consistently missing or infrequent in settings which do not encourage discussion or debate of moral issues (Edwards 1986; Snarey 1985; Snarey and Keljo 1991). It must be noted, however, that research on moral reasoning among adolescents in hunter-gatherer cultures which lack social class structure and formal political systems and in complex nation-states such as those of Eastern Europe still remains to be done. Snarey (1985) identifies major empirical assumptions underlying Kohlberg's claims and finds striking cross-cultural empirical support for the invariance of stage sequence and the existence of the full range of stages; major cautions regarding the range and general applicability of stages across cultures are also noted, based on a review of some forty-five studies of moral reasoning conducted in various cultural settings. From longitudinal and cross-sectional data obtained in twenty-seven countries, stages 1 to 4 were virtually universal; stage 5, though rare in all populations, was evident in two-thirds of subcultures which included adults in the sample. However, evidence for post-conventional reasoning was found only in urban cultural groups or middle-class populations and was absent from folk cultures. Snarey argues that Kohlberg's stage scheme and scoring system may misinterpret the presence of higher stages of reasoning in some cultural groups.

With information now accumulated from the Americas, Asia, Africa, Europe and the Pacific, it appears that moral stage development is stimulated by three conditions:

(1) an individual's contact with a *diversity of personal or cultural values;* (2) an individual's ability to reason in formal or school-like ways about moral issues; and (3) an individual's tendency to *take as one's reference group a complex society.*

(Edwards 1986: 427)

If these conditions are met, advancement to higher stages of moral reasoning is more likely to occur, regardless of cultural setting. However, some cultures may not find post-conventional logic to be relevant or appropriate to their value systems.

A number of cross-sectional and longitudinal studies have addressed Kohlberg's claim of an irreversible and invariant stage sequence in the development of moral reasoning; virtually all have found an increase in more advanced stages of reasoning associated with increasing age – to a point. With few exceptions, all have also indicated a lack of any major regression over time (Edwards 1986; Snarey 1985; Colby and Kohlberg 1987; Walker 1989). From Kohlberg's own work, moral judgments become more advanced with increasing age for pre-adolescents and adolescents in industrialized western nations, regardless of social class or sex (Kohlberg 1958, 1969). In his twenty-year longitudinal follow-up, the use of stages 1 and 2 decreased markedly from age 10, while stage 5 did not appear until the age of 20 and was not a stage attained by more than about 10 per cent of the sample beyond that time (Colby *et al.* 1983). Furthermore, no cross-sectional or longitudinal studies have found any stages to be 'missing' within the sample's age range (Edwards 1986). On the question of sex differences in stage acquisition, the only research showing consistent results of difference are with adults; however, such sex differences have disappeared when education level and job status have been controlled (Kohlberg 1984). Strong evidence exists for the claim to an irreversible and invariant stage sequence, particularly with the Standard Issue Scoring procedure (Walker 1989).

Family and personality variables associated with stages of moral reasoning have been explored in numerous investigations. Speicher (1992) has examined the relationship between adolescent moral judgment and perceptions of family interaction. Her findings show a consistent relationship between adolescent moral judgment and reports of positive intrafamilial relationships and cognitive stimulation of moral reasoning. Similarly, Kennedy *et al.* (1988) have examined adolescents' perceptions of family interaction patterns in relation to their own moral reasoning and interpersonal cognitive problem-solving skills; adolescents who perceived parents to be high on personal growth and system maintenance dimensions had more advanced scores on both moral reasoning and problem-solving tasks.

Research based on the work of Piaget, Erikson, Loevinger, and Kohlberg suggest strong interrelationships between the processes of cognitive functioning, identity formation, ego development, and moral reasoning. Numerous results have pointed to a link between the use of formal operational thought and the use of more advanced stages of moral reasoning (for example, Carroll and Rest 1982; Tomlinson-Keasey and Keasey 1974; Walker 1980). What has also emerged from such work is the finding that cognitive level appears as a necessary but not sufficient condition for one's mode of moral reasoning. In other words, one must generally attain formal operational thought to be able to reason at post-conventional levels; however, attaining formal operations does not necessarily ensure that one will use post-conventional reasoning in making moral decisions.

Measures of identity status based on Erikson's framework and ego development using Loevinger's model have also shown strong links with stage of moral reasoning. Podd (1972) presented evidence from work with late adolescent males to show a strong relationship between identity status and moral logic; identity achievement subjects used post-conventional reasoning, while pre-conventional and transitional moral reasoning was used most frequently by diffusions. Numerically, more subjects classed as foreclosed were using conventional modes of moral logic, though such results did not differ statistically from other identity statuses. Work by Hult (1979) and Rowe and Marcia (1980) has produced similar results. Skoe and Diessner (1994) have used Skoe's (1993) newly developed, care-based measure of moral reasoning to find a strong relationship between moral reasoning, ego identity status and Kohlberg's moral judgment interview. One conclusion from Skoe's research is that an ethic of care plays a role in identity development for men and women, but that the care ethic may be more important to women than men in terms of identity development. '[G]ender differences in psychosocial development are more subtle and complex than simple main effects in response to standardized dilemmas' (Skoe and Diessner 1994: 285). From Loevinger's stage sequence in the development of the ego, longitudinal research has also indicated links between current stage of ego structure and that of moral reasoning; however, ego stage in early adolescence has not been able to predict a later stage of moral reasoning (Gfellner 1986b; Kitchener *et al.* 1984).

The relationship between moral reasoning and moral behavior is complex and has raised some interesting questions. A review by Blasi (1980) has indicated that there does seem to be a fairly strong correlation between stage of moral reasoning and type of moral action. The question of what constitutes a virtuous moral act, however, has generated much debate and obviously is crucial to define before addressing any relationship between the two variables. According to Kohlberg, the definition of a moral act must include the actor's conception of right action and judgment of responsibility to perform the act. In other words, one who acts morally, 'practices what she preaches'. Considerable evidence from the literature does support the closeness of association between judgment and action; as one develops towards higher modes of moral logic, one's actions become more 'moral' (in reflecting a concern for basic human rights) and are more likely to take place. For example, Krebs and Rosenwald (1979) found moral stage to predict very accurately the likelihood that a subject would return a questionnaire if a verbal commitment to do so had been made. Nelson *et al.* (1990) found the moral reasoning of adolescent delinquents to be significantly lower relative to that of non-delinquents. One very thorough investigation by Haan *et al.* (1968) arose from the naturalistic setting provided by the Berkeley Free Speech Movement. Questioning subjects as to their activities during the demonstrations as well as administering Kohlberg's moral dilemmas, those individuals within each of Kohlberg's three moral decision-making levels evidenced very distinctive behaviors. More than half of all subjects reasoning at the lowest and highest levels participated in sit-ins and were often arrested; by contrast, only 11 per cent of subjects at the conventional level took part in the sit-ins. With a recent re-analysis of these data using the

Standard Issue Scoring system, however, a monotonic pattern emerged; that is, 'at each higher stage of moral reasoning represented in the sample, a greater proportion of subjects sat-in' (Candee and Kohlberg 1987: 554). In general, recent studies of moral judgment and action have indicated reasonably consistently a monotonic relationship between moral reasoning and moral action (Kutnick 1986).

Current directions in moral development research

Research aimed at refining Kohlberg's theoretical formulations continues. Questions concerning the relationship between hypothetical moral dilemmas and moral judgments made in typical everyday life situations are currently being explored by a number of researchers (for example, Skoe and Gooden 1993; Krebs *et al.* 1991; Carpendale and Krebs 1992). Krebs' work demonstrates that, although moral judgments are structured in terms of Kohlberg's stages, people use different structures to respond to different types of situations. People do not always respond at their highest level of moral competences; rather, there appears to be a wide range of within-person stage usage. Social situation may play a more important role in stage utilization than the constructivist model of Colby and Kohlberg suggests. Gilligan *et al.* (1990) furthermore show how moral reasoning in real-life contexts relies on cognitive structures other than those based solely on formal operational logic. The relationship between Kohlberg's theory of moral development and moral motivation is currently being explored by Blasi (1990). Questions regarding the relationship between moral judgment, action, and development are being refined by Turiel (1990), who believes that Kohlberg's almost exclusive emphasis on moral aspects of social interactions kept him from addressing other important social domains that may be related to moral action. Enquiries into how people acquire their moral goals, how goals change and grow over the years, and how people sustain their faith and certainty in the face of serious difficulties have been the subject of recent qualitative studies by Colby and Damon (1992). Many questions remain to be explored in understanding the development and demonstration of moral maturity and the process of change. Darley (1993) suggests a return to basic questions of what issues people consider to be moral issues (or what domains do we regard as being domains of morality), what are the sources for people of moral imperatives, and how are internal representations of moral rules coded in an array of different cultural settings. He argues that Kohlberg's legacy can be best respected by considering the conditions that arise from the moral problem or question at hand rather than automatically assuming an analysis of moral reasoning provides the correct approach.

IMPLICATIONS FOR SOCIAL RESPONSE

Kohlberg himself devoted enormous energy to researching the implications of his moral reasoning stage scheme for social response. 'My own interest in morality and moral education arose in part as a response to the Holocaust, an event so enormous that it often fails to provoke a sense of injustice in many societies' (Kohlberg 1981: 407). The field of education has been the greatest beneficiary of Kohlberg's efforts at application. Although some might argue that the family would provide the best target for intervention, studies addressing family correlates of moral stage development do not support such a view; it seems that conditions for moral development within the home, school, and wider community are similar and that the educational system offers an opportunity equaling that of the family for facilitating moral reasoning development (Kohlberg and Wasserman 1980: 562).

Kohlberg (1980a) has outlined what he believes to be basic requirements for an approach to moral education. Such intervention must meet the following prerequisites:

> (a) of being based on the psychological and sociological facts of moral development, (b) of involving educational methods of stimulating moral change, which have demonstrated long-range efficacy, (c) of being based on a philosophically defensible concept of morality, and (d) of being in accord with a constitutional system guaranteeing freedom of belief.
>
> (1980a: 17)

Kohlberg's care in stating the foundations for his proposed educational interventions are intended to bring to light what he regards as two very dangerous and destructive avenues to moral education operative in the majority of US schools – the 'hidden curriculum' and the 'bag of virtues' approaches.

The 'hidden curriculum' approach refers to the unconscious shaping of children's moral attitudes by teachers and schools unaware of their roles in moral education – without explicitly stating, discussing, and formulating their educational purposes and practices. 'The *hidden curriculum* refers to the implicit values governing rewards, discipline, grading, and teacher–student interaction in the school' (Kohlberg and Wasserman 1980: 559). Kohlberg cites a conversation with his young son to illustrate the subtle yet powerful impact of the hidden curriculum:

> For example, my second-grade son one day told me that he did not want to be one of the bad boys in school, and when asked 'who are the bad boys?' he replied 'the ones who don't put their books back where they belong.' His teacher would probably be surprised to know that her trivial classroom management concerns defined for children what she and her school thought were basic moral values, and that as a result she was unconsciously miseducating them morally.
>
> (1980a: 18)

Even the hidden curriculum of Neill's liberal Summerhill does not escape Kohlberg's attack; at Summerhill, unquestioning loyalty to the school, to the collective is the unstated yet determining force guiding the school's socialization of students.

The second, 'bag of virtues' tack is an explicit moral education; here the school clearly dictates values it regards as 'right', and the institution proceeds to instill such beliefs in its young and captive audiences. For example, children attending such schools are commonly taught that the practice of certain 'virtues' will bring happiness, good fortune, and good repute forever more. The problem with such 'character building' programs is that reality does not abide by such rules. Kohlberg (1981) points to the fate dealt virtuous Charlie Brown, captured in the theme song of his show, 'You're a Good Man, Charlie Brown'. Charlie Brown, it seems, has a character of innumerable virtues – humility, nobility, cheerfulness, bravery, courtesy, and honor, with a heart of gold to boot; in short, here is the embodiment of all the noble qualities one could imagine wrapped up in one small, boy-shaped package – if only Charlie Brown weren't so 'wishy-washy'! Kohlberg argues that a 'bag of virtues' approach to moral education, in which aims are taught as virtues and vices through the praise and blame of others, produces youngsters like Charlie Brown – a wishy-washy mix of all things to all people with no sense of an autonomous self.

Kohlberg defines his alternative goals of moral education in the statement below:

> Following Dewey and Piaget, I shall argue that the goal of moral education is the stimulation of the 'natural' development of the individual child's own moral judgment and capacities, thus allowing him to use his own moral judgment to control his behavior. The attractiveness of defining the goal of moral education as the

stimulation of development rather than as the teaching of fixed rules stems from the fact that it involves aiding the child to take the next step in a direction toward which he is already tending, rather than imposing an alien pattern upon him.

(Kohlberg 1980a: 72)

The ultimate aim of Kohlberg's moral education, that of advancement to higher stages of moral reasoning, is the only type of moral education which does not violate a young person's moral freedom; it is the only approach respecting individual autonomy and rejecting indoctrination. Implicit in this educational goal is the principle and promotion of a self-determined identity. To the question of parental rights in objecting to the teaching of values other than their own, Kohlberg replies, 'Respect for the parents' rights [in this case] is not respect for the child's autonomy, a more legitimate concern' (Kohlberg 1980a: 74).

With the foundations of Blatt's (1969) and Turiel's (1966) work, it has become clear that advance to a higher stage of moral reasoning is possible to induce; this process, however, involves not simply a matter of adding more information but rather providing conditions that will facilitate a qualitative reorganization of moral reasoning structure. The first 'Kohlbergian' moral education program consisted of introducing hypothetical moral dilemmas into the classroom for discussion (Higgins 1991). Activities such as debates and challenging discussions with teachers, parents, and peers as well as role-taking activities all become potential sources of disequilibrium and possible catalysts for movement to a more advanced mode of reasoning. It is only through such destabilization that new and higher stages of orientations to justice can occur.

From the research of Kohlberg and associates (Colby *et al.* 1977), several concrete steps appear necessary to facilitate moral reasoning development in such programs of moral education. The first involves that of developmental match. Teachers or counselors must begin by carefully listening to the moral judgments and ideas actually being expressed by individual youths under their supervision. An accurate assessment of a young person's current stage of moral logic is critical to further intervention. Once a student's present stage of moral reasoning has been discerned, teachers then present arguments drawing from the *next* higher stage of reasoning.

Our experiments have indicated that students understand not more than one stage above their own, and they reject reasoning at all stages below their own. Accordingly, a stage 3 student may induce movement in a stage 2 student by dialogue, whereas the reverse does not occur.

(Kohlberg 1975: 254)

An atmosphere of openness and exchange is essential to this change process. Through such activities as moral discussions, classroom debates, and opportunities for role play, one is exposed to ideas and situations that pose contradictions to one's present mode of cognitive functioning, creating a state of disequilibrium and dissatisfaction with the old structure. A school counselor relates her personal experiences about the impact of such a moral education program at her school:

> I had many unanswered questions [prior to the program]. Why were the students in my peer counseling seminar so tuned into their own needs that they found it difficult to help others in a sustained effort? Why did large group school meetings about serious events like stealing produce little student concern beyond telling victims not to bring anything of real value to school? Why did huge efforts toward creating a functioning, effective school government prove unsuccessful?
>
> What the cognitive-developmental approach to moral education offers me and other counselors is a framework for understanding 'where students are' rather than imposing some predetermined theory onto the content of the individual, class, or group discussion .... Understanding the research on moral education interventions gives the counselor a guide for structuring experimental activities to aid students in their development and for creating a school environment characterized by the conditions for moral growth.
>
> (Kohlberg and Wasserman 1980: 564)

Such programs for moral education have been implemented in a number of educational environments. Blatt and Kohlberg (1975) report results of teacher-led discussions about moral dilemmas in four classrooms of early and mid-adolescents over the course of one term. Students' moral stages were assessed and the teacher then began systematically introducing dilemmas and supporting arguments at a stage one step beyond that of lowest-functioning students. As such arguments became comprehensible to these students, the process was repeated so that all class members were exposed to reasoning one stage beyond that used initially. At the term's end, significant changes in stage of moral reasoning had occurred; one-quarter to one-half of those in these classrooms increased their mode of moral reasoning by one stage, while essentially no change had occurred for control classes, who received no such teacher-induced intervention. Furthermore, change for the experimental group was maintained over a period of at least one year. Later work by Colby *et al.* (1977) obtained similar results with larger samples of adolescents. An additional important point that emerged from this latter study was a suggestion that age (length of time at a particular stage of reasoning) may be related to the potential for change.

> We interpret this interaction as an indication that it may be easier to stimulate development in children who have been at a particular moral judgment stage some intermediate length of time than in those who have just entered a new stage or those who have remained at the same stage beyond some optimal period.
>
> (Colby *et al.* 1977: 102)

There may be an optimal period for change to the next stage of moral reasoning. This result warrants further research. Regardless of an adolescent's social class, intelligence, social and verbal skills, over forty studies of such educational interventions have demonstrated effectiveness in advancing the development of moral reasoning for participants (Leming 1986). Change has been demonstrated to hold up over at least a one-year interval and moral discussions led by students have shown to be as effective as teacher-led discussions in promoting stage advancement (Higgins 1991).

However, recent self-destructive actions such as drug usage in the day-to-day lives of many adolescents caused Kohlberg to shift to a broader and potentially more forceful vision of moral education in the late 1970s. The moral atmospheres of social institutions and their impact on moral development have now become the focus of more recent writings on moral education. Institutional climates may stimulate or retard moral growth (Jennings and Kohlberg 1983; Higgins 1991). Rules, norms, and justice structures within educational or other community institutions have their own stage of morality (as judged by a majority of participants). Furthermore, such moral atmospheres are capable of advancing over time. A 'just community' alternative high-school program was found to develop to a higher stage as judged by community participants (Leming 1986). Social role-taking opportunities provided by such organizations as well as the level of justice within that setting are directly related to one's stage of moral reasoning; a higher stage of institutional justice appears to be a condition for an individual's development to a more advanced understanding of justice (Leming 1986). Thus, community settings responsible for the welfare of adolescents may do much to facilitate the development of moral identity by, themselves, operating according to principles inherent in advanced levels of moral decision-making. This new and broader 'just community' perspective on moral education has been the focus for much recent research and discussion. Findings such as the following illustrate the critical importance of community climate in facilitating or arresting moral reasoning development:

> Since normal moral reasoning development seems to advance about one-half stage every 3 years (Colby and Kohlberg 1987) the lack of a moral culture in the large high schools actually seemed to be a drag on the development of their students, locking them into preconventional or early conventional thinking throughout their high school tenure.

> (Higgins 1991: 132)

Ultimately, Kohlberg extended his 'just community' interests beyond the school and began to use real-life dilemmas in prison settings (Hickey and Scharf 1980). Here, too, efforts to advance moral reasoning and create a more just and concerned community have been demonstrated.

SUMMARY

Kohlberg has viewed the development of moral reasoning as qualitative change, occurring in a universal, hierarchical, and invariant sequence of six stages by which one resolves moral conflict. Although Kohlberg does not directly address the formation of identity, he views the development of moral reasoning as one aspect of ego functioning. Kohlberg's stages, strongly related to indexes of cognitive development, identity formation, ego development, and moral behavior, reflect the increasing internalization of rules and principles. Kohlberg's twenty-year longitudinal study indicates that conventional reasoning dominates adolescent and adult modes of moral decision-making. It is possible to induce stage advancement by exposing adolescents to role models, debates and discussions, or institutional climates reflecting a mode of reasoning one step higher than their present stage of functioning.

5 Ego development in adolescence
Loevinger's paradigm

Since I cannot remain sane without the sense of 'I', I am driven to do
almost anything to acquire this sense. Behind the intense passion for
status and conformity is this very need . . . people are willing to risk
their lives, to give up their love, to surrender their freedom, to sacrifice
their own thoughts for the sake of being one of the herd, of conform-
ing, and thus of acquiring a sense of identity, even though it is an
illusory one.

(*Erich Fromm,* The Sane Society)

Erich Fromm (1955) has pointed out that we, as human beings, are the
only animals capable of saying 'I' and thus being aware of ourselves as
separate entities. He also adds that we are the only species finding our
own existences a problem, presenting an inescapable demand for attention. Looking at the development of the human race, Fromm sees that
the degree to which we are aware of ourselves as separate beings depends upon the degree to which we have emerged from the clan. In the
medieval world, feudal lords and peasants were identified with their
social roles in a hierarchy. One was not a person who happened to be a
peasant; rather, one *was* his or her social station, thereby obtaining a
definition of 'I'. When, however, this social system broke down so that
'lords' and 'peasants' were no more, our forebears had a problem. A
response to self-definition other than through prescribed roles became
necessary, and the Renaissance brought great opportunities and new-
found freedoms for individuals to create their own, unique personal
identities. Over the next few centuries, however, people gradually
found many different substitutes to solve the riddle of the 'I', for the
act of self-definition did require some effort. Indeed, by the early twentieth century in the western world, totalitarian regimes were often welcomed; the thought did occur to some observers that maybe human
nature was not really all that averse to tyranny after all – at least the

problem of identity was averted. Indeed, Fromm (1955: 63) sees self-definition through such identity substitutes as nationality, religion, and social class to be 'the formulae which help a man [and woman] experience a sense of identity after the original clan identity has disappeared and before a truly individual sense of identity has been acquired'. While no longer maintaining feudal structures, we nevertheless find identifications with social roles to be convenient, and conformity to norms of the surrounding clan is often the means by which the riddle of the 'I' is bypassed. Jane Loevinger (1976) offers us a hierarchical vision of solutions to the problem of 'I' in her model of ego development. Like Fromm, she finds conformity to be the most common means by which late adolescents and adults deal with the problem of identity; unlike Fromm, she bases this conclusion on data supplied by thousands of respondents.

In contrast to most other identity theorists described in this volume, Loevinger's model has arisen from an empirical base of evidence. Whereas other writers on identity have initially looked to theory for guidance in their construction of an identity paradigm, Loevinger's model has been derived from statistical analysis of empirical data; paradigm revision for Loevinger has occurred in response to anomalies in the data themselves. While some have argued that Loevinger has not constructed an explanatory theory of identity development, she has been one of the few social scientists studying identity to generate her claims from a solid, empirical base.

Also in contrast to Blos and Kohlberg described in previous chapters, Loevinger postulates an ego more holistic in form; ego, to this social scientist, assumes a meaning markedly different from that understood by psychoanalytic ego psychologists and some cognitive-developmental theorists. Rather than *having* a collection of functions such as reality-testing and impulse control, the ego to Loevinger *is* the 'master trait of personality', the frame around which the tent-like canvas of personality is stretched, the basis of identity. Furthermore, the ego, according to Loevinger, is a structure which develops over time, not necessarily bounded by tasks related to chronological age; though adolescents and adults will most frequently find their solutions to the meaning of the 'I' from that framework of conformity suggested by Fromm, Loevinger's work indicates the existence and possible attainment of other more mature and autonomous ego structures during late adolescence and adulthood.

LOEVINGER, THE PERSON

In 'Confessions of an Iconoclast', an invited address to the American Psychological Association's Committee on Women, in 1982, Jane Loevinger describes her commitment to the belief that every human being must find his or her own way, resisting the pressure to become a role model for others. Both the successes and failures of another may serve as sources of both inspiration and discouragement for one's own course of development. As Loevinger neared completion of her undergraduate work from the University of Minnesota prior to World War II, she was strongly discouraged by others from pursuing a career. As a Jew with radical political sympathies, she found her first job offer with a child welfare institute withdrawn when this background became known. Loevinger also applied for an assistantship in her alma mater's Psychology Department, but her dismal employment prospects as a Jewish woman in academic life were pointed out by the department's head, who did not evidence any personal prejudice but advised that she marry a psychologist and thereby resolve her professional aspirations! Loevinger conveys these circumstances to give a perspective on the times and social context from which her career began.

During World War II, Loevinger worked for two years in academic settings before resigning to complete her PhD. With men returning to their careers following the war, she found that opportunities for women in all professional fields had suddenly evaporated. A series of part-time teaching and research posts marked her career until she received an appointment at Washington University in St Louis, Missouri. It was from her post at that university's Psychology Department and Social Science Institute that Loevinger's research and writings on ego development emerged. Now professor emeritus, Loevinger still maintains active writing and research interests; she is currently completing a revision of her ego development coding system. Her works are contained in numerous articles and four major books: *Measuring Ego Development*, vols 1 and 2 (1970); *Ego Development* (1976); *Paradigms of Personality* (1987). Furthermore, Loevinger's model of the ego has served as the impetus for numerous longitudinal, cross-sectional, and cross-cultural studies of the ego in formation.

THE NATURE OF THE EGO

On the nature of the ego, Loevinger has been reluctant to offer a precise and concise definition. When pressed to do so, she has preferred to point to stages she has delineated in the development of the ego, saying the ego is that entity which undergoes qualitative change as one moves through the developmental sequence (Loevinger 1979a). Loevinger finds no term really appropriate to capture the breadth of functions falling under the 'ego' rubric.

> The concepts of ego and ego development remain useful, the former to cover, among other things, the person's striving for meaning and self-consistency, which is the cornerstone of all psychotherapy, and the latter to cover aspects of character formation, interpersonal relations, and self-conception, which ought to be part of diagnosis.
>
> (Loevinger 1979a: 4–5)

In an earlier work, Loevinger (1976) elaborates the ego's screening property, which works to exclude observations and information that do not fit its frame of reference. We selectively perceive (or misperceive) 'reality' to meet the structure of our own ego stages, thereby keeping anxiety at bay.

> Let me put the theory into my words: What Sullivan calls the 'self system' acts as a kind of filter, template, or frame of reference for one's perception and conception of the interpersonal world. Any observations not consonant with one's current frame of reference cause anxiety; therefore, to avoid or attenuate the anxiety, such perceptions are either distorted so as to fit the pre-existing system or they are 'selectively inattended to', in Sullivan's phrase.
>
> (Loevinger 1976: 49)

This quality of selectivity is what gives one's stage of ego maturation remarkable stability during late adolescent and adult life.

Most recently, Loevinger (1994: 5) indicates that the term *ego development* was selected to denote the many factors involved in personality development, such as motives, moral judgment, cognitive complexity, ways of perceiving oneself and others; '[p]erhaps the word *outlook* captures something of the core idea'. She rarely uses the term *ego*, preferring instead to avoid confusion with the psychoanalytic concept and to focus on the broad meaning of her own conceptualization of ego development. Loevinger differentiates ego development from the term *self* by reserving self to describe an internal, subjective experience accessible only to the individual, while ego development denotes an aspect of the person that is more or less public and classifiable by an outside observer (Loevinger and Blasi 1991).

Where Kohlberg saw separate and distinct subdomains of functioning as contributing to ego development, Loevinger sees the ego as a more holistic entity which *is* these functions. While Kohlberg and his colleagues preferred to delineate and assess separate ego subdomains such as moral reasoning in the social sphere and natural (physical) worlds, Loevinger finds the ego to be an indivisible, unitary structure engaged simultaneously in the activities of impulsive control, interpersonal style, conscious preoccupation, and cognitive functioning. The ego, to Loevinger, is that which gives one a general framework through which to view the world. Perhaps Loevinger's most succinct description of the ego's task is 'the search for coherent meanings in experience' (Loevinger and Wessler 1970: 8).

Somewhat easier for Loevinger is defining what the ego is not. The term *ego* has been interpreted in at least four different ways through the rise of psychoanalysis, and Loevinger (1976) finds only that meaning used by Erikson to be somewhat compatible with her own conception of the term. One current notion – for example, of Spitz (1959) – looks at the ego and its development only during the early stages of life as the self comes into being. Loevinger finds this definition problematic, for not only does she see the ego developing in the years beyond infancy but also Spitz's definition makes it impossible to differentiate ego development from psychosexual or intellectual development which are, to her, important distinctions that need to be made. A second usage of *ego* – for example, Hartmann (1958) – refers to all development within the 'conflict-free ego sphere'. However, Loevinger finds conflict in all her stages of ego development; indeed, the ultimate acceptance of internal conflict is the hallmark of her highest ego states. A third and commonly used referent for the ego – for example, by Bellak *et al.* (1973) – is that multitude of functions contributing to personality; furthermore, ego can also refer to any one of these functions. Loevinger sees some, but not all, dimensions of personality developing as a unit. Only in Erikson's (1963) psychosocial model of ego development does Loevinger find some similarity with her usage of the term. However, the developing ego Erikson describes occurs within normative age groupings (defined by different psychosocial tasks which must be met for development to proceed). Loevinger, on the other hand, finds enormous variability of ego stages within any single age group (particularly during late adolescence and adulthood). Furthermore, Erikson does not necessarily take the ego to be a unitary system of functions as does Loevinger (Snarey *et al.* 1983). Thus, Loevinger's concept of the ego – a unitary framework from which we generate meaning and coherence – is a notion differing markedly from most other uses of the term *ego* within psychoanalysis. (Indeed, one well-known ego psychoanalytic writer advised professional audiences not to read Loevinger's work because of this discrepancy.) Ego development is seen by Loevinger as only one of four different developmental channels; in her major volume on the meaning of ego, she also explores the relationship of ego development to other physical, psychosexual, and intellectual development streams (Loevinger 1976).

THE EGO: ASSESSMENT AND DEVELOPMENT

Loevinger's fascination with the ego and its maturation arose in trying to make sense of puzzling results from a test she had constructed to measure mothers' attitudes towards problems of family life (Loevinger 1987). Test items were designed to assess women's attitudes to small-scale domestic concerns for the purpose of assessing the explanatory power of various psychological theories; however, results were confusing. Despite psychometric care in test construction, no psychological theories were confirmed. However, as Piaget had become interested in the reasoning behind incorrect answers children gave to Binet's early tests of intelligence, Loevinger became intrigued by the more general ways in which people responded to the items of her instrument. In particular, a number of those from her sample appeared to be answering in stereotyped, socially approved ways, though items were devised to minimize that possibility. Examining how items clustered in factor analyses, Loevinger found the test seemed to be measuring how authoritarian a family was in its ideology (as construed by the mother). Although the measure provided no evidence supporting the influence, for example, of psychosexual stages in determining attitudes to family problems, it did point towards a more general way in which people organize their attitudes – in short, Loevinger's paradigm of the ego was born.

From the original instrument, a new thirty-six item Sentence Completion Test (SCT) was devised, allowing people to project their organizing frames of reference onto cues that would give the tester some means of understanding respondents' varied constructions of 'reality'. In a two-volume series, Loevinger and Wessler (1970) and Loevinger, Wessler, and Redmore (1970) published a hierarchical model of the developing ego along with Sentence Completion Test forms, suitable for men, women, boys, and girls, to assess ego stage. Some typical test items are as follows: 'What gets me into trouble is . . .'; 'Being with other people. . .'; 'I feel sorry . . .'. The two volumes also provide a manual for intensive training in the scoring procedures for ego development test items. In addition to Loevinger's initially detected authoritarian (conformist) mode of dealing with the problem of the 'I', a variety of other modes (ego stages) have appeared in her data. More recently,

Loevinger (1985) has presented a new, shortened, eighteen-item version of the original thirty-six-item Sentence Completion Test. Loevinger and Blasi (1991) note that while psychoanalysts generally focus on the period of infancy to describe the process of ego development, the SCT assesses development only after speech has begun.

Results of studies using Loevinger's model have generally pointed to an ego developing through a hierarchical and invariant sequence of stages. Although evidence for sequentiality is not conclusive, mean ego stages in both longitudinal and cross-sectional studies have generally increased with age (Loevinger 1979c; Loevinger *et al.* 1985). Like other developmental theories of identity formation, it is not possible to appreciate the most common ways of making the self and outer world cohere during adolescence without understanding preceding and succeeding possibilities. Unlike other theorists of identity, however, Loevinger has been silent regarding the mechanism(s) driving those qualitative ego stage reorganizations and the principles governing connections between stages.

Accepting the relevance of Piaget's hierarchical model of cognition to the study of ego development, Loevinger has also been heavily influenced initially by the psychoanalytic literature and later by the writings of Sullivan (1953). Each stage in Loevinger's sequence to follow addresses characteristic modes of impulse control, interpersonal style, and conscious preoccupations. In her early work on the SCT, Loevinger (1976) originally identified four ego stages; since that time, raters have become aware of additional stages and levels of ego structure intermediate between stages. Loevinger reserves the term *level* to describe states which seem to present mixtures of responses from immediately preceding and succeeding stages. In a recent review, Loevinger (1987) indicates that further levels may still await identification. In the pages to follow, all of Loevinger's current stages are identified and described, along with those transition levels most germane to adolescence. It is likely that some striking parallels will be noted between Loevinger's stages and those of Kohlberg, described in the preceding chapter.

It is perhaps most clearly through the early diaries of Anaïs Nin that we are allowed to glimpse during adolescence Loevinger's ego stages in development. Nin's diaries during her second decade move from concrete, vivid descriptions of her life as an 11-year-old Parisian immigrant to New York to those of a 17-year-old young woman with a complex and differentiated internal life. We will look to Nin for illustrations of those ego stages and transformations commonly occurring during adolescence.

Presocial stage (I–0)

This stage characterizes the state of affairs for the newborn infant, as yet unable to discriminate self from not-self, as yet not having an ego (let alone impulse control!). In differentiating the self from its surroundings, an infant comes gradually to achieve a sense of object constancy. Discovering the non-self is the main conscious preoccupation during this stage. One who remains unable to differentiate that which is self from that which it is not is said to be *autistic.* Loevinger's presocial stage of development is identical to that referred to by Mahler *et al.*'s (1975) description of the autistic self.

Symbiotic stage (I–1)

This stage corresponds to Mahler *et al.*'s (1975) description of the symbiotic infant, in which the primary care-taker and infant are perceived by the latter as one entity. While able to discriminate the self from its surrounding environment, the infant cannot yet distinguish itself from the main care-taker. The infant here is ruled by impulse, is symbiotic in its form of relatedness, and is consciously preoccupied with the self. It is during this symbiotic stage that language begins to develop, assisting the differentiation process. Loevinger (1976: 16) notes an interesting phenomenon: 'Partly for that reason [lack of language in life's earliest stages], the remnants of the Presocial and Symbiotic stages do not appear to be accessible by means of language in later life, as remnants of all later stages are'. Because ego stage is assessed by language on the SCT, these earliest two phases of development remain uncharted by Loevinger.

Impulsive stage (I–2)

It is only from the threshold of the impulsive stage that it is possible to assess ego development by SCT items. The preschool child is governed by impulses and is fearful of retaliation; other people are strongly needed, but as objects of dependency, to be manipulated and exploited. (Additionally, others are viewed either as all-good or all-bad, with no mixture of extremes.) The present, with all the problems it insistently presents, is the focus of this stage's dealings with time. Past or future are not of any immediate value, for what they bring is not happening *now.* Bodily feelings, particularly the sexual and aggressive, are conscious preoccupations. Gradually, external constraints help to curb the child's impulses, later to come under the self's control.

However, those at the impulsive level have no awareness of self as such and there is little distance from impulses themselves. (Impulses are most frequently described in the present tense, for example.) A child or adolescent who remains at this stage too long is often labeled incorrigible or uncontrollable.

Self-protective stage (Delta)

This stage is marked by the child's first attempts to control its own impulses; there is now sufficient distance from the impulses to make possible their control. In learning to anticipate short-term rewards and punishments, the child's fragile and guarded efforts at impulse control become apparent, enabling greater autonomy from external agents; the self-protective stage receives its name from this very characteristic quality of vulnerability. Self-interest (or opportunism) remains the primary motivator, as rules are used in the service of one's own desires; it is getting caught that labels an act 'bad'. The self-protective child understands, however, that there are rules which have some function, a point lost on the impulsive child. For the self-protector, blame is conveniently externalized so that other people or circumstances rather than one's own actions are at fault and responsible for one's present predicament. Interpersonal relations, while not strongly dependent, are characterized by a wary, manipulative mode, and control is the primary conscious preoccupation.

Conformist stage (I–3)

The state of conformity, captured eloquently by Erich Fromm, marks a developmental milestone for the ego; now, for the first time, there arises the ability to identify one's own welfare with that of a group (family or, later, peer group). At the same time, however, 'the self is not much different from others in the group, whatever one's group may be' (Loevinger and Blasi: 1991). Such a step requires trust in one's self and the world; where trust is lacking, the world is viewed as a community of 'enemy agents', and foundations are thus laid for an opportunistic, exploitative, deceptive self-protective adolescent and adult ego state. For the conformist, rules are obeyed because they are approved by the group and not because punishment lurks on the horizon; the group's disapproval, in and of itself, is enough to regulate the conformist's behavior. Impulses are similarly controlled through desire for social acceptance. Such is the state of development for Eric Hoffer's 'true believer', who does not endure solitude easily and is attracted to mass movements. 'Though stranded on a desert island, he must still feel that he is under the eyes of the group. To be cast out from the group should be equivalent to being cut off from life' (Hoffer 1951: 61). People within the conformist's group are liked and trusted, though those of other groups are often mistrusted, stereotyped, and flatly rejected. Living according to stereotyped roles prescribed by the group is the conformist's *modus operandi*. While he or she values cooperation rather than competition (the latter value characteristic of those in the preceding stage), others are evaluated by the conformist in terms of external appearances and material possessions rather than through highly differentiated internal feelings, characteristic of more mature ego stages. Inner life tends to be described by the conformist in rather bland, banal, concrete clichés, with social acceptability, reputation, and status serving as primary preoccupations. The conformist stage normally emerges during early adolescence and may be retained through late adolescent and adult life.

Through a framework of conformity at the age of 11 years, Nin uses her diary to confess the secrets of her soul, a young soul seemingly eager to please while at the same time limited in the vocabulary to describe its inner life. Events are described in vivid although concrete terms, and feeling states have a clear, albeit banal, ring:

> January 2 . . . I have made a resolution to keep my diary all year long. Nothing comforts me like being able to tell all my sorrows, my joys, my thoughts to a silent friend. . . . Now let's talk seriously. In February I will have a birthday, 12 years old. I am so old! It's high time for me to become a little woman. I have tried so often to do that, and then for the least thing I get angry, and I must start over again. I get back on my feet, but the road is slippery, be careful. Yes, I am a big girl and I must become perfect. Afterward it will be too late. Maman is calling me. I shall go, I don't want to slip down the path of disobedience.
>
> (Nin 1978: 39–40)

Though normally assessing ego structure in a different manner, Loevinger would likely find such lines typical of the conformist adolescent. Here, an enormous developmental milestone has been achieved as the ego regulates itself via the norms for 'womanly behavior' determined by the prevailing reference group. That path of obedience to mother seems desirable for the approval it brings, rather than the punishment it avoids; such is the logic of the conformist individual, orientated to others and giving somewhat banal descriptors of inner life.

Self-aware level: transition from conformist to the conscientious stage (I–3/4).

This transition level is probably the easiest to study, for it is the modal state of adult ego development within the United States (Loevinger 1976). Unlike the transition phases of ego structure described by Kegan in the chapter ahead, Loevinger's transition levels can remain as stable structures through adolescent and adult life. Notable features of the self-aware level are an 'increase in self awareness and the appreciation of multiple possibilities in situations' (Loevinger 1976: 19). Vaguely defined feelings, often self-conscious, come to mind in descriptions of inner life by an ego functioning at the self-aware level. Now there is an awareness of the self as a self and a separation from total identification with the norms of the group (Loevinger and Blasi 1991).

> Perception of alternatives and exceptions paves the way for the true conceptual complexity of the next stage. For example, at this [Self-Aware] level a person might say that people should not have children unless they are married, or unless they are old enough. At the next [Conscientious] stage, they are more likely to say unless they really want children, or unless the parents really love each other.
>
> (Loevinger 1976: 19)

Awareness of individual differences begins to emerge at the self-aware level, in contrast to the stereotypic thinking of the conformist; at the more mature ego stages of development, a premium is placed on individual differences. At the self-awareness level, the self can be aware of itself, distinct from (though still related to) the group; multiplicity is the conscious preoccupation of this ego state.

Several years further into her second decade, Nin begins to evidence a more self-aware ego structure in descriptions of her own qualities and behaviors; as the age of 14 years approaches, greater ability to reflect on the complexity of her inner life is becoming apparent. There is a change of focus in her diary now from what she does to how she feels.

> February 17. My birthday is coming on the 21st. There are only a few days left until then, and as I see the beginning of another age for me drawing near, I reflect, I feel sad at times, and other times I am happy. I am sad when I think that time goes by so quickly and that I don't do anything. I feel happy sometimes when I think that

this 14th birthday brings me a little closer to being a young lady, which is the theme of all the beautiful stories of adventure, real misfortunes, love. Because I hope that in growing up, I am going to find the young man of my dreams.

(Nin 1978: 157)

As Loevinger states, 'Untying what-I-am from what-I-ought-to-be opens the way for beginning to differentiate one's real and ideal self' (Loevinger 1987: 228). Nearing the age of 14, Nin appears to be differentiating her feelings more clearly and describing inner life in somewhat more complex and varied terms, though her dreams may still be those of the surrounding clan rather than her own individually secured desires. Loevinger indicates that those at the self-aware level are still basically conformists with somewhat greater ability to differentiate emotions; this description would seem to reflect Nin's life framework as she approaches her fourteenth birthday.

Conscientious stage (I–4)

At this stage, qualities such as the ability to generate long-term, self-evaluated goals are present, coupled with the ability for critical self-evaluation, a sense of responsibility, and an ability to describe individual differences in traits. Loevinger (1976) notes that only a few youngsters have attained this stage by early adolescence (13 or 14 years). In the conscientious stage, rules are internalized so that what is considered right or wrong depends upon one's personal evaluation of the circumstances. While the self-protector obeys rules to avoid punishment and the conformist does so to receive group approval, the conscientious individual evaluates rules and standards, long-term goals and ideals in accordance with her own ethical principles.

A person at this stage is less likely than the Conformist to feel guilty for having broken a rule, but more likely to feel guilty if what he does hurts another person, even though it may conform to the rules. At this stage a person is his brother's keeper; he feels responsible for other people, at times to the extent of feeling obliged to shape another's life or to prevent him from making errors.

(Loevinger 1976: 21)

In general, conscientious individuals see themselves as authors of their own destinies, intensive and responsible in their interpersonal relationships.

Additionally, a rich inner life of far greater conceptual complexity characterizes the ego at this conscientious stage of maturity. One's own behavior, as well as that of others, is viewed in terms of patterns having underlying motives, more vivid and realistic than such descriptions by those at less mature stages of ego development. Achievement tends to be measured against one's own standards rather than by recognition from the surrounding social environment (for the conformist) or competitive advantage (for the self-protector). Differentiated inner feelings are predominant conscious preoccupations at this stage of development.

By age 16, Nin's capacity for self-examination is even more evident. As she rereads pages of her earlier diary entries, she reflects on the changes she has experienced in herself and the oncoming transition she senses.

> June 13 ... During the last two hours I have been busy rereading several of my diaries. ... I have gone through so many impressions. ... Around me, the natural and inevitable tragedy of life unfolds. My personality is developing, my handwriting is changing, my spelling is a little better, my ideas are becoming clear and precise. I am neither naive nor shy, and am less ignorant. At 16 I have changed so much that right now, when I analyze my feelings, I understand that the little eleven-year-old girl and *her* character exist only in the notebooks. This transformation, which is so normal, is like an abyss that makes me dizzy. It is a deep mystery of nature that takes my breath away. Even now, I may be on the threshold of another transformation, on the threshold of another being that will be added to or will replace the one that I am about to leave behind, as one gets rid of an old worn coat. ... Each of us is a book without an Epilogue, an unfinished book whose Author reserves the right to write the ending, since He wrote the beginning.
>
> (Nin 1978: 250–1)

This new self-conscious quality apparent in Nin's self-analysis is characteristic of what Loevinger finds at the conscientious stage of ego maturity. Actions are now described in psychological terms; absolute statements are replaced by comparatives and contingencies. Self-critical, the conscientious stage individual also has the self-respect evident in Nin's diary entry. A beginning sense of self-authorship is also apparent. By her eighteenth year, Nin struggles with the conflicting demands of a literary life-style and family responsibilities; such perceived polarities, however, must await further integration and possible transcendence during more mature ego stages.

Individualistic level: transition from conscientious to autonomous stages (I–4/5)

An increased sense and appreciation of individuality and concern for emotional independence are hallmarks of this level (in contrast to excessive responsibility for others at the preceding stage of ego functioning). Close relations with others, however, are often viewed as incompatible with achievement strivings. An awareness of inner conflict dawns, but such conflict is frequently externalized (for example, if only God, spouse, children and so forth, were more accommodating, there would be no conflict between my career, marriage, and motherhood roles). At the next higher autonomous stage, such internal conflict is accepted as a way of life, with increasing ability to tolerate paradox and ambiguity.

> To proceed beyond the Conscientious Stage a person must become more tolerant of himself and of others. This toleration grows out of the recognition of individual differences and of complexities of circumstances at the Conscientious Stage. The next step, not only to accept but to cherish individuality, marks the Autonomous Stage.
> (Loevinger 1976: 22)

Like earlier and later transition levels, this state may be relatively static during late adolescence and adulthood. Conscious preoccupation lies with individuality, development, and roles.

Autonomous stage (I–5)

The ability to cope with conflicting needs and responsibilities is the distinguishing feature of this stage of ego development. Loevinger (1976) indicates that the autonomous individual probably has no more conflict than those at less mature stages of ego maturation, but acknowledges and deals with it rather than projecting it onto the environment or denying it. Greater tolerance for ambiguity and increased cognitive complexity mark the autonomous individual's frame of reference. 'He [the autonomous individual] is able to unite and integrate ideas that appear as incompatible alternatives to those at lower stages' (Loevinger 1976: 23). In terms of interpersonal relatedness, there is a respect for another's autonomy coupled with desire for interdependence. Conscious preoccupations are self-fulfilment and psychological causation. The autonomous stage of ego development is the highest found in most samples and probably in most populations (Loevinger and Blasi 1991).

Integrated stage (I–6)

The highest stage of ego development yet identified by Loevinger is defined by the ability to transcend conflicts of the autonomous stage. In addition to the qualities of cognitive complexity, more mutual interpersonal relations, and respect for autonomy which were all present in the preceding stage, there is now a new consolidation of identity and a savoring of individuality. Loevinger equates this stage of ego development to Maslow's description of the self-actualizing person. The integrated individual is difficult to study, in part because so few exist and in part due to limits in the ego maturity of the test interpreter. 'Moreover, the psychologist trying to study this stage must acknowledge his own limitations as a potential hindrance to comprehension. The higher the stage studied, the more it is likely to exceed his own and thus to stretch his capacity' (Loevinger 1976: 26). The integrated individual holds identity as the primary conscious preoccupation.

In order to assess ego stages more in line with Loevinger's method, let us turn to examples of how an adolescent at different stages might respond to one of the SCT items. Table 5.1 illustrates the varied types of responses given by individuals at different stages of ego development to the same sentence completion item. These responses indicate a sequence of shifts towards greater internalization of responsibility and increasingly complex differentiation of experiences. Results from some US surveys indicate that the conscientious-conformist (self-aware) level is the most commonly occurring state of ego maturity in the general adult population; however, those without tertiary (college) education are usually functioning at or below that level, while those with tertiary education are generally functioning at or beyond that level (Holt 1980; Loevinger *et al.* 1985).

Hauser (1978) notes that the developmental sequence of progress through ego stages can be interrupted at any point. The result of such interruption is a consequent 'character style' which corresponds to features of the stage when development ceased. Loevinger has not detailed the mechanisms which may assist or halt progress though stages of ego development, though Hauser *et al.* (1984) point to family interaction patterns which may play a role in an adolescent's ultimate stage of ego functioning.

On the issue of behavioral prediction from ego stage, Loevinger has been reluctant to make categorical statements. As she points out, 'The question really is not, Can we predict perfectly? but, Can we predict any better than chance?' (Loevinger 1984: 44). Obstacles to predicting behavior include the stubborn originality and creativity

Table 5.1 SCT responses at different ego levels relevant to adolescence

Stem: When they avoided me . . .

Stage	Response	Comment
Self-protective	I laughed because my intentions were to avoid them.	Need to protect the self through hostile humor
Conformist	I felt as if I wasn't wanted.	Feelings of rejection by the group
Conscientious-conformist	I felt very self-conscious.	Feeling conscious of the self
Conscientious	I took stock of myself to find possible reasons.	Evaluation of the self
Individualistic	I found I had been rather snobbish to them, although unintentionally.	Taking responsibility for one's actions, though unintended
Autonomous	I wondered why they did – was it me? or was it them? or something else?	Indicates conceptual complexity with three possibilities contrasted

Source: Adapted from Loevinger (1987: 230)

among human subjects and the design problem of using samples large enough to show statistical relationships in clinical research. From validational studies of the SCT, Loevinger has found certain behaviors to characterize lower ego levels, but no such characteristic behaviors have emerged at higher stages. What one can predict for those functioning at higher stages and levels of ego maturation are certain attitudes and values. The common observation of high conformity to peer pressure during early and middle adolescence fits well with what one might predict of behavior for those at the conformist stage of ego functioning; this observation also is in accord with results from validational studies for those at lower stages of ego development. Loevinger and Blasi (1991) do note that conceptual complexity is related to ego development, but while some may argue that a measure of ego development stage is nothing more than a poor measure of intelligence, they suggest otherwise:

[W]e have seen a few examples of people relatively low level, conformist or self-aware, among intellectually superior individuals. Almost a fourth of the distinguished men in Vaillant's ... Grant study, selected during their college years as men of exceptional potential, tested at the self-aware level in their mid-fifties. An unpublished Washington University study of educable retarded high school students found some of them also at that level.

(Loevinger and Blasi 1991: 165)

AN OPTIMAL LEVEL OF EGO DEVELOPMENT

Loevinger makes no claim that a higher stage of ego development is necessarily a healthier stage (Snarey *et al.* 1983). While Kohlberg, through his programs of educational intervention, demonstrates the premium he places on more advanced levels of moral reasoning, Loevinger has not embarked on any similar venture to attempt the raising of one's ego development stage. Furthermore, she does not attempt any philosophical justification of why a higher stage is better (as does Kohlberg). Loevinger, however, like Kohlberg and Kegan, does provide a means for assessing normative developmental patterns; again, like those theorists covered in adjacent chapters, health versus illness is not at issue in Loevinger's model of ego functioning.

Loevinger (1976) takes great care to avoid any association of ego stage with good adjustment or positive mental health. She points out that an individual at almost any stage of ego functioning can be well or poorly adjusted. While a low (for example, impulsive) stage of ego functioning maintained long past its normative demise may make functioning in the larger social order marginal, it nevertheless can be done. Indeed, some adults at the self-protective (Delta) stage of development may have very profitable and successful careers. Up until recent decades, academic psychology curricula placed great emphasis on a 'psychology of adjustment'. Gradually, writers such as Fromm, Jahoda, Maslow, and Schachtel have questioned adjustment and conformity to social norms as the epitome of development. Individuals at Loevinger's higher stages of ego functioning may be very 'poorly adjusted', refusing to sacrifice their own values and goals to the dictates of the larger social order. With regard to the issue of psychotherapy, Loevinger (1976: 427) cautions the clinician to 'keep his patient's problems and adjustment conceptually distinct from ego level; a person of any ego level may become a patient, though there may be differences in the kind of pathology or presenting symptoms characteristic for different levels'. Early and mid-adolescents might be expected, normatively, to operate from a self-protective or conformist framework; whereas a greater range of ego stages can be observed during late adolescence, the conscientious-conformist (self-aware) position is modal. Any association between stage of ego functioning and good social adjustment or positive mental health should be avoided during any phase of the lifespan, according to Loevinger. This view, however, has been recently challenged through empirical work by Noam and his colleagues (Noam 1992) and will be described in a subsequent section.

CRITICISM OF LOEVINGER'S CONSTRUCT

In the first major independent review of Loevinger's ego development construct, Hauser (1976) raised several issues in need of clarification – issues which have been re-echoed by critics in the decades since that time. Of primary concern has been the lack of attention paid by Loevinger to mechanisms driving development through her stage sequence, giving rise to ego stages in the first place. Hauser voices such questions in the following passage:

> Two important theoretical questions implicit in such a model are the following: What is the mechanism of change? And, what principle is at the core of the 'qualitative levels of organization'? . . . In more deeply analyzing the model itself, it would be important to propose explicitly more abstract formal principles that govern both the 'vertical structure' (connection between stages) and 'horizontal structure' (organization within stages' . . .).
>
> (Hauser 1976: 952)

Because an organizational principle has not been delineated, Hauser also questions the means by which affect and cognition are related in each of Loevinger's stages and how motivation influences development. At present, these theoretical and conceptual issues remain unresolved and have also raised further protest from critics.

There appears still to be a lack of underlying logic to the ego development sequence (Habermas 1975; Broughton and Zahaykevich 1977, 1988; Kegan 1986c). Snarey *et al.* (1983) raise queries related to this problem; they note that while other structural theorists such as Kohlberg and Piaget have carefully articulated the structure which organizes and drives development, Loevinger appears to define her stages as 'ideal type characterological portraits'. In fact, it is rare to meet any such 'pure' characterological individual in reality; yet such cases form the basis for description of and classification into ego stages. Where a stage conceptualization of the self is organized by theory, one is not stuck with the problem of having to label as a 'typical character type' any child or adult, who may be quite atypical of the reality they supposedly represent. In one of her few and very recent comments on the issue of mechanisms underlying development, Loevinger (1994: 4) has noted that 'there is no generally accepted theory of what accounts for progress in ego development'. She does suggest that movement from the conformist stage may occur when the person becomes aware that he or she does not always conform exactly to the socially prescribed role; however, she has remained silent on more general principles that may drive the overall developmental process. Loevinger has, however, been one of few identity theorists to develop a statistically rigorous base for delineation and assessment of her ego stages.

A second issue which has generated critical discussion is Loevinger's suggestion of an indivisible ego. Snarey *et al.* (1983) have found it necessary to postulate an ego having various subdomains, each separately amenable to empirical study. When the ego has been approached in this way, *décalage* relationships between subdomains have appeared. (For example, a certain stage of cognitive development appears as a necessary but not sufficient condition for a more advanced stage of moral reasoning.) Snarey *et al.* believe that Loevinger is unable to recognize and account for such differential developments in her ego development scheme. Loevinger (1983: 339) responds that such a view of the divisible ego is 'not absurd. It is neither grossly at variance with nor strongly supported by the fragmentary data presently at hand.' She counters the claim for *décalage* relationships among subdomains on mathematical grounds, indicating problems such as lack of the necessary precision in measuring instruments to justify *décalage* notions. A further problem Loevinger finds in the divided ego construct is failure by its researchers to specify interrelationships among all subdomains by providing age norms and matching of ego subsystems on rigorous empirical grounds.

Loevinger's approach to the study of ego development lies in contrast to the approach taken by trait psychologists, and these differing orientations have been the subject of several recent interchanges between Loevinger and her critics (for example, Loevinger 1991, 1993a, 1993b; Costa and McCrae 1993). Loevinger's approach to personality suggests that the development of the ego occurs through qualitatively different levels of reorganization; this orientation is in contrast to a trait approach that views personality as comprised of basic traits which remain relatively stable over time. Costa and McCrae (1993) and Goldberg (1990) have been leading proponents of the trait-factor approach. Both of these latter research teams suggest there are five basic dimensions of personality. Costa and McCrae have labeled these N-neuroticism, E-introversion/extroversion, O-openness to experience, A-altruism, and C-conscientiousness (degree of impulse control), while Goldberg's (1990) labels are Surgency, Agreeableness, Conscientiousness, Emotional Stability, and Intellect. Costa and McCrae (1993) argue that all of their five major personality factors can be seen as 'master traits of personality', while Loevinger (1993a) does not believe such a trait-factor approach can reveal important qualitative differences – for example, between the conformist and conscientious stages in individual ego development. The distinction between a person conscientiously following the authority of others or conscientiously living according to their own conscience is blurred in a Costa trait approach.

Further criticism has been leveled at Loevinger's SCT test scoring scheme, with alleged confusion between content and structure (Broughton and Zahaykevich 1988; Josselson 1980; Snarey *et al.* 1983). Broughton and Zahaykevich suggest that this fusion makes it difficult to assess the extent of class and cultural bias on the SCT. Josselson argues that beyond the conscientious stage, ego functioning seems to be defined by particular social values rather than any structural elements. She cites the 'cherishing of individuality' characteristic of higher ego stages as a feature having more to do with cultural values rather than maturational form. Snarey *et al.* cite the following example to illustrate what they believe to be Loevinger's confusion between content and structure:

> For instance, for the sentence stem, 'My conscience bothers me if . . .' the response 'I steal' is classified as a self-protective Delta stage response. The Loevinger manual notes that stealing is a more concrete content of moral valuing than lying or cheating. But in our terms, it is clearly content, a statement of what *is* wrong or right, not a direct expression of structure or form of reasoning about *why* something is wrong or right. The response 'I steal' has no clear face validity as reflecting a self-protective stage.
>
> (Snarey *et al.* 1983: 321)

These writers argue that a brief statement of content does little to indicate underlying logical processes which govern a stage of ego development. Noam (1992) furthers the argument by suggesting that complexity and maturity are fused in Loevinger's stage model of ego development. From his work with clinical populations, Noam argues that complexity often exists in stark contrast to integration; with such

groups, scoring at a higher stage of ego development does not mean
that an integration has been attained. Both Snarey *et al.* (1983: 321)
and Mitchell (1993) also question Loevinger's assumption that empirical evidence should constitute the highest law of the land. Snarey *et al.*
conclude that Loevinger's ego development construct has been 'a
trade-off between significant empirical gains and obvious philosophical shortcomings' (Snarey *et al.* 1983: 321), while Mitchell questions
whether methods of study might sometimes lose touch with meaning
in personality development. Nevertheless, Loevinger's paradigm has
become an increasingly popular pathway to assessing identity (ego
development) in adolescence and adulthood.

RESEARCH FINDINGS ON EGO DEVELOPMENT

Loevinger's Sentence Completion Test for measuring ego development
has generated research on wide-ranging related issues since the instrument was first published over two decades ago. Hauser (1976) and
Loevinger (1979c) have offered thorough coverages of investigations
using the SCT during the 1970s, and more recently *Psychology Inquiry*
(1993) has devoted a special issue to a review and discussion of Loevinger's ego development model. Loevinger's paradigm has sparked
enquiry into such issues as refinement of the SCT, sex differences and
developmental patterns of ego change during adolescence and adulthood, links with related personality variables, and attempts to promote
ego growth in contexts ranging from families to school classrooms and
prison settings. In this section, the focus will be on a brief review of
research related to developmental patterns of and variables associated
with ego maturation during adolescence for a non-clinical population,
while intervention programs to enhance ego development will be
addressed in the following section.

Investigations into developmental patterns of ego maturation during
adolescence have been the primary focus of a number of studies into
the formation of adolescent identity. Both longitudinal and cross-sectional designs have been used to explore developmental trends, though
Hauser (1976) notes the limitations of cross-sectional research for testing an hypothesis of invariant order in stage sequence.

> Put most simply, there is no way to discover whether stages have
> been skipped or moved through consecutively by individuals unless
> one studies the same subjects over a period of time. By following,
> with a repeated measures design, a varied group of subjects over
> some years, one can potentially determine the following: (a) the

presence or absence of change in ego development level; (b) the direction of the change; (c) the ego development level stages through which the change occurred; and (d) factors associated with the change.

(Hauser 1976: 949)

It has been possible to examine these issues raised by Hauser in the longitudinal studies of Adams and Fitch (1982), Gfellner (1986a), Kitchener *et al.* (1984), Loevinger *et al.* (1985), Redmore and Loevinger (1979), Redmore (1983), Novy (1993), Dubow *et al.* (1987), and Allen *et al.* (1994). Most, though not all, of these longitudinal designs have pointed to change in ego development stage over at least a one-year span during adolescence; most, though not all, have similarly indicated a generally steady progression in stage development during the course of adolescence. Upon closer examination of results from these studies, it would appear that greatest gains in ego development emerge during the secondary school years, with greater stability occurring in late adolescence and young adulthood (Adams and Fitch 1982; Gfellner 1986a; Kitchener *et al.* 1984; Redmore and Loevinger 1979; Redmore 1983). Longitudinal studies of late adolescents differ, however, in indicating whether there is any significant gain or regression during the post-secondary school years. Loevinger *et al.* (1985) found significant regression over the university years for women; whether this result was an artefact of the SCT as a measuring instrument or a genuine indication of regression in personality functioning remains an unanswered question. Longitudinal results have generally indicated a half ego-stage increase from Delta/conformist level to the conformist stage from grades 8 to 12; patterns of movement from mid to late adolescence have not been consistent across longitudinal studies. Addressing Hauser's fourth point, some environments (such as those university contexts with a narrow curriculum focus) may be associated with regression in ego maturity (Loevinger *et al.* 1985; Adams and Fitch 1983). Additionally, socio-economic status has predicted acceleration in ego development (Gfellner 1986b); students in higher socio-economic groups generally attained ego stages one to two years in advance of their counterparts from lower socio-economic backgrounds. Browning (1987) has also noted a statistically significant relationship between ego development and education, with greatest impact of parental educational level coming before age 18 years for the offspring. Finally, parental child-rearing styles have predicted ego development during adolescence and adulthood. Child-rearing styles characterized by acceptance, a non-authoritarian approach to punishment, and identification of the child with the parent have been associated with higher levels of ego development some twenty-two years later in adulthood (Dubow *et al.* 1987). Fathers' displays of autonomy and relatedness towards their adolescents (such as providing challenging interactions within a broader context of autonomy-relatedness) were predictive of greater gains in adolescent ego development over a two-year interval (Allen *et al.* 1994).

Several cross-sectional investigations have also enabled us to observe frequently occurring ego stages during the course of adolescence. Browning (1987), Gfellner (1986b), Kishton *et al.* (1984), and Loevinger and Wessler (1970) all present cross-sectional studies of ego development during early, middle, and late adolescence in which the ego stage distributions shift upwards with age. At least two unpublished doctoral dissertations using comparable cross-sectional designs also report similar patterns in the distributions of ego development stages during adolescence (Coor 1970; Hoppe 1972).

The relationship between sex, sex role identity, and ego development have been the focus for a number of investigations into ego development during adolescence and young adulthood. Adolescent girls or women have been slightly in advance of their male counterparts in stage of ego maturation (Bailey and Cohn, cited in Loevinger *et al.* 1985; Gfellner 1986a,b; Kitchener *et al.* 1984; McCammon 1981); mixed results have appeared in other investigations, though findings have generally favored females (Redmore 1983; Redmore and Loevinger 1979; Loevinger *et al.* 1985). Loevinger *et al.* summarize the controversy regarding differential ego development patterns for the two sexes:

> Our results suggest only that in ego development, as in many other kinds of development, women reach maturity a little sooner than men. Neither in the present or in previous studies has there been support for mean differences between men and women at maturity.
>
> (1985: 959)

When we turn to the relationship between sex role identity and ego development, some interesting though mixed findings again emerge. A number of studies have examined relationships between sex role identity and ego development (for example, Costos 1986, 1990; Nettles and Loevinger 1983; Prager and Bailey 1985; Schwarz and Robins 1987; Snarey *et al.* 1986). Perhaps the most consistent thread running through such findings is that ego stage seems positively related to androgynous role expectations but not to androgynous self-conceptions. Ego development may be related to some sex-role attitudes and to self-conceptions of agency and communion; however, an association between ego development and self-conception of masculinity and femininity has received minimal support.

Additional personality variables of identity status, moral reasoning, and cognition have been related to Loevinger's ego development stages. Consistent findings have come from those studies examining the relationship between ego identity status and ego development. Achievement and moratorium subjects have scored significantly higher in ego development than foreclosure and diffusion subjects (Adams and Shea 1979; Ginsburg and Orlofsky 1981); when identity has been assessed on a self-report high to low continuum, moderate positive correlations have been attained between ego identity and ego development stage (Adams and Fitch 1981). When identity status and ego development have been studied longitudinally over a one-year time-span in late adolescence, movement of subjects into higher stages of both identity constructs has been noted, though the relationship between identity status and ego development for individual subjects was not reported (Adams and Fitch 1982). In exploring the predictive relationship between ego identity (measured on a self-report high to low continuum) and ego stage over time, knowledge of either variable has been equally effective in predicting the other over a one-year time interval (Adams and Fitch 1981).

The relationship between moral reasoning and ego stage as well as cognition and ego stage have also been explored. Gfellner (1986b) found low positive correlations between ego stage and moral reasoning stage in early but not late adolescence in a cross-sectional investigation of the two variables; in a longitudinal investigation of these variables over a four-year interval from early to mid adolescence, ego development and moral reasoning related at fixed points in time, but ego development stage in early adolescence did not predict subsequent moral reasoning stage (Gfellner 1986a). Kitchener *et al.* (1984) reported increases in use of principled moral reasoning over a two-year span during late adolescence and young adulthood; no change in ego stage was observed, however. Low to moderately strong relationships between ego development and moral reasoning have been reported by Rest (1979a) even when the effects of age have been removed.

The relationship between cognition and ego stage has been the focus of a small number of studies. Hurtig *et al.* (1985) reported relationships between ego development and measures of both physical-mathematical cognitive functioning as well as social-interpersonal cognitive functioning. Cognitive functions contribute significantly to ego functioning during mid adolescence, but the type of cognitive function and its degree of impact depend upon the subject's sex; ego functioning was predicted by interpersonal reasoning for females and by physical-mathematical reasoning for males. The authors question the assumption of a necessary link between higher levels of cognitive structure and ego maturation unless there is an expansion of the concept of cognitive structure beyond that of formal operational thought. Significant relationships between different measures of intellectual development and ego stage have been observed by Alisho and Schilling (1984) and Ginsburg and Orlofsky (1981). In exploring adolescents' concepts of marriage, Tamashiro (1979) noted that adolescents were more advanced in ego development stage than in their developmental concept of marriage. Generally too few studies have been conducted to assess adequately the validity of Loevinger's claim to a unitary ego.

The relationship between ego stage and interpersonal interaction during adolescence has been the focus of a limited number of studies based on Loevinger's model. Hauser (1978) directly investigated interaction styles of pre-conformist, conformist, and post-conformist female high-school students; on factors assessing warm/available and active/spontaneous, post-conformist subjects had the highest scores during an initial interview with a young adult male interviewer; pre-conformist subjects showed significantly higher scores on the sexy factor (assessing sexually provocative behavior). Earlier work by Frank and Quinlan (1976) had also noted relationships between ego stage and interactional style consistent with expectation; conformists evidenced more conforming behavior, while more incidents of impulsive and acting-out behaviors occurred for pre-conformist adolescents. In family contexts, adolescent ego development has been related to parental behavior (Hauser *et al.* 1984; Leaper *et al.* 1989; Novy *et al.* 1992; Allen *et al.* 1994). Adolescents who elaborated their ideas and increased their contributions to family discussions were at higher levels of ego development; correlational findings suggested the possibility that some families enhance adolescent discourse through acceptance of and empathy with their adolescents, while families who promote a repressive atmosphere (through parental judging, devaluing, constraining) are associated with regressive and repetitious adolescent speech patterns. Parents' affective enabling and accepting behaviors were strongly related to higher levels of adolescent ego development in Hauser *et al.'s* (1984) work. From this study, however, it was not possible to discern whether a parent's behavior was reactive to rather than responsible for the adolescent's speech pattern. Examining adolescents' perceptions of parenting styles, Gfellner (1986a) found higher ego stages of adolescents related to perceived parental loving and supporting, while perceived parental demanding was associated with lower stages of adolescent ego development. In an interesting study of problem marriages, Nettles and Loevinger (1983) found that different attitudes and expectations about sex roles and divisions of labor rather than characterological differences in ego stage of development created difficulties for couples. A later longitudinal study of the relationship between adaptation to divorce and ego development in adult women found that marital separation or divorce might be a disequilibrating event but serve to foster ego development (Bursik 1991). Results of studies addressing ego stage and interaction style point towards a picture generally consistent with expectation that adolescents at higher stages of ego development behave in warmer, more responsive ways and come from families which support and enable, while adolescents at lower stages of ego development evidence more impulsive and acting-out behaviors and come from families in which parents are demanding and judgmental in interaction with their teenagers.

Current directions in ego development research

Recent studies utilizing the SCT have included psychometric investigations of the instrument's construct validity (Novy 1993; Vaillant and McCullough 1987), effects of scoring instructions (Jurich and Holt 1987), the development and construct validation of a shortened form of the SCT (Loevinger 1985; Picano 1987), and explorations of the relationship between ego development and adaptive/maladaptive adjustment in adolescence (Jennings and Armsworth 1992; Noam, Recklitis, and Paget 1991). Blasi and his colleagues (Blasi and Milton 1991; Blasi and Glodis in press) have been examining the more subjective aspects of identity experienced by those in each of Loevinger's ego development stages. Furthermore, Helson and Roberts (1994) have examined the ability of mid and late adolescent cognitive and personality traits to predict ego development in middle adulthood. They found ego level at age 43 to be predicted by verbal aptitude in high school, psychological-mindedness in college, and challenging life experience during the young and middle adulthood years. These researches all suggest the need for further examination of factors affecting ego development over time.

IMPLICATIONS FOR SOCIAL RESPONSE

A brief statement at the conclusion of Loevinger's (1976) volume on ego development only hints at the important implications her scheme may hold – not only for psychotherapy but for other forms of social response: 'the appropriate kind of therapy may be related to the patient's ego level, with organic and manipulative therapies more appropriate at lower levels, insight therapies more appropriate at higher levels' (Loevinger 1976: 427). Some four years later, Loevinger again raised the implications of her model for counseling:

> Not only the choice of therapy method but the entire mode of address to the client should take into consideration the client's ego level – among other things, of course. Similarly, the mode of teaching counseling students should take their current level into account.
>
> (Loevinger 1980: 389)

However, Loevinger's energies have remained with the refinement of measuring techniques for ego development, and she leaves the applications of her model to be explored by other writers and researchers.

In contrast to Kohlberg, Loevinger questions the use of interventions to attempt to advance the present stage of ego functioning. While Kohlberg justifies, philosophically, his belief that 'higher is better' and aims to promote more mature forms of reasoning through educational means, Loevinger is cautious about the goal of raising ego development as an appropriate therapeutic or educational aim:

> To what extent should advance in ego level itself be an aim of therapy? One should admit that, particularly with adults, this may be too high an aim to set, for it is both the strength and the weakness of the ego that it is remarkably stable. . . . It is almost paradoxical that the higher the client's ego level, the more open he or she is likely to be to further advance during therapy.
>
> (Loevinger 1980: 389)

Indeed, writers who have begun to examine the social implications of Loevinger's model in educational and counseling arenas have not directed energies towards advancement of ego stages as much as towards ways in which adolescents or adults can be appropriately met in their current modes of ego functioning. Although Kegan, described in the next chapter, is very much concerned with the process of structural change, even he places high premium on client readiness for any transition. Indeed, any attempt to alter an existing structure before readiness of the client may be a form of cruel and misguided therapeutic effort (Kegan 1982).

Writers exploring the applications of Loevinger's model of ego development have focused primarily on clinical, judicial, and educational spheres; investigations within all these realms have indicated that recog-

nition and appreciation of an individual's current stage of ego maturation is crucial to effective intervention. Swenson (1980) has described,
from a theoretical base, what he believes to be the implications of
Loevinger's model for the field of counseling. Drawing attention to
the importance of both individual and environmental variables on
client behavior, Swenson sees responses of those at less complex
stages and levels of ego development to be more subject to environmental influences, while those at higher stages are more capable of either
changing or transcending their environments. Swenson finds two transition periods in Loevinger's model important for counseling interventions that would have relevance for adolescents – the transition from
behaving according to self-interest (for example, finding out about
likely rewards and punishments) to regulating one's interests with
those of others and the transition from this latter organization to the
internalization of rules (like behaving in accordance with one's own
inner standards) and at the same time experiencing greater mutuality
in relationship. Swenson finds it necessary to recognize the impact of
the environment before, during, and after these transitions in the
planning of therapeutic interventions.

For adolescents (and adults) below the conformist stage, the environment is having enormous influence on behavior, and therapy should
be directed towards changing environments or changing the
reward/punishment system operating within the adolescent's environment. At the self-protective stage (where we might expect to find some
younger adolescents), Swenson suggests the utility of either behavior
therapy with a cognitive orientation or Glaser's reality therapy; both
these approaches recognize the individual's capacity for some degree
of self-control and would seem suited to that framework of the less
mature self-protector ego structure.

> Behavior [of the self-protector] is calculated to gain the rewards the
> individual seeks from the environment without incurring punish-
> ment. A therapy that helps the person to gain the sought-after re-
> wards without simultaneously provoking punishment or retaliation
> would be applicable.
>
> (Swenson 1980: 386)

For the adolescent (or adult) conformist whose actions are guided
by the opinions and rules of a reference group, Swenson recommends
Ellis's rational-emotive therapy to help differentiate rational from irrational beliefs. A conformist is likely to be grappling with conflicting
role demands and be unable to please everyone; this conflict is likely to
cause much distress, for the conformist's ego structure thrives on the

group's approval. Ellis's approach could assist the conformist to resolve conflicting demands from such role requirements, as well as point the way to a more self-aware orientation in the resolution of incompatible demands.

Adolescents (and adults) at the self-aware level are in the process of shifting from external to more internal sources of behavioral standards and belief systems as well as developing greater authenticity in relationship. Ellis's approach, in Swenson's view, offers most to individuals at this stage of ego organization, for rational-emotive therapy aims at helping people to question many irrational beliefs derived from the *status quo* and focus on more personally satisfying values and beliefs. For example, Ellis (1962) encourages people to question the irrational belief that 'I must be liked by everyone in my group', the *raison d'être* for the conformist and an appropriate challenge for one at the self-aware level.

For those at the conscientious, individualistic, and autonomous stages, therapies shifting from environmental manipulation to greater personal focus on self-fulfilment and existential issues would be most appropriate, in Swenson's view. The client-centered therapy of Rogers might be particularly valuable for those (primarily late) adolescents and adults at the conscientious stage, with a newly emerging awareness of their own internal standards and more differentiated inner life. Client-centered therapy, in particular, encourages self-exploration and resolution of conflict on one's own terms, seemingly useful for the client at the conscientious stage. Humanistic and existential approaches, concerned with more philosophical issues, might be particularly appropriate to individualistic and autonomous stage clients, with their greater abilities to accept the individuality of other human beings and all the issues this capacity raises.

Swenson concludes by cautioning that adolescents at higher stages of ego functioning may, nevertheless, appear at university counseling centers with problems such as test-anxiety, more characteristic of the lower stage self-protector; for such situations, a behavioral strategy that recognizes and aims to reduce the anxiety would be appropriate. However, even under such circumstances the client's ego stage must be recognized and addressed. Thus, an exam-anxious, self-aware student might best be helped by the counselor's presentation of a behavioral strategy as one that can assist people to gain greater control over impulses and reactions to stress. Eventually, the aim would be a therapy of 'self-help' which this self-aware student self-administers.

Kirshner (1988) and Noam (1992) have addressed the relationship between psychopathology and Loevinger's stages of ego development.

Kirshner (1988: 222) argues from a theoretical base that early experience may generate later conflicts that exist independently from ego developmental stage: '[S]pecific conflicts, for example, ones relating to libidinal, aggressive, and response-seeking experiences with objects, could easily occur in individuals without regard to the stage of ego development finally achieved'. From an empirical base, however, Noam and his colleagues have found a definite relationship between ego development and symptom expression during adolescence and adulthood (Dill and Noam 1990; Noam, Powers, Kilkenny and Beedy 1991; Noam 1992). In their study of treatment requests, Dill and Noam (1990) discovered that higher ego stage patients in an outpatient setting were more likely to request insight therapy, while lower ego stage individuals were more likely to request reality checks and behavioral intervention. The Harvard/McLean Laboratory of Developmental Psychology and Developmental Psychopathology has been monitoring inpatient samples of more than 1,200 children and adolescents suffering from affective, conduct, anxiety, and attention-deficit disorders in addition to normative and outpatient samples (Noam 1992). Results of this work point towards a strong relationship between ego development and symptomatology, with adolescents at pre-conformist stages of ego development evidencing more externalizing behaviors (impulsivity, acting out, delinquency) and conformist adolescents consistently more prone to directing aggression against the self (feeling guilty and/or depressed). At higher, post-conformist stages of ego development, however, research linking ego development and internalizing symptomatology has been less conclusive; some findings, however, do indicate that with increasing developmental complexity, psychopathology becomes more internalized.

Further clinical issues raised by Loevinger (1976) are the relationship between client and therapist ego level as a factor in therapy as well as the optimal relationship between ego stages of supervisor and trainee. With regard to the first issue, there may be differential effectiveness among therapists at different stages of ego development. This suspicion has been confirmed by work with young offenders by the California Youth Authority (Palmer 1974) and with juvenile delinquents (Warren 1969). Young persons high in ego maturity have responded best to teams high in predicted efficiency (high ego level), while the relation has been reversed for those young offenders at lower stages of ego maturity. Loevinger suggests that therapists have a 'pacer' function and that therapy may work best when the therapist functions at a stage of ego development just beyond that of the client. Carlozzi *et al.* (1982) and Carlozzi *et al.* (1983) have found therapists' counseling efficacy to be related to higher stages of ego development. Several recent publications have examined the optimal relationship of ego stages between supervisor and counselor-trainee. Swenson (1980) has suggested that great difference in stages of ego development between the two is likely to reduce effectiveness of supervision. Trainees may be assisted most by supervisors at their same stage of ego development or one stage beyond. (Supervisors should never be at a stage of ego maturity lower than their trainees.) Cebik (1985) proposes a model of matching trainees and supervisors so that the latter are in close proximity to trainees and thereby able to serve as pacers. More recent work by Borders and Fong (1989), however, has produced inconclusive results regarding the relationship between ego development among counselor-trainees and their effectiveness with clients.

Further research on the impact of ego development stage between adolescent and counselor and between counselor and supervisor has begun to appear. Stage of ego development does appear related to skill acquisition and performance by counselors. Simpler, more concrete descriptions of clients are used more frequently by counselors at lower stages of ego development, while those at higher stages use more complex and interactive descriptions (Borders *et al.* 1986). Additionally, those counselor trainees at higher stages of ego development have evidenced fewer negative thoughts about their clients and reported a more neutral, objective approach to the counseling process (Borders 1989).

Some attention has been given to the kinds of secondary and tertiary curricula that may be associated with higher stages of ego development, though any definitive summary is at present unavailable (Loevinger 1987). Through curriculum efforts (for example, learning to listen and social-role-taking exercises, cross-age teaching experiences) to stimulate interpersonal maturity, adolescents have shown significant gains in stage of ego maturity (Dowell 1971; Rustad and Rogers 1975; Erickson 1975; Exum 1977; Kessler *et al.* 1986; Sprinthall *et al.* 1992). Additionally, Loevinger's model has been the inspiration behind a scheme of career education which recognizes different career decision-making strategies likely to be used by self-protector, conformist, self-aware, conscientious, and autonomous adolescents (Miller-Tiedeman and Tiedeman 1972). Tiedeman and Miller-Tiedeman (1977) have introduced school curriculum efforts aimed to shift adolescents from other-directed to self-generated career decision-making styles through exercises focusing on 'I-power'; increases in ego development from conformist to conscientious stages were observed, along with decreases in impulsive decision-making strategies. More

recently, the relationship between ego development and teacher education has also been examined (Cummings and Murray 1989). Adult
learners have differed by stage of ego development in their views on
educational issues such as the role of the teacher and sources of knowledge; however, ego development stage of the learner was not related to
instructor ratings or course grade. The application of Loevinger's
model to educational and therapeutic arenas remain rich avenues for
further investigation; to date, application studies have generally
pointed to the critical nature of addressing the adolescent, at least
initially, at his or her current stage of ego development.

SUMMARY

The ego, according to Loevinger, is that 'master trait of personality'
which serves as an organizing framework for one's customary orientation to one's self and to the world. Ego development is but one of four
lines of development (ego, physical, psychosexual, and intellectual)
which are conceptually distinct; in contrast to Kohlberg, however, Loevinger views the ego as a unitary entity, rather than being comprised
of various subdomains having *décalage* relationships. Ego development proceeds through a series of stages, believed to be hierarchical
and invariant in sequence, which mark a continuum of increasingly
complex and differentiated means by which one perceives oneself, the
world, and one's relationships in it. Loevinger has developed a Sentence Completion Test composed of thirty-six items, which enables
people to project their organizing frameworks onto the instrument.
Individuals are assessed according to ego stage or transition level
through their responses; adults in the general US population have a
modal level at the conformist/conscientious transition. Greatest gains
in ego development occur during early and mid adolescence, with girls
generally reaching higher ego stages earlier than boys; no sex differences in stage of ego development have regularly appeared at maturity,
however. Recognition of an adolescent's ego stage has important implications for counseling, psychotherapeutic, and educational purposes.

6 Identity as meaning-making
Kegan's constructive-developmental
approach

> Peter: *I . . . I don't understand what . . . I don't think I . . . I DON'T*
> *UNDERSTAND!. . . .*
> Jerry: *What were you trying to do? Make sense out of things? Bring*
> *order?*
>
> (*Edward Albee,* The Zoo Story)

Peter and Jerry live in the same city and visit the same park, yet they
inhabit different worlds. Transcending contrasts in social class and
years of accumulated schooling, Peter and Jerry construct meaning in
clearly distinct ways, each hanging in an evolutionary balance that
gives rise to a different sense of personal identity and construction of
the 'reality' of their chance afternoon meeting in Central Park. Peter
makes meaning of his life and encounter with Peter through a conventional, 'law and order' orientation. Life must be lived according to
society's rules, and Jerry's disregard for the norms of social interchange and demand for Peter's park bench bring the latter to the very
edge of his evolutionary stability: 'People can't have everything they
want. You should know that; it's a rule; people can have some of the
things they want, but they can't have everything' (Albee 1962: 136).

Meanwhile Jerry has returned from the zoo, insistent upon telling
this stranger his story: 'I've been to the zoo. (*Peter doesn't notice.*) I
said, I've been to the zoo. MISTER I'VE BEEN TO THE ZOO!' he
opens, and slowly manipulates Peter into a relationship meeting his
own desired purposes (Albee 1962: 113). Alongside Albee's intended
Zoo Story message regarding the violence lurking within the confines
of both the literal and metaphorical zoos of the play, Kegan might
argue that life is also a zoo in the colloquial sense of the term – in that
experience of confusion which exists prior to the human activity of
successful meaning-making.

Identity to Kegan is a matter of making (or, more accurately, creating) sense, the way in which Peter and Jerry and everyone interpret and make their worlds cohere. The 'same' view can be seen in many ways, the same sound heard in many forms. 'How we will understand what we hear – or better put, *what we actually do hear* – will be settled there where the event is made personal sense of, there where it actually *becomes* an event for us' (Kegan 1982: 3). That 'there' for Kegan is the machinery of identity construction and evolution which has been tapped until now primarily through social scientists' cognitive or affective probes. Aldous Huxley's (1972) axiom that experience is not what happens to you but rather what you do with what happens to you, is the foundation upon which Kegan's identity (or meaning-making) theory is built. A self struggling to organize and make sense of its experience, with evolutionary constraints during each stage in this process, is what Kegan's constructive-developmental theory is about.

Kegan's work, to a greater or lesser degree, draws from all identity theorists discussed in this volume – from the more affectively orientated ego psychoanalytic psychology and object relations traditions to the cognitive developmental approaches of Piaget and Kohlberg; yet Erikson, Blos, Mahler, Kohlberg, or Loevinger, each considered in isolation, does not allow one to address that underlying 'zone of mediation where meaning is made', the essence of the self in Kegan's view. Each cognitively or affectively based approach we have examined to this point would seem to tap only one facet of identity, rather than portray the subtending structure which initially brings cognition and affect into existence. Having begun our enquiries into the nature of adolescent identity with Erikson, the first writer to attend carefully to its formation process, it is perhaps most appropriate now to conclude with the synthesizing work of Kegan, the most contemporary and integrative identity theorist to consider identity's evolutionary process. Over the past twenty-five years working as a teacher, researcher, and clinician, Robert Kegan is currently Senior Lecturer in the Human Development and Counseling area at Harvard University, a senior faculty member at the Massachusetts School of Professional Psychology, Chair of the Institute for the Management of Lifelong Education, and Co-director of the Clinical Developmental Institute in Massachusetts. Kegan also lectures widely to professional and lay audiences.

KEGAN'S VIEW OF IDENTITY

Impressed with the contributions Piaget had made to understanding the development of logical thinking in children as well as object relations theorists' delineation of the ego, Kegan's bold new construct of identity has emerged from the marriage of these two traditions. How-ever, rather than addressing the marital relationship *between* cognition and affect (a time-honored developmental pursuit), Kegan has shifted psychological orientation completely by attending to the possible developmental process that *underlies* cognition and affect and initially brings both into being:

> We begin by asking not 'What is the relationship between affect and cognition?' but 'What is the relationship that "has" cognition and affect?' . . . If we begin by assuming that cognition and affect are not separable – that neither leads to or governs the other, that they are actually aspects of a common process – then we shift our atten-tion from the relationship between them to the common process that subtends them.
>
> (Kegan *et al.* 1982: 105)

By analogy, Kegan considers a cylinder with two openings – if atten-tion is focused on the openings, one could consider this geometric form as two holes connected by a glass tube. Yet such a construction of 'reality' does not really capture the essence of the cylinder – that entity which creates the two openings in the first place. 'Cognition and affect, similarly, might not have a relationship so much as they are created out of a bigger context that has them' (Kegan *et al.* 1982: 106). It is this larger context which Kegan addresses in defining identity.

Kegan's construct draws particularly upon cognitive-developmental notions of Piaget and Kohlberg as well as object relations theory in describing identity (or meaning-making) as the way 'the organism and the environment in which it is embedded keep reconstructing their relationship . . . . [Meaning-making is] a series of qualitative reconstruc-tions of the relation between the subject and the object of experience' (Kegan *et al.* 1982: 107). Development, that process giving rise to both cognition and affect, is an activity that brings into being structures which define the boundaries between self and other. In other words, identity formation (or meaning-making) is an ongoing process in which the boundaries between self and other become structured, lost, and reformed. The activity of meaning-making, of organizing and making sense of the world, and then losing that coherence and sense of self to a newly emerging way of being and making sense are the foundations of the constructive-developmental approach; questions re-garding the form and process of meaning-construction are this orienta-tion's preoccupation.

More now about the meaning of 'self' and 'other' before addressing their changing relationship. 'Self' (or subject) to Kegan refers to that intrapsychic framework in which one is embedded and from which one is unable to create distance; it is not possible to have or to be aware of one's framework when embedded in it. For example, a young child *is* his or her impulses and perceptions; rather than *having* impulses and perceptions under the self's control, the 2-year-old's self *is* that which he or she perceives and desires. As for the meaning of 'other' (or object), Kegan's usage differs somewhat from that of object relations theorists reviewed in Chapter 3. To the latter, *object* refers to an image or internalized representation of a person important to us that guides much of our present behavior. For Kegan, *object* refers not to our internalized representation of another person at all but rather to more general phenomena that we come to relinquish – 'to those feelings, thoughts, constructs, and relationships that we can step out of, observe, and thus manipulate' (Noam *et al.* 1983: 101). The term *object* means literally 'thrown away from'; for Kegan, identity or meaning-making is about the way in which we come to 'throw away' something that once was a part of the self and make it an object to a new, restructured self so that what we once *were* we now *have*. Subject (self) and object (other) are in an ongoing process of change that may continue over the course of the life-span.

For Kegan, understanding the balance (or lack thereof) between subject and object is crucial to untangling the process by which identity or the making of meaning evolves over the course of the life-span. Development through the eyes of constructive-developmental theory is about the systematic way in which people change boundaries between that which is taken as self and that which is taken to be other, about that which gets thrown away; furthermore, it is about how that which gets thrown away is later re-integrated into a new kind of relationship with the self. As development proceeds for the 2-year-old described earlier, perceptions and impulses move to the object side of the subject–object balance and come under the control of a more differentiated self. And so the 5-or 6-year-old is said to *have* rather than *be* his or her perceptions or impulses; that which was self has become object to a new self structure. While an old self (one which *was* its perceptions/impulses) has been 'thrown away', a new and more differentiated self, *having* its perceptions/ impulses, is gained. Thus, identity formation (meaning-making) is the process of balancing and rebalancing following a shift from the subject to object side of the subject–object relationship. Rather than occurring only during adolescence, it is a process having regularity in sequence, form, and movement that may continue its motion over the life-span.

Kegan refers to a subject–object (self–other) relationship in balance

as an *evolutionary truce*. More accurately, '[e]volutionary truces establish a balance between subject and object' (Kegan 1982: 28). Truces are
a time when the world 'makes sense', though that sense it makes differs
markedly for individuals in different subject–object balances. Such is
the situation faced by Peter and Jerry in making sense of their afternoon chance encounter from different self–other balances. And such is
the situation responsible for an exasperated mother's ultimate realization in dealing with her young son in an example to follow. Kegan
anecdotally tells the tale of a mother with two sons squabbling over
their allocation of a dessert pastry. It seems the younger, a 4-year-old,
has received only one portion because he is smaller, while his 10-year-
old brother has received two. In total frustration following her failed
efforts to assure the younger child of his 'just dessert' when he is older,
the mother cuts her 4-year-old's pastry in half.

> 'You want two pieces? Okay, I'll give you two pieces. Here!' – where-
> upon she neatly cut the younger boy's pastry in half. Immediately
> all the tension went out of him; he thanked his mother sincerely,
> and contentedly set upon his dessert. The mother and the older son
> were both astonished. They looked at the boy the way you would
> look at something stirring in a wastebasket. Then they looked at
> each other; and in that moment they shared a mutually discovered
> insight into the reality of their son and brother, a reality quite
> different from their own.
>
> (Kegan 1982: 27–8)

For this 4-year-old, no error or inconsistency is present in his judgment. 'The deep structure of the [evolutionary] truce, simply put, is
that the perceptions are on the side of the subject; that is, the child is
subject to his perceptions in his organization of the physical world'
(Kegan 1982: 28-9). This youngster is unable to separate his self from
his impulses or perceptions; rather than *having* impulses and perceptions, he *is* them. Embedded in his perceptions, this pre-operational
child has no self capable of organizing changed perceptions; thus it is
the world (and the two pieces of pastry it now appears to offer) rather
than his perceptions of it that change through mother's actions.
'Distinguishing between how something appears and how something *is*
is just what one cannot do when one is subject to the perceptions'
(Kegan 1982: 29). This child's evolutionary truce, however, should
soon change when that which was self (impulses/perceptions) is
'thrown away' to become the object in a new balance or evolutionary
truce. Then and only then will mother be foiled in her plot to provide
'more' dessert by cutting one portion in half.

In contrast to many stage theorists, Kegan is also interested in the transitions between stages of meaning-making. We spend much of our lives being developmentally 'out-of-balance', moving from one state of subject–object balance to another, and it is to those who accompany another on such a journey of transition that Kegan's theory speaks particularly well. Implications for clinical as well as more naturalistic modes of intervention emerge from this constructive-developmental view and will be described in a later section. Rather than 'breakdown' in one's meaning-making efforts, Kegan prefers the alternative concept of 'breakthrough' to capture the essence of change from an old to a new balance. Transition involves loss, a mourning of that loss, and experiencing a sense of vacuum prior to rebalance. 'All growth is costly. It involves leaving behind an old way of being in the world. Often it involves, at least for a time, leaving behind the others who have been identified with that old way of being' (Kegan 1982: 215). All transitions involve a period of time in which the self is not yet sufficiently differentiated from its old context of embeddedness to take that context as its new object. In a recent pilgrimage through files of old notes, I came across a poem, hand-scrawled, by a late adolescent student. It reflects very clearly that state of suspension between old and new equilibra, where it seems that 'nothing is, is now'; like the commonly used analogy of an adolescent swinging in space between bars of two trapezes, this teenager has no framework between evolutionary balances from which to make the world cohere:

How to endure the space beyond time's next dot
Where nothing is
Is now
And all that was
Is no more
And that that is, isn't.

(Janine, aged 19)

The essence of transition between states of subject–object equilibrium is a 're-cognition', an awareness that 'all [the me] that was, is no more'. When the balance as to what 'self' is 'me' shifts sufficiently to the object side of the subject–object balance, the new self takes as object its old framework of embeddedness, thereby granting 'me' the ability to reflect upon it. Thus, a poem by Janine in her new evolutionary truce might end, 'And all that was, *is* no more, but now I've grown to *have* it'.

Most recently, Kegan (1994) has turned to examine the fit between contemporary western culture's demands on its adolescents and adults and their developmental capacities actually to meet those demands. Kegan has argued that for at least some significant part of our lives, there is a gross mismatch between the complexity of our culture's 'curriculum' and our mental capacity to 'grasp it' in the arenas of schooling, working, parenting, partnering, and psychotherapy. He suggests that it is necessary to make explicit our culture's 'hidden curriculum', its expectations for adolescents and adults, in order both to increase sensitivity to subject–object balances individuals may need to reach in order to satisfy cultural expectations as well as to provide appropriate supports for the evolutionary process. These issues will be examined more fully in the section on the implications of constructive-developmental theory for social response.

THE EVOLUTION OF MEANING-MAKING

Kegan (1982: 81) proposes that the making of meaning evolves through a sequence of qualitatively different stages: 'I suggest that human development involves a succession of renegotiated balances, or 'biologics', which come to organize the experience of the individual in qualitatively different ways'. The questions that might now well be asked are, 'What are these qualitatively different ways that give rise to cognitive and affective structures, and what brings such ways into being?' Here, Kegan turns to Piaget and Kohlberg for their work on the development of meaning-making in the physical and social worlds; it is through these 'ways of knowing' that clues exist regarding a possible underlying organization that gives rise to developmental differences in children's logic in the first place. We, too, will turn briefly to these writers for a reinterpretation of meaning-making through Kegan's constructive-developmental lens. Following such excursions, we will journey in some detail through Kegan's subsuming stages of subject–object organization that he holds responsible for Piagetian and Kolbergian observations.

Believing Piaget to be a genius finding more than he sought, Kegan (1979; 1982) views the implications of Piaget's stages of cognitive change during childhood and adolescence as pointing the way towards a concept of personality (not merely cognition) as revolutionary as that of Freud. Each stage of cognitive understanding in Piaget's framework signifies that very underlying cylinder of self which makes the world cohere. In Piaget's sensori-motor infant, who uses a logic based on reflex action, Kegan finds a child living in its first developmental truce – that of *being* rather than *having* its reflexes and sensations. Here the child does its thinking by moving and sensing. As the subject–object balance tilts, the child comes to *have* rather than *be* its reflexes, and a new subjective is thereby created. Reflexes and sensations now are object for a self which is able to reflect upon its own sensations. 'When the child is able to have his reflexes rather than be them, he stops thinking he causes the world to go dark when he closes his eyes' (Kegan 1982: 31). This new self structure is that of Piaget's pre-operational child, now embedded in her perceptions and impulses but able to organize which sensations are me and which are not-me. The 4-year-old described earlier who received his 'just dessert' exemplifies a self embedded in (subject to) his perceptions. For the concrete operational child, Kegan asserts that perceptions/impulses (the old subject) have 'moved over' to become the object to a self now embedded in a concrete construction of the physical world. Within the limits of this truce, physical properties of the self and world are explored; finding solutions to games of skill and knowledge become guiding quests. Through Kegan's framework, the final evolutionary truce Piaget describes is that of formal operational thought. When this new truce is negotiated, there appears the ability to reflect on that which *was* the concrete operational thinker – a self embedded in (or subject to) the 'actual'. Through the evolution of formal thought, the adolescent self is one which can now reflect upon the 'actual' as only one (rather boring) instance of a far greater range of 'possibles'. '... this new balance makes 'what is' a mere instance of 'what might be' (Kegan 1982: 38). And so hypothetico-deductive reasoning appears. The subject (self) has once again become the object of a new subjective, as the 'actual' becomes object to a subjective of the 'possible'.

The extension of Piaget's work by Lawrence Kohlberg (described in Chapter 4) also provides a lead into that underlying cylinder of the self, according to Kegan. As with Piaget's developmental account of meaning-making in the physical world, it is similarly possible to reinterpret Kohlberg's developmental scheme of moral meaning-making; both accounts, Kegan argues, point to that process underlying and giving rise to both schemes in the first place. Young children's constructions of social meanings (morality) would appear governed by the same forces allowing them to make sense of the physical world. Kohlberg's first evolutionary truce (heteronomous morality) can be viewed as one in which the child's perceptions (both social and physical) are subject; the child's self here is embedded in its perceptions, thereby making impossible any understanding of another's intention. (This balance is Piaget's description of the pre-operational child.) As perception becomes object during the second evolutionary truce (individualism, instrumental purpose, and exchange), we find a self able to appreciate that other people have perspectives of their own. Now, however, the self is embedded in its own needs and unable to orientate one perspective to another. Those operating from the next balance, Kohlberg's stage 3 (interpersonal concordance) orientation, now have their needs as objects 'thrown from' the former self. Here, however, the self is not yet differentiated enough to *have* its relationships; rather, the self *is* its interpersonal affiliations. Early formal operations are required for reciprocal role-taking. As subject 'moves over' in the transition to Kohlberg's 'law and order' orientation of stage 4, relationships now become object to the new 'me', a me *having* rather than *being* its interpersonal affiliations. Stage 4, however, also has its own self-embeddedness context. No longer bound to pleasing others in the immediate social group in order to construct one's notions of right and wrong, one now is embedded in a larger social order. Or, more accurately, one creates a larger social order of embeddedness. Here, one *is* one's organizational affiliations. In transcending embeddedness in these social or ideological groups, the subject of post-conventional moral reasoners (stages 5 and 6) has once again 'moved over' – that organizational context defining the self of stage 4 individuals now becomes object to a new subjective *having* rather than *being* its corporate commitments. 'The result is that one comes to distinguish moral values apart from the authority of groups holding those values' (Kegan 1982: 67). Thus Kohlberg's stages of moral meaning-making may also be created by that underlying cylinder of personality giving rise to Piaget's stages of making sense of the physical world.

Kegan's constructive-developmental view holds that it is the individual's inability to satisfy itself which drives development. By attending to discrepant experiences found through exposure to different situations, the organism strives not to return to its old homoeostatic state of subject–object balance but rather to create a new and more complex self (subject) able to make sense of and respond to the new reality. While no easy feat, each hard-won balance brings with it a new kind of recognition of how the world and the self have become more distinct while at the same time more related.

Self–other balancing is not something one pursues in isolation. The constructive-developmental framework suggests that a 'holding environment' or 'culture of embeddedness' with its own particular features and functions is crucial to one's successful emergence from embeddedness with what will become 'object' in the next balance. 'The infant, I have said, is embedded in its sensing and moving, but there is a real human environment in which it lives, with which it confuses its own sensing and moving' (Kegan 1982: 115). While, from the infant's view, mother is part of the self, she is also its holding environment, that 'real human environment' in which the child's self–other balancing takes place. Mother (or primary care-taker) provides the external medium for the infant's evolution, for its efforts at making the world cohere. Having learned something of the cylindrical openings observed by Piaget and Kohlberg leading to a vision of their underlying generator, let us now view that which may constitute the cylinder of identity itself, according to Kegan, and gives rise to the normative adolescent experience of 'I'.

The growth and loss of the incorporative self (stage 0)

Infants join us equipped with reflexes which have been adaptive in the prenatal environment; most of these responses are rather useful during the early months of terrestrial existence, too. At this time, the infant *is* its reflexes and sensations, without awareness of a world separate from its self; the infant *is* its reflexes, all self and no object. Since there cannot yet be a subject–object balance, Kegan *et al.* (1982) have termed this incorporative phase, stage 0. This is the stage which gives birth to the object, and such is the structure underwriting Piaget's stage of sensori-motor intelligence.

Kegan (1982) turns to Erikson's young patient, Jean, for an interpretation of her predicament in the framework of constructive-developmental theory. Although 6 years of age when Erikson meets her, Jean's meaning-making system is closer to that of an incorporative infant. Separated from her mother between 9 and 14 months to allow the latter to recover from tuberculosis, Jean failed to differentiate and emerge from embeddedness with her reflexes and sensations; as a result, other people have failed to come into being in her meaning-making system. At the very time Jean would have been separating from her culture of embeddedness in transition to the next evolutionary balance, that culture left her. Jean's emergence from this incorporative stage may have been thwarted by the collapse of the very 'holding' context for her budding self–other evolution. Compounding the loss of some part of herself which was only just beginning to become object, Jean lost the very ground supporting this transition itself. In the process, she appears to have thrown both herself (subject) along with the budding object (her sensations) completely away.

For those more fortunate than Jean, a self *having* rather than *being* its reflexes will gradually emerge from the incorporative balance. Such is the status of meaning-making for the stage 1 impulsive self; however, now the subject–object relationship is embedded in a new intrapsychic framework – that of perceptions and impulses.

The growth and loss of the impulsive balance (stage 1, or first order of consciousness)

Kegan (1982: 139) says of the child hanging in the stage 1 balance, 'An infant discovers that there is a world separate from him; but not until years later does the child discover that this separate world is not subject to him'. This summary is a beautifully simple yet eloquent description of life through the eyes of the 2- to 5-year-old child embedded in his or her perceptions and impulses. A world separate from the child has been created in its evolutionary process; yet at the same time, that world is at the mercy of the child's perceptions – with different views of something, it is the world (and not the child's perceptions of it) that changes.

Here it is just not possible to coordinate two or more differing views of the same thing, for there has not yet evolved a self differentiated from its perceptions to do the organizing of them. Thus, one is unable to take the role of another. Cognitively, there is no ability to reverse operations; affectively, there is no ability to experience ambivalence. The self or others can only be experienced as all good or all bad but not a mixture of both. A child now believes everyone sees things from his or her point of view. This ability to take the role of another, to see that others have perspectives of their own, involves a further reconstruction of the subject–object balance which lies a few years down the road for the preschooler in her present meaning-making truce.

Cognitive-developmental and psychoanalytic theory have noted important milestones occurring during the 2- to 5-year-old's life-span. Kegan continues by reinterpreting cognitive-developmental observations of how the child learns to take the role of another as well as the psychoanalytic account of the Oedipus complex. Both phenomena can be read as a self subject to its own impulses and perceptions evolving within the holding environment of the family. We have earlier seen the results of a pre-operational child subject to his own perceptions – the world (and not his perceptions of it) changed when a dessert pastry was cut in half. The Freudian family romance may be no more than that – a child, embedded in its own impulses playing them out within the context of its natural culture of embeddedness, the family. Kegan does not find it enlightening to consider the young child as wishing to have a parent as a lover; rather, it is the holding environment of the family that becomes the protector of the child's impulses and the recipient of its mode of loving. Indeed, the very fact that one parent often becomes the source of impulse gratification and the other an inhibitor really results from the child's inability to integrate 'hero and villain' in one person. Oedipal issues may so often arise in the free associations of adult patients, for the very practice of psychoanalysis itself encourages that fantasy-filled, representational, imaginative mode of thought characteristic of the pre-operational preschooler. Again, an underlying evolutionary cylinder giving rise to both cognitive and affective phenomena appears as a distinct possibility.

Transition from the balance of the impulsive self finds the child bringing impulses and perceptions under his own control; that which was the impulsive self becomes the object of a new subjective. In an anecdotal account of an expedition with several 6-year-olds to see the Disney film *Pete's Dragon,* Kegan (1985) captures the essence of the children's evolutionary transition. The film, partly fantasy and partly 'real' (like thought in the pre-operational to concrete-operational transition), depicts the adventures of a young boy, Pete, and a dragon friend who eventually helps Pete obtain a pretty decent set of parents. Mission accomplished, dragon takes leave of Pete and parents, who live happily ever after. Not so, however, for the children under Kegan's charge. In tears, one little girl cries, 'Why do these movies always have to end so sad? . . . Why can't he have both? Why can't he have the dragon *and* the nice parents? Why can't he have both?' (Kegan 1985: 180). For Kegan's young companions, pre-operational and Oedipal stages are in their final days; the world of concrete reality takes over as dragon life fades and the child comes to coordinate his or her impulses and perceptions to take on a more defined role within the family unit. One cannot, it seems, have both dragon and real world drama in the next evolutionary truce. Beyond the age 5 to 7 transition, a new balance with its own form of self-embeddedness once again appears; while *having* rather than *being* its impulses, the imperial self of stage 2 is now embedded in its own needs, interests, and wishes.

The growth and loss of the imperial balance (stage 2, or second order of consciousness)

That imperial self of the concrete operational child comes to take over the function of impulse control previously exercised by the family. Both internal and external experience are now conserved. Stability of needs and habits becomes more evident in contrast to the whimsical lability of the preschooler's impulse life. Children hanging in the imperial balance become more self-sufficient, evidencing a 'self-containment' and sense of agency. In coordinating perceptions, the realization comes that others truly do have their own perspectives, and one's own is not automatically read and shared by all. Now one's own needs, interests, and wishes *are* the self. That self cannot yet coordinate different needs of others, for such capability comes only when subject (needs, interests, wishes) differentiates and becomes the object for a new interpersonal subjective in transition to stage 3's interpersonal balance.

In another anecdote, Kegan (1982) tells of his teaching experiences with a class of 12-year-olds, most of whom were embedded in this imperial balance. They were asked one day to describe the moral of Murray Heyert's short story, 'The New Kid'. In the story, it seems Marty is clumsy, always chosen last for the neighborhood's baseball team and always relegated to the outfield. During a game, Marty has his opportunity for glory – and, of course, blows it by failing to catch the ball and save his team from defeat, once again becoming the recipient of much scorn and abuse. Then one day a new kid arrives who, it seems, is even more of an oddity than Marty. He follows in Marty's footsteps, failing spectacularly at the crucial ball-catching moment. And lo and behold, it is Marty who leads the humiliating attack on this new-found object of derision. Even more startling, however, were responses to what the story meant by the children in Kegan's classroom:

> The story is saying that people may be mean to you and push you down and make you feel crummy and stuff, but it's saying things aren't really that bad because eventually you'll get your chance to push someone else down and then you'll be on top.
>
> (Kegan 1982: 47)

In the imperial balance, these 12-year-olds could only make meaning from an embeddedness in their own needs and interests; the ability to coordinate their own interests with those of another is just what the imperial self cannot do, for the self has not yet differentiated to the point of being able to reflect upon its needs, taking them as object to be coordinated with others. Most children in Kegan's classroom evidenced simple reciprocity; yet, they could not consider how both Marty and the new kid felt, orientating one to the other. Such limits of meaning-making underlie Kohlberg's stage 2 hedonistic orientation towards morality.

The school and peer group become the culturing environment to those making meaning from the imperial balance; both can provide the supportive structure of expectations and response appealing to many young souls. Schools concerned about education without failure are providing a vital 'holding' function that helps set the tone for the child's evolutions to come. In the world beyond the family unit, it is the school and peer group which can now supply the respect and esteem due to children in the process of making sense according to their own needs and interests. Such is the balance and culture of embeddedness for most children of primary school age; such may also be the balance for the child behind the mask of the adult sociopath (Kegan 1986a).

The growth and loss of the interpersonal balance (stage 3, or third order of consciousness)

The adolescent is expected to be interpersonally trustworthy. This expectation arises from a long history of evolutionary activity and is possible only as the self–other balance tips so that needs and interests become the self's new object; now the self *has* (rather than *is*) its needs and is able to reflect upon them and coordinate them with those of others. Here, one is expected to be able to uphold a promise and generally become orientated towards mutuality in relationship. While reciprocal role-taking seems to be the triumph of transition to this new balance, the interpersonal is its constraint. For the stage 3 interpersonal self, one does not *have* one's interpersonal relationships; the self *is* its relationships and very vulnerable to attitudes within the immediate social context.

> A white teenager living in a liberal northern suburb may espouse values of racial egalitarianism if that is the prevailing peer ethic, only to become a holder of racist views among racist friends if her family relocates to a school and neighborhood in the South or closer to the action in the North. The prevailing wisdom here will be that the teenager has changed as a result of new friends and new influences; it would be as true to say, however, that the teenager's way of making meaning has remained the same.
>
> (Kegan 1982: 57)

Kohlberg's interpersonal concordance orientation would seem to reflect this new balance, wherein the self is embedded in its need for another's approval and unable to step out of this shared reality.

Kegan (1982) notes that it is often the person embedded in the interpersonal balance whom the assertiveness trainer inappropriately targets. Assertiveness courses, with their emphasis on skills for declaring 'more independently' one's needs and wishes, misses the predicament of the interpersonal self. With no self yet differentiated from the inter-personal, there is no subject to do the asserting; it is thus to a vacuum that the assertiveness trainer speaks when addressing the stage 3 self. Similarly, it is often difficult for the interpersonal self to express anger, for such behavior threatens disruption of the very relationship which *is* the self. Often individuals in this balance may be victimized in relation-ships yet be unable to experience anger (or relinquish the relationship), for such action threatens that very self–other balance which one is. Qualitative differences in the way the self coheres must be appreciated and addressed for therapeutic intervention to be effective.

The interpersonal self is the normative subject–object truce of early and mid-adolescence; transition to a new form of independence from the interpersonal is the hallmark of late adolescent and young adult identity. During such transformation, however, the individual must once again undergo the loss of an old balance; this time, it is one's relationships which become object to the new self, now embedded in its institutional or ideological affiliations.

The growth and loss of the institutional balance (stage 4, or fourth order of consciousness)

In differentiating from the medium of the interpersonal, the institu-tional balance gives birth to a sense of self-authorship. *Having* rather than *being* its relationships, the self evolving to stage 4 again experi-ences the ability to internalize that which was previously external. Now the interpersonal is regulated by a self differentiated from others; here, it is threats to personal autonomy rather than relationships which bring about defensive operations. 'The strength of stage 4 is its psycho-logical self-employment, its capacity to own oneself, rather than having all the pieces of oneself owned by various shared contexts' (Kegan *et al.* 1982: 115).

A young man, Jonathon, whom I interviewed as part of a longitudi-nal study of identity formation during late adolescence, reflected on the changes he saw in himself during the two years covered by the study. He seemed unable to pinpoint very specifically just what had happened to him in his own development, but had the following to say:

> Well, they've changed [my beliefs and values], but in subtle ways. Whereas before I believed what I believed because I didn't know any different, now it's because I have some much more well thought-out ideas about why I believe what I believe, even though what I believe may not have changed tremendously.

Kegan might argue that what has happened to Jonathon is the very emergence of a self coming to author itself. The old balance of 'believing what I believed because I didn't know any different' was limited by that form of knowing which *was* its interpersonal context. What was subject (the interpersonal) has shifted to the object side of the subject–object balance, enabling Jonathon now to reflect upon his former structure from the self-authorship balance of his present way of making sense.

Kegan quotes one of his clients, whom he feels very clearly lies in this stage 4 balance. There is a sense of self-ownership coming through Rebecca's words; yet it is the very rigidity of this self-ownership which limits this stage 4 evolutionary truce:

> I know I have very defined boundaries and I protect them very carefully. I won't give up the slightest control. In any relationship I decide who gets in, how far, and when.
>
> What am I afraid of? I used to think I was afraid people would find out who I really was and then not like me. But I don't think that's it anymore. What I feel now is – 'That's me. That's mine. It's what makes me. And I'm powerful. It's my negative side, maybe, but it's also my positive stuff – and there's a lot of that. What it is, is me, it's my self – and if I let people in maybe they'll take it, maybe they'll use it, and I'll be gone.'
>
> (Kegan 1979: 16)

Rebecca's self *is* the psychic organization it is trying to run smoothly. In the stage 4 balance, the self derives meaning from the organization rather than deriving the organization from one's own meaning or valuing system. Here, one *is* one's career, citizenship, religion. There is no broader or more encompassing framework within which to relativize one's organizational commitments, no self to organize its organizations. Piaget's stage of full formal operations and Kohlberg's 'law and order orientation' are the observables resulting from this evolutionary balance.

The culture of embeddedness for the institutional self is the larger social order – that public arena in which one is normatively received and recognized during late adolescence and adulthood. Without adequate recognition by such institutional holding environments, the evolutionary process is once again under threat. Transition to the interindividual balance sees the self with an increasing desire to question that which motivated its affiliations to those institutions with which it has been identified; there is thus a gradual and increasing differentiation from the value generator itself.

The growth of the interindividual balance (stage 5, or fifth order of consciousness)

The last evolutionary truce for which there is evidence is one in which the self is differentiated from its institutions – there is now a self which *has* rather than *is* its institutional affiliations. The new interindividual balance coordinates institutional selves and, in turn, is embedded in inter-individuality. Now, it is possible to have an interdependent self-definition, for a self is 'brought to, rather than derived from, others'. While one can feel manipulated by the stage 2 imperial self, devoured by the stage 3 interpersonal self, and 'mediated' by the stage 4 institutional self administrating its business, the stage 5 interindividual self is there, open to its own re-creation through ongoing contact and exchanges with other individuals and systems, also open to change and redefinition.

From this last balance, one comes to *have* rather than *be* one's career, religion, nationality or other institutional affiliation. Institutions are no longer upheld as ends in themselves, for they no longer reign supreme (for example, career performance is no longer ultimate). Rather, a new structure of the self exists which looks to ways in which institutions might better serve the self's own purposes in growth. Kohlberg's post-conventional level is characterized by a self dislodged from its societal lodgings; at this stage, the legal system lies at the foot of a self capable of creating (rather than merely upholding) the law. This moral reasoning level Kegan finds governed by that deep structure of the interindividual balance. Similarly, there is evidence of a fifth Piagetian stage beyond formal operations, wherein there is the ability to stand outside a system and reflect on it, rather than using the system to be the means of one's reflecting; Kegan and his colleagues again find this stage of cognitive understanding governed by that deep structure of the interindividual balance (Souvaine *et al.* 1990).

Themes of differentiation and integration, of separation and inclusion spiral throughout the balances and transitions of the evolving self; however the relationship of these themes or *stylistic preferences* to one's actual *structure* of meaning-making has been clarified by Kegan in his more recent writings (Kegan 1994).

> Moreover, I confused *style* and *structure* throughout *The Evolving Self* by using an organizing metaphor or image I have since come to 'repent' (literally, 'to think again'). . . . I equated certain orders of consciousness (the first and the third [subject–object balance]) with the style of *connection* and other orders of consciousness (the second and the fourth [subject–object balance]) with the style of

separateness. Unconfusing these sets of distinctions involves seeing that each order of consciousness can favor either of the two fundamental longings [for connection or separateness].

(Kegan 1994: 221)

Thus, in any of Kegan's subject–object balances, one might adopt a 'relational' or 'separate' style of approach to the developmental task of meaning construction.

While Mahler *et al.* (1975) and Blos (1967) have emphasized experiences of intrapsychic separation and connection, the birth and adolescent rebirth of the self, Kegan argues that the process not only of differentiation but also of integration occurs again and again over the course of the life-cycle.

> Mahler understands her work to suggest that the person is not born only once, as it were, but is psychologically born a second time as it emerges from an *extra*-uterine symbiosis. My reading of the structural-developmental research, in concert with my own clinical work and clinically oriented research, suggests that we are psychologically born *again and again.*

(Kegan 1983: 294)

Each renegotiation of the evolutionary balance between self and other means not only the death of an old subject but the birth of a new self. This process normatively occurs during early and late adolescence in transitions to stages 3 and 4, respectively; however, meaning-making to Kegan is a lifelong activity with rebalancing not restricted to the years of adolescence alone.

AN OPTIMAL MODE OF MEANING-MAKING

Like others before him, Kegan, too, has shifted from a health/illness model of identity to one which views identity formation as a developmental phenomenon. For Kegan, definition of healthy identity holds dangers similar to that 'bag of virtues' approach to moral education described by Kohlberg; there can be no absolute model of good mental health. All definitions, from traditional psychiatry to humanistic psychology, are biased, reflecting attitudes of a particular reference group. An orientation towards development, on the other hand, provides a framework from which to generate more justifiable goals for intervention in that norms of growth can be addressed. During early and middle adolescence, one would expect to see youngsters generally making meaning from the imperial (stage 2) or interpersonal (stage 3) balances (or not making sense from the stage 2–3 transition). Late adolescents present a greater range of possibilities for meaning construction, and Kegan refrains from specifying normative age ranges for stages beyond the imperial-interpersonal transition. However, one might generally anticipate late adolescent meaning-making from the interpersonal or institutional balances (based on Kohlberg's longitudinal data) or not so doing from the stage 3-4 transition. Certainly the educational system requires of all adolescents simple role-taking skills, and intervention will be needed if a young person is unable to make sense from at least the imperial balance by early adolescence.

CRITICISM OF KEGAN'S CONSTRUCT

In its relatively short life-span, constructive-developmental theory has not attracted a large body of criticism. One body of protest has come from those concerned with its lack of empirical verification (Loevinger 1979b, 1983; Snarey *et al.* 1983). Though derived from research based on cognitive-developmental and object relations' models, constructive-developmental theory is now beginning to validate its proposals by research from within its own ranks – see Kegan (1994) for a more thorough review of current empirical research.

Loevinger (1979b) has raised additional conceptual and methodological criticisms. She has questioned Kegan's claim to one underlying logic of development from which other domains of cognitive and ego functioning spring. Additionally, she questions the neatness with which Kegan seems to suggest that individuals fall into evolutionary truces and transitions. She notes that in developmental schemes, interviewees regularly fail to fit existing rating criteria for stage placement. Loevinger concludes that if one recognizes this empirical phenomenon, 'the belief that one's deductions are so logically compelling as to require no empirical support may fade' (Loevinger 1979b: 40). Kegan himself, however, fully endorses the need for empirical verification and does not make statements to the contrary in his theoretical writings (Kegan 1982, 1994).

Kegan has been criticized by feminist writers on the grounds that his hierarchical developmental model arbitrarily places women in a position of disadvantage; the stage 3 interpersonal balance may simply characterize a women's way of organizing experience, while the stage 4 institutional balance may more aptly portray the experience of men. Kegan's recent (1994) clarification of stylistic and structural differences in meaning construction, however, greatly illuminates the ways in which the sexes may or may not adopt stylistic differences in the development of their actual structures of meaning-making.

Further questions have been raised regarding details of the theory itself. Snarey *et al.* (1983) point to many questions raised by the constructive-developmental approach. They ask whether the hierarchy of biological and social organizing principles are genuinely structural and developmental rather than merely parallel processes (for example, do impulses change into needs or do they come from different starting points?). They also question the lack of distinction Kegan makes between thought and action, an important boundary in Piagetian and Kohlbergian theory. Noam further questions the viability of Kegan's unified self model and has attempted to develop a more comprehensive model of development by examining the role played by individual biography in potentially limiting structural change (Noam 1988, 1990, 1992). Barrett and Harren (1979) suggest the need to account for unconscious processes in the evolution of the self, while Soldz (1988) argues for consideration of the phenomenon of regression in Kegan's constructive-developmental approach. Other critics have questioned what it is that is generally common to a given subject–object balance that is shared by elements from different cognitive, affective, interpersonal, and intrapersonal domains; for example, how are impulses and perceptions similar in their underlying meaning-making structure? In his latest volume, Kegan (1994) has addressed many of these criticisms, and the constructive-developmental model appears as an exciting approach to integrating cognitive and affective forces within a single life-span framework of identity evolution.

RESEARCH FINDINGS ON THE EVOLVING SELF

Constructive-developmental theory has been used to account for a variety of naturalistic, clinical, and laboratory phenomena; however, the work of Kegan and colleagues is still in its infancy and requires the necessary complement of empirical study to verify more fully what a reinterpretation of existing research has begun to unravel. (See Kegan 1982, 1985, and 1994 for empirical bases of the evolving self model.) While this section will overview existing research based specifically on Kegan's model, it will also discuss that which is still needed to validate further this constructive-developmental approach.

The first empirical study making use of constructive-developmental concepts examined the relationship between depression and subject–object balance. Kegan (1979, 1982) has argued that depression is the companion of a subject–object balance in the process of transition; different forms and experiences of depression might therefore be associated with transitions between different evolutionary truces. Based on a pilot study with thirty-nine individuals during their stay on a hospital psychiatric ward, Kegan believed he and his colleagues had detected three qualitatively different forms of depression in descriptions patients provided of their predicaments.

These three types of depression all involved a self under threat. Type A ('self-sacrificing') depression was felt by those concerned over loss of their own needs or the increasing cost of keeping them at bay. Feelings of being constrained, controlled, deprived, interfered with or, alternatively, a mixture between feeling 'a slave to my own interests' and a 'loss of my own distinct personality' were often expressed by these individuals. 'With loss of the satisfaction of my wants, I may no longer be' seemed to be the root of this existential dilemma. Type B ('dependent') depression was felt by those experiencing a relationship under threat. Feelings of being abandoned, betrayed, forsaken, and unbearably lonely were often experienced, as were alternations between feeling fused with another and then guilty for 'putting myself first'. The fundamental issue here seemed to be that with the loss of my relationships, I may cease to exist. Type C ('self-evaluative') depression was experienced as a blow to self-esteem, a failure to live up to the expectations people held for themselves. Subjectively, people here spoke of feeling humiliated, empty, and out-of-control in an unfair world where life was meaningless; sometimes a mixture of emotions appeared, from identification with performance and feeling isolated to feeling weak, evil, or unbounded. Here, the void looming large was that with the loss of my self-authorship, I may cease to be.

Each individual was rated according to one of these depression types by researchers blind as to the person's self–other differentiation rating. When depression types were compared with self–other differentiation ratings, a very strong association appeared. Those experiencing depression Type A were rated as stage 2 or 2-3 transitional; those experiencing depression Type B were rated as stage 3 or 3-4 transitional; and those experiencing depression Type C were rated as stage 4 or 4-5 transitional. Although small, this pilot study does point to a possible relationship between type of depression and way of making meaning (or, more accurately, failing to do so). These results fit in well with related studies of depression, countering criticism of Kegan's tautological thinking (Kegan 1983). Kegan (1982) also suggests that 'abandonment depression', characterized by separation anxiety, accompanies the stage 0-1 transition, and 'disillusioning depression', characterized by feelings of being shut out, sent away, distressed that others have gone into business for themselves, reflects the concerns of those in the stage 1-2 transition.

Research since this initial study has focused on several important issues in construct assessment and validation. One important advance has involved the development of a reliable instrument and training manual to assess an individual's stage of meaning-construction (subject–object balance). Kegan and his colleagues (Lahey *et al.* 1987) have developed a semi-structured interview, lasting approximately 1– 1½ hours, for the purpose of giving individuals the opportunity to demonstrate the limits of their meaning-making capacities. An individual is asked to select for further discussion several items that evoke memories of recent events from a series of ten key emotional experiences. These key emotional experiences (angry, success, anxious or nervous, strong stand or conviction, sad, torn, moved or touched, lost something, change, important to me) all contain elements of self-reference and boundary. The interviewer then carefully probes the interviewee's experiences to determine not *why* the particular emotion was felt but rather *how* the self must be constructed in order to feel the particular boundary violation the individual has expressed. In addition to identifying the predominant meaning-making stage, the interview rating systems also identifies four transition points along the continuum between all adjacent subject–object balances. Lahey *et al.* (1987) report four studies of interrater reliability, one of test-retest reliability, and one of inter-item consistency. When interrater agreement of subject–object balance is defined as falling within one discrimination unit (1/5 stage), agreement percentages between two raters were 82 per cent, 100 per cent, 100 per cent, and 100 per cent across the four studies. The one study of test-retest reliability reports a Pearson $r = .834$ ($p < .001$) when agreement is defined as falling within one discrimination unit (1/5 stage). The correlation of scores between two forms of the interview was .96 as reported in the one study which addresses the question of inter-item consistency. The subject–object interview has provided the means for assessing structures of meaning-making in the research which is described below.

A crucial move toward construct validation of Kegan's model has come by investigating the claim that progress through meaning-making stages occurs in a hierarchical and invariant sequence. Empirical support for this proposition has now emerged from a nine-year longitudinal study by Kegan and his colleagues (Kegan 1994). In this investigation, twenty-two adults were interviewed annually for four years and then re-interviewed again five years later. With few exceptions, intra-individual change from one data collection point to the next has involved movement in the direction of increasing complexity; without exception, changes were very gradual with no individual demonstrating a shift of more than two discrimination units (2/5 of a stage) over the course of one year. Although further research is needed to verify the claim of an hierarchical and invariant sequence, results from this initial study have been promising.

Over the past decade, the subject–object interview has been used in research to address a number of issues. The question of structural consistency in different domains of life has been examined in Lahey's (1986) research with adult men and women. Lahey conducted forty-four subject–object interviews with twenty-two adults (eleven men and eleven women) to examine the degree of consistency among participants' constructions of the realms of work and intimacy. She found that subjects were no more than one discrimination unit (1/5 stage) apart in eighteen of twenty-two cases – a remarkable show of consistency. The question of gender differences in subject–object scores has been examined by Bar-Yam (1991), who failed to find any significant differences between the sexes in levels of self-evolvement for a sample of adults ranging in age from mid-twenties to mid-fifties. The study concluded that the tendency towards separateness or inclusion may be more related to individual differences in style or the social and cultural environment than underlying meaning-making structure, supporting Kegan's (1994) elaboration of the difference between structure and style. Further research from a constructive-developmental perspective has focused on issues as varied as constructions of partnering (Jacobs 1984; Higgins 1985; Allison 1988), parenting (Kaufman 1985; Osgood 1991), work (Hsia 1992), future time perspectives (Seymour 1991), friendships (Beykema 1990), autobiographical writing (Hodgson 1990), and social perspective-taking (Dixon 1986).

In an interesting secondary analysis of comparable, randomly drawn research samples who had been given subject–object interviews, Kegan (1994) has made the point that at any given moment, it is likely that around one-half to two-thirds of the adult population in the United States has not fully reached the fourth order of consciousness (the institutional balance); given the cultural demands on late adolescents and adults for a fourth order of consciousness, Kegan observes this gap between demand and capacity and points to the enormous mental burden of modern life for the majority of late adolescents and adults in contemporary western culture.

Current directions for constructive-developmental research

In order to continue validation of Kegan's constructive-developmental model, how should assessment be undertaken? Kegan (1985) himself has suggested that individual studies might seek appraisals on a variety of relevant measures for subjects within varying age groups. A study by Pratt *et al.* (1991) has examined the relationships among four systems for thinking about two personal life dilemmas. Adults aged 35–85 each were assessed via the coding schemes for Kohlberg's moral judgment interview, Kegan's subject–object interview, Gilligan's moral orientation interview, and a measure of integrative complexity; the Kohlberg, Kegan, and integrative complexity codings of the dilemmas were positively related to one another. Thus, within at least one larger age range, there is empirical support for Kegan's model. Further, such work towards validation might include measures of cognitive performance on Piagetian tasks, Kohlberg and Selman assessments of social cognition, and various other tests more relevant to specific developmental levels.

Within other age groupings, Kegan has reflected on appropriate means to explore the issue of consistency and further validate his model. For the 4-to 8-year-old child, he suggests the use of measures such as reality or fantasy-orientated play, impulsivity versus impulse control, involvement with parents versus involvement with own projects, and an open or closed boundary orientation in the home to examine consistency across developmental systems. With adolescents, one might assess such issues as ability to regulate impulses, early memories (as an indicator of current world view), self versus parental reference in self description, and ego identity status in addition to Piagetian, Kohlberg, and Selman measures of physical and social cognition. In so doing, one would predict that single subjects should show some consistency across measures, and that one cluster of indicators (pointing towards a less mature form of meaning-making) would characterize younger sample subjects, while another cluster (indicative of more advanced levels of meaning-making) would appear for older subjects sampled. Additional longitudinal assessments also need to be undertaken to confirm the hierarchical and invariant nature of the truce and transition sequences.

IMPLICATIONS FOR SOCIAL RESPONSE

We live in an age when counseling and psychotherapy are often regarded as the panacea to life's ills. With all the complexities and divergences of current psychotherapeutic views and practices, Kegan offers some very simple advice – observe the wisdom of nature and the supports she optimally provides through the family, peer group, work settings, and love relationships. Then let these cultures of embeddedness serve as models not only for psychotherapeutic practice but also for more naturalistic models of intervention. Kegan looks to nature in attempting to specify requirements of optimal 'holding environments' or 'cultures of embeddedness' for assisting a self in its evolutionary business.

> Not only does an understanding of 'natural therapy' – those relations and human contexts which spontaneously support people through the sometimes difficult process of growth and change – offer 'preventative psychology' a sophisticated way to consider a person's supports, it offers a new guide to therapeutic practice by exposing some of the details of those interactions which it is quite possible successful therapy is replicating, whether it knows it or not.
>
> (Kegan 1982: 256)

With these thoughts, Kegan sees several characteristics and functions provided by natural holding environments. When it is functioning optimally, each culture of embeddedness (1) holds securely (confirms and recognizes), (2) lets go at an appropriate time (contradicts and assists differentiation), and (3) remains in place to see its guest through the transition to a new balance. A holding environment must begin by 'holding securely', acknowledging that self which is its guest and participating actively and intimately with the individual in his or her present meaning-making experience. But that environment must also provide contradiction to encourage differentiation. As we have seen, evolution of the self is driven by contradiction which cannot be integrated by the existing self–other balance. That contradiction must be at a level appropriate to its guest in her or his present meaning-making balance, however. In this way alone can the evolving self eventually take over the host's current functions in the next balance. Such contradiction often appears in the form of limit-setting. Finally, the host culture must be there and remain available to support its guest's passage to a new self–other balance. It is primarily the job of the main care-taker, parents, family and school, school and peer group, work context or other public arena, and love relationship to act as holding environments for the incorporative, impulsive, imperial, interpersonal, institutional, and the inter-individual selves, respectively, and thus assist the developmental passage of its guest by remaining intact and available throughout his or her evolutionary passage.

An example of one such culture of embeddedness, with the holding functions it successfully provides, might help us appreciate more fully the supports and contradictions which facilitate identity development. Kegan (1980) met 20-year-old Richard on a special program designed to prepare persons previously regarded as unemployable for jobs. Richard had given others the impression that he did not care about the program and was only in it for the money. Initially arriving late or irregularly, he would comment that he just could not make it and did not understand why he was being treated unfairly; a program that worked on a premise of cooperative decision-making made little sense to Richard. Making meaning from the imperial balance, Richard found that people just got in his way and made life inconvenient. Earlier cultures of embeddedness had failed to meet this young man in the balance that he was. Fortunately this time, however, the special program gradually filled the three holding functions Richard needed for evolution from this balance. It began by *meeting him in his balance and confirming him*. Tasks leading to financial reward and other personal gain were introduced to Richard by instructors teaching the necessary technical skills for completion of a marketable product. Richard's self-interested self was recognized and confirmed through the presentation of skills that would better his financial position. Once hooked into a task, however, Richard eventually met some *contradiction* in the instructor's expectation that Richard would soon regulate his work with others. The special program furthermore *remained in place* for the young man as he gained more than he bargained for. Through the course of the program, Richard actually underwent reconstruction of his self; acknowledgement of his initial meaning-making state followed by contradiction had caused his old subject–object balance to become unhinged. Once successfully established in the interpersonal balance, Richard was able to reflect upon how he had changed. Kegan (1980: 378) gives the following account: '[A]t the beginning of the program he used to worry when he screwed up about what would happen to him, and now, when he screws up, he worries about other people being worried'. The holding environment had successfully fulfilled its three functions, though this match between Richard and the job program had occurred by accident. The implications from constructive-developmental theory, however, are that such provisions for growth can be planned and do not need to be a matter of chance occurrence at all.

When a holding environment fails in any one of its functions, its guest is in trouble. Terry, at 16, was not as fortunate as Richard. Kegan (1980) came to know Terry when she was brought to a psychiatric unit by her exasperated parents, who considered their daughter to be out of control. The final straw had come when Terry skipped school and flew into a rage at her mother's confrontation about the incident. Terry felt her mother was intrusive and nagging, always blocking her desires.

Stealing money from her mother's purse to run away, Terry initially barricaded herself in her room and later led various authorities on a grand chase around town. Once resident on the psychiatric ward, Terry found that this community held expectations of cooperation in group therapy and participation in ward life. Like Richard, Terry was also meaning-making from the imperial balance, which was nearing the end of its life. The ward, however, did not even attempt to meet and confirm Terry in her initial balance. Operating according to her own interests, Terry did not yet possess a self capable of that very mode of meaning-making that the ward assumed – one able to regulate its own impulses and achieve mutuality in relationship. Eventually violating the inviolable (confidentiality of therapy group disclosures and unprescribed drug use), Terry was thrown out of the ward community. Failing to meet Terry where she was, the ward added further insult to injury by not only declining to offer contradiction at a level appropriate to its guest but by ultimately refusing to remain in place for her possible evolution. Had Terry been met and confirmed in her balance, contradicted, and 'held' through the evolutionary process, a far different outcome might have been possible.

What would be features of optimal holding environments for adolescents in the interpersonal and organizational balances? Kegan (1982) suggests that for the interpersonal self, the host culture of embeddedness (natural or psychotherapeutic) must initially recognize and confirm the adolescent's capacity for mutual, self-sacrificing, idealized relationships by sharing her feelings and internal experiences. Following such recognition, it must gradually insist on the recognition of its guest as a distinct and independent agent, responsible for her own self-authorship while still valuing closeness and remaining emotionally available through the transition process (for example, friend or therapist does not leave, the family does not shift locale and disrupt its teenager's relationships). For the organizational self, the environmental host (again natural or psychotherapeutic) must begin by recognizing and confirming its guest's own authorship in providing opportunities for expression, achievement, and responsibility. Gradually, the host must promote differentiation by insisting on relationship with the *person* running the show, refusing mediated, non-intimate forms of response. And finally, organizational supports must remain in place for the guest undergoing the process of intrapsychic separation from them (for example, one is not dismissed from work or a relationship at the very time of transition). Ultimately, the culture of intimacy meets the interpersonal self and enjoys that 'counterpointing of identities' which Erikson describes.

If we want to know another in any fundamental way, we as potential evolutionary hosts must recognize and confirm that balance in which our adolescent guest hangs. The act of joining another in his or her meaning-making system is the base from which subject–object differentiation can later spring. Kegan (1982) believes that Carl Rogers is a master of 'joiners'. The latter's client-centered approach of reflecting feelings at the 'cutting edge' of client awareness goes far beyond a simple parroting reply (an attack sometimes leveled at this technique). Rogers' empathic responding allows host intimately to join guest in the latter's unique as well as more universal way of making sense. Rather than making meaning from the host's agenda (for example, through interpretation of client attitudes), the constructive-developmental approach strongly advocates confirming and joining the guest's meaning-making system as the first order of business, followed by stimulating and accompanying the guest on its journey of self-evolution. Failure of a host environment to join and fully value its occupant's present meaning-making balance, later to let go and encourage differentiation while remaining in place to provide support can only serve to miscarry another's evolutionary life project.

Recently, Kegan (1994) has turned to examine the demands placed upon adolescents and adults by contemporary western culture, and has suggested some specific strategies that society and interested individuals may provide to assist teens into and through the process of structural transition. Demands for the interpersonal balance abound in the expectations schools, families, employers and other social agents hold for adolescents. Adolescents are expected to take the needs and interests of others into account in their families and communities. In school, they are expected to think in connotative and denotative ways, to provide definitions rather than just examples; in employment they are expected to be reliable, loyal to the company, and able to make commitments. In all of these arenas, there appears to be a common demand for a single, underlying (interpersonal) third order of consciousness; however, very few adolescents are likely to be constructing their realities in this way the moment they turn 13. Thus, teenagers are likely to be 'in over their heads' for at least a portion of their adolescent years. This situation is not necessarily bad, in Kegan's view, provided teens also experience effective support along the lines noted above. Such support can come through a variety of ways, but ideally it will foster developmental transition by anchoring the bridge from the second to third order of consciousness firmly at both ends. It is thus necessary within social contexts to build in features that will support this type of transition, without distain for those at different points on the 'consciousness bridge'.

In the arena of education, for example, Henderson and Kegan (1989) and Kegan (1990) argue for a curriculum that will work to address the growth of the student's mind rather than providing merely a set of skills and information. A teacher might facilitate movement from the imperial to interpersonal balance (second to the third order of consciousness) in the following way. In an attempt to get across the concept of irony from an O. Henry story, a teacher might ask students for a definition. A student constructing from the second order of consciousness is likely to respond with an example. The teacher who responds that this is a good example of irony with a request for further examples and gradually asks what all these examples have in common does much to assist rather than discourage students in their struggle towards the interpersonal balance.

In late adolescence and young adulthood, cultural demands shift and the fourth order of consciousness (institutional balance) becomes a prerequisite for meeting societal expectations. Within the arena of employment, individuals are expected to be more self-initiating, self-correcting, and self-evaluating, guided by their own visions or goals coordinated with those of their employer. In the family, people are expected to be psychologically independent of partners, transcending an idealized notion of love, and managing boundaries between the generations to support the development of others. As citizens, individuals are expected to be able to look at and evaluate the values and beliefs of cultural inheritance rather than be captive of them. Even within the arena of psychotherapy, Kegan observes that the approaches of Rogers, Perls and Ellis all demand greater self-support and self-direction. Such expectations require a fourth order of consciousness, and again, the gap between cultural expectation and the capacity for many looms large. From research noted earlier, Kegan (1994) estimates that approximately one-half to two-thirds of adults in the United States have not fully reached the fourth order of consciousness. Institutional demands for fourth-order construction may do much to encourage the developmental process, but again, Kegan (1994) argues for the provision of necessary social supports to assist in the transition.

One specific activity in the arena of work has been developed by Kegan (1991) to facilitate the move to a more complex order of consciousness. Initially, one is asked to consider the question 'How could your work be going better than it is now?' Then one is asked to reflect on the following issues: (1) my present beliefs or convictions that undergird responses to the question; (2) the competing, contradictory, or hidden beliefs that maintain the *status quo*; (3) their contributions to the less than optimal expression of beliefs noted for the first point. Such an activity encourages one to reflect on the contributions the self makes to defining present circumstances with the ultimate goal of taking as object that which is currently understood to be 'given'.

Postmodern demands in some arenas of contemporary society place additional burdens on the many individuals who have not even fully attained fourth-order meaning-construction. However, since few individuals do reach the fifth order of consciousness (inter-individual balance), and if they do, it is rarely before age 40, discussion of its facilitation is beyond the scope of the present volume.

SUMMARY

Robert Kegan has proposed a constructive-developmental view of the identity formation process. This integrative theory suggests a process which drives cognitive and affective developments and is responsible for generating logics tapped by Piaget and Kohlberg in the realms of physical and social cognition. The theory describes a sequence of balances and transitions in the relationship between that which is considered self and that taken to be other. Balances give rise to the meaning one makes of the world; transitions involve the loss of an old way of knowing. Adolescents gradually make meaning from the interpersonal balance, in which one *is* rather than *has* relationships, and later from the organizational balance, in which one *is* rather than *has* one's institutional affiliations, or from transitions to or from each of these balances. A self optimally evolves to a new balance in a holding environment which has three characteristics: holding securely, letting go, and remaining in place. Any intervention through natural or psychotherapeutic means must come to know an individual in his or her initial meaning-making balance, contradict at an appropriate time with an appropriate response, and remain in place during its guest's evolutionary passage for optimal development to proceed.

7 Towards integration and conclusions
They tell their stories

I was losing myself. The ground, once so firm beneath my feet, now quivered; the path below disappeared. And then I met the abyss, where my own name and possessions became strangers, unfamiliar baggage in this formless place. But this very abyss, where all was lost, somehow, somewhere gave rise to what I now dare to call 'me'.

(*A 16-year-old voyager*)

I once overheard a well-liked teacher in a quiet moment of reflection comment to a distraught soul in a 16-year-old's form that there is no map when it comes to matters of maturing; even Frost's road less traveled, described in his well-known poem by that name, is more defined in form than the course this teenager must plot. Although there are undoubtedly no detailed relief maps laying out the finer contours of our individual identity pathways, there do appear to be some major, general thoroughfares in the identity formation process that, when recognized, might have given both the adolescent wayfarer and sympathetic bystander above some assurance of a teenage future that would once again cohere, albeit in a new way. Plottings of general normative routes provided by Erikson, Blos, Kohlberg, Loevinger, and Kegan not only allow us to glimpse the next developmental roadside resting point (identity stage) but also provide guides as to the most useful means of unblocking developmental arrest as well as assisting the already engaged traveler on his or her own life journey.

Having studied the maps of five identity theorists to chart the evolution of the 'I', one might now wish to collate such plottings in search of common ground. While theorists have converged on the phenomenon of identity from somewhat different approaches, the stage features of Erikson, Blos, Kohlberg, Loevinger, and Kegan do lend themselves to ready comparison. Though each theorist uses somewhat different mechanisms to account for the developmental process of identity formation during adolescence, it is instructive to trace commonalities in stage features across the five chartings.

Erikson's more generic probe of the identity versus role confusion task of adolescence has been elaborated by both Kegan (1982) and Marcia (1966) in such a way as to allow more detailed comparisons with other frameworks. Kegan has noted that Erikson's identity versus role confusion stage, with its orientation to a solitary self in search of vocational, ideological, and sex role commitments, captures the energy of late adolescents but does not adequately describe the adolescent of earlier times. Following Erikson's childhood stage of industry versus inferiority, Kegan suggests a stage of affiliation versus abandonment to encompass the pursuits of 'connection, inclusion, and highly invested mutuality' more characteristic of younger adolescents. Marcia's foreclosure and diffusion identity statuses, most prominent in early adolescence, describe individuals concerned with maintaining or attaining identificatory relationships; interesting parallels exist between these statuses and the psychosocial dilemma of the affiliation versus abandonment stage suggested by Kegan. With Kegan's addition to the Erikson scheme, identity models viewed in this volume suggest stages which fall into rather intriguing alignments when plotted across theories; such patterns, in turn, point to what may be different underlying intrapsychic organizations or 'deep structures' of adolescent identity development. Table 7.1 gives an overview of the course of identity development from the five orientations presented in this volume.

From this table, we can see how the Eriksonian industry versus inferiority conflict of the later primary school years, with its focus on individual mastery, is described psychodynamically by Blos in terms of latency, with its time of Oedipal consolidation, and pre-adolescence, with increases in sexual and aggressive drives; these two theoretical maps both depict a self in the process of seeking and serving its own interests. For Kohlberg, Loevinger, and Kegan, strong parallels exist between the instrumental orientation of moral logic and the self-protective stage and imperial balance of ego functioning. All of these stages again blueprint a self whose own needs are primary, whose interests are self-protective. All five models sketch a pre-adolescent self with a sense of agency, striving to meet its own needs, taking over the function of impulse control previously exercised by the family but not yet capable of coordinating its own needs with those of other people.

With the addition of Kegan's affiliation versus abandonment conflict to Erikson's stage scheme, the five theoretical thoroughfares again coincide to point towards a new state of intrapsychic organization. Where isolated self-interest marked the structure of preceding times,

Table 7.1 The normative developmental course of identity during adolescence from five theoretical perspectives

Identity theorist	Stages of development				
	Industry/Inferiority	(Affiliation/Abandonment)*	Identity/Role Confusion	Achievement	Intimacy/Isolation
Erikson	Industry/Inferiority	(Affiliation/Abandonment)*	Identity/Role Confusion	Achievement	Intimacy/Isolation
Marcia		Foreclosure/Diffusion	Moratorium	Achievement	
Blos	Latency, Pre-adolescence	Early adolescence	Adol. proper	Late adolescence	Post adolescence
Object relations adaptation		Adolescent symbiosis	Differentiation Practicing Rapprochement	Object constancy	
Kohlberg	Instrumental orientation	Interpersonal concordance orientation		Social system orientation	Principled orientation
Loevinger	Self-protective stage	Conformist stage		Conscientious stage	Autonomous stage
Kegan	Imperial balance	Interpersonal balance		Institutional balance	Inter-individual balance

* It is the opinion of Kegan (1982) that Erikson overlooks a stage between 'Industry' and 'Identity' in the identity formation process. Kegan terms this stage 'Affiliation vs. Abandonment' to capture the period of 'highly invested mutuality' which occurs in early adolescence, prior to the late adolescent quest for individual identity.

early adolescence marks a time of affiliation. With an underlying structural organization which now enables young people to orientate to others, Marcia's foreclosure status denotes the formation of an identity through identification, a distinct style of other orientation. (The diffusion status reflects a non-normative failure in this process.) Blos's early adolescence, with its object relations counterpart of adolescent symbiosis, captures a self embedded in its internalized object representations and only later coming to differentiate from them. Kohlberg, Loevinger, and Kegan also describe a self embedded in some way in an interpersonal matrix. The moral logic of Kohlberg's interpersonal concordance orientation finds right action to be that which pleases others and brings their approval. Loevinger's conformist stage depicts a self bound to the dictates of the immediate social group, while Kegan's interpersonal balance describes a self unable to distance from or step out of a shared reality. Across the five identity maps, early adolescence seems to reflect a focus on affiliation, in both the intrapsychic and external object relations realms.

Mid to late adolescence has been the main focus of Erikson's writings on identity; across all five identity thoroughfares, we can now see a self distancing from the affiliative organization of early adolescence and once again more focused on pursuing its own interests while at the same time coordinating such needs with those of a larger social reality. Marcia's moratorium and achievement identity statuses reflect states of searching for and finding satisfying vocational, ideological, and sexual commitments within a social order. Adolescent differentiation, practicing, and *rapprochement* subphases of disengagement from internalized object ties would seem to underlie the moratorium identity status, with the achievement status reflecting an intrapsychic organization of adolescent self–other constancy. Kohlberg, Loevinger, and Kegan all describe a corresponding state of late adolescent self organization as one bound by a sense of duty to uphold the larger social order while at the same time able to experience a sense of self-ownership and authorship. A heightened sensitivity to questions of 'Who am I?' are concomitant features of late adolescence. Again, all five models in some way depict a self loosened from its earlier interpersonal moorings, more self-aware than ever while remaining orientated towards a larger social order.

It is not until post-adolescence that the self may attain yet another stage of structural organization to become more affiliative in form. Erikson's stage of intimacy versus isolation, Blos's post-adolescence, Kohlberg's principled orientation, Loevinger's autonomous stage, and Kegan's inter-individual balance all detail a self orientating to others from a more differentiated intrapsychic position. As Erikson describes intimacy to be a counterpointing of identities (possible only when identities have become reasonably well established), so, too, does Blos suggest post-adolescence to be a time of character consolidation as boundaries between self and others firm; then and only then does Blos suggest that mature and intimate extra-familial love relationships can form. Kohlberg, Loevinger, and Kegan all describe a young adult self more autonomous in its organization which, at the same time, is more capable of instigating community reform on issues of social justice as well as experiencing mutuality in relationship. Young adulthood, for all reviewed theorists, can be a time in which a more differentiated-than-ever sense of 'I' makes possible a more intimate-than-ever sense of 'we'.

With such commonalities in the contours of theoretical approaches, can we find any similarities among their varied calls for social response to the identity formation process during adolescence? Perhaps the most crucial common denominator is the importance all approaches attach to the need for accurate identification of the young person's present stage of identity development in planning effective support or intervention to facilitate change. Marcia, Blos and object relations theorists, Kohlberg, Loevinger, and Kegan all begin by stressing the importance of differential social response to adolescents in various stages of the identity formation process. As intrapsychic organizations differ through the normative stages of development, so, too, must social response vary to meet the very unique demands presented by each phase of structural organization.

Beyond this common denominator, theorists vary in the emphasis placed on the desirability of facilitating movement to more mature stages of organization. While the advantages of facilitating development for those with identity structures arrested in childhood seem clear, Loevinger, in particular, questions the ultimate value of interventions designed to advance functional ego stages to more mature forms in late adolescent and adult life; for her, designing educational and psychotherapeutic responses tailored to meet a client in his or her current ego stage of functioning without necessarily facilitating further structural development are appropriate end goals.

Among those theorists who do place high premium on interventions to promote more mature forms of identity organization, all acknowledge the importance of adolescent readiness before attempting to stimulate change. Even Piaget, on whose work Kohlberg and Kegan are based, suggests an optimal time of readiness for change:

I have a hypothesis which I am so far incapable of proving: probably the organization of operations has an optimal time. . . . It is probably possible to accelerate intellectual development, but maximal acceleration is not desirable. There seems to be an optimal time. What this optimal time is will surely depend on each individual and on the subject matter. We still need a great deal of research to know what the optimal time would be.

(Piaget 1967: 1)

It is the research of Kohlberg and colleagues which has offered some guidelines on recognition of readiness. As indicated in Chapter 4, development (at least to a higher stage of moral reasoning) appears most easily stimulated in children 'who have been at a particular moral judgment stage some intermediate length of time than in those who have just entered a new stage or those who have remained at the same stage beyond some optimal period' (Colby *et al.* 1977: 102). In his theoretical writings, Kegan, too, emphasizes the importance of timing in efforts to stimulate further development; promoting differentiation too soon can sabotage another's life project. In reporting the experiences of a first-year university student still hanging in the interpersonal balance, Kegan illustrates the critical role of timing in social response:

The subtle and overt messages a college freshman gets that he is on his own in the conduct of his academic and private life can serve to honor that newly emerging voice in the development of personality. But for a person who has not yet begun this emergence, the same messages – which professors and advisers may think of as confirmations of the student's adulthood – can be experienced as an abandonment, a refusal to care and a disorienting vacuum of expectation. This new embeddedness culture is not yet called for, and the old one has been lost.

(Kegan 1982: 186)

Mahler and other object relations theorists have also stressed the ill effects on infant and later adolescent and adult personality organization when the primary care-taker expedites differentiation before that optimal time of readiness on the part of the individual in his care.

With these cautions in mind, how might progress to a more mature stage of identity organization be best promoted? A common thread weaving its way through approaches concerned with this issue seems to be the bystander's introduction of dialogue aimed at creating a state of intrapsychic disequilibrium in the youthful traveler while at the same time remaining in place to provide a supportive relationship. Kohlberg and his associates have advocated exposure to reasoning at the next stage of moral logic, while Kegan and object relations theorists similarly suggest the provision of experiences which both refuse to confirm the old intrapsychic balance and at the same time recognize and meet the new. Marcia likewise aims gradually to facilitate progress to a more mature identity status for foreclosure and moratorium adolescents by promoting a degree of unstructuredness within a supportive framework that permits freedom for the adolescent's experimentation and exploration. If stimulating a more mature identity organization is a desired aim, it would seem that initially meeting a structure growing ready for change and then deliberately contradicting this organization while remaining supportively in place as the new comes into being are the most facilitative means of promoting further identity development.

THEY TELL THEIR STORIES

Having examined five major theoretical thoroughfares to the identity formation process, it is now time to learn from adolescent wayfarers themselves something of their own experiences in the development of 'I'. As part of a pilot project to examine developmental change in the underlying structures of identity organization, I assessed a small number of adolescents at four age levels (intermediate school: age 13 to 14 years, n = 6; high school: age 15 to 16 years, n = 5; beginning university: age 17 to 18 years, n = 7; established at university: age 19 to 20 years, n = 6) in several ways. The following measures were given: the Marcia 'ego identity status' interview to determine style of psychosocial commitment along with extended questions to probe the nature of psychosocial commitment that might reflect varying subject–object balances within Kegan's constructive-developmental paradigm; Kohlberg's moral dilemmas to detect stage of moral reasoning; Loevinger's Sentence Completion Test to identify ego stage; and the Hansburg Separation Anxiety Test to identify attachment profile as a potential indicator of intrapsychic organization underlying object relationships. With regard to the ego identity status interview extension, efforts were made to understand the adolescent's construction of meaning through his or her relationship to commitments. How identity alternatives were conceptualized and explored and how chosen values were justified and given meaning formed the basis of the extended interview. Rather than offering a statement of definitive patterns, the following case examples of individuals in each of Marcia's four identity statuses were selected to illustrate typical features of identity structure which may underlie this more overt psychosocial measure of commitment.

Diffusion – Daniel, aged 14

In the fourth form (grade 9) at high school, Daniel has not thought too much about what he would like to do when he leaves school (possibly at age 15), though the idea of being an auto mechanic holds some appeal. When pressed as to the attractiveness of this occupation, he is unable to articulate any satisfying features: 'Don't know. I just don't want an office job where I'm stuck inside'. (His father had an 'office job'.) Despite further efforts to learn what Daniel might like to do, he is unable to articulate vocational possibilities other than 'maybe be an electrician or something. [What might appeal to you about being an electrician?] My grandad was an electrician and he is always good at fixing things'. He would 'probably' be willing to change his mind if something better came along. In terms of parental reactions, 'I told them a year or so ago that I would like to be a mechanic. [How did they react?] They didn't seem to mind'.

Religion has never played any role in Daniel's life and he can't see that changing. His parents hold similar attitudes of lack of interest, and they do not discuss religion at all at home. Daniel does not think much about political issues, except when he sees news broadcasts on television – then he thinks about political issues 'sometimes – but only because they are there and there is nothing else on television'. He has given no thought to the issue of sex roles.

Daniel's reasoning is conceptually very simple. Despite probings to the limits of his comfort, Daniel is unable to articulate any clear interests on any of the four ego identity status interview components. Daniel presents a picture of depression and resigned hopelessness to a life in which the self is powerless. Dearth of response to conceptions of the self give some clues regarding the possible subject–object balance underlying Daniel's psychosocial identity diffusion; however, it is this same lack of response which prohibits any comfortable classification.

On Kohlberg's Valjean Dilemma, Daniel is rated at Stage 3(2), with reasoning primarily reflecting the interpersonal concordance orientation. He believes the tailor should not report Valjean to the police because 'he was looking after people. He had done a lot for the village community'. A citizen, in Daniel's view, does not have to report an escaped convict 'because they could still be dangerous or still do stuff. [Still do stuff?] To people or things'. People who break the law in Daniel's view should be punished 'so they won't do it again'. He describes Valjean's 'generally being a help to other people' as the justification for 'not too hard a sentence'.

On Loevinger's Sentence Completion Test, Daniel's responses reflect an impulsive stage of ego development. Dichotomizing the world into good or bad, happy or sad, there is conceptual simplicity in those stems he does complete:

> WHEN I AM CRITICIZED . . . I feel sad.
> WHEN THEY AVOIDED ME . . . I feel mad.
> WHAT GETS ME INTO TROUBLE IS . . . when I am up after bed time.
> BEING WITH OTHER PEOPLE . . . is fun.

On the Hansburg Separation Anxiety Test, Daniel has a profile of severe anxious attachment. His attachment scale score is very high, while the individuation scale score is extremely low; responses to both mild and strong stimulus cues on attachment and individuation scales are nearly equal. All other psychological system scale scores are extremely high, with the exception of painful tension. Self-love loss greatly exceeds self-esteem preoccupation. With such a profile, Hansburg (1980b: 16) indicates an unconscious symbiotic need to feel 'fully and completely attached to an attachment figure'. It may be that Daniel's orientation to others on Kohlberg's scheme (which I found surprising given his Marcia and Loevinger ratings) may be a further reflection of this unassuaged symbiotic need.

Foreclosure – Felicity, aged 19

In her second full-time year of a university law degree, Felicity has identified strongly with an older brother (who did not complete his law degree) in adopting her vocational plans; her father was a manager in a large financial corporation before his death nine years earlier. Her vocational commitment is firm: 'If I pass all my law courses I wouldn't give it up, because that's what I've always wanted to do. Now I've started it, there's no point in changing.' She will consider alternatives if and only if she fails her exams; no 'contingency plans' have been seriously processed at present. When pressed as to the appeal of law, Felicity responds:

> Well, I've had a lot of advice to do a law degree and everyone says it's a good background type of thing. But I also quite like the elite kind of thing. It's a real kind of achievement if you do actually get through the whole degree.

Status, rather than the intrinsic appeal of the profession, seems the prime motivator for Felicity in her career aspirations.

On religion, Felicity regards herself as a non-practicing Christian. She attended church and Sunday school as a child, but once she had shifted to a new district at the age of 12, she never went again:

> I think it was that all my friends went [in a former neighborhood]. I wasn't really committed. I just went because all my friends went. But when I went to [a new locale] I made friends but none of them went to church or anything so I think that's why I stopped going. And also I used to go to church occasionally with Mum but she stopped going after my father died, so I did too.

When pressed as to any conflicts about religion, she had the following to say:

> I like the idea of getting married in a nice, big church wedding, but on the other hand, I think it's a bit hypocritical of me having that when I have no interest in religion at all. [How do you think you might respond?] I probably will get married in a church and then forget about it.

Conflict is over concrete events rather than abstract ideological principles, resolved simply by shutting off the pressure at its source.

On political and social issues, Felicity labels herself conservative. Quite certain how to vote, she indicates the rationale for her decision: 'I think a lot of it has to do with how you were brought up, what your parents believed in. That will always be with me; I'll always think that way'. It is only with regard to the issue of sex roles that Felicity diverges in her views from those of the family tradition.

Felicity's world is conceptually simple and solid. A career path is followed not by a self finding pleasure in expressing its talents and interests but rather by a self gaining pleasure in conforming, attaining status, and 'making it'. For Felicity, identity seems a matter of just 'being there'; any self active in the process of selection is absent ('I've had a lot of advice to do a law degree and everyone says it's a good background type of thing'). Kegan might argue that Felicity's relationship to her commitments is that of a self not yet disembedded from its interpersonal matrix; the self *is*, rather than *has*, its identificatory relationships and is unable to distance from or reflect upon them. For the most part, Felicity shuts out any potential for conflict, unable to tolerate ambiguity ('Now that I've started law, there's no point in changing'). Such a defensive maneuver is necessary for a self as yet unable to distance from its identifications. If conflicts are experienced at all, they appear as clear, categorical alternatives over concrete issues (to be or not to be married in a church) rather than as considerations of less clearly defined ideological alternatives. Felicity appears to be hanging in the interpersonal balance.

On Kohlberg's Valjean Dilemma, Felicity is rated stage 3(4), primarily using the interpersonal concordance orientation, while still evidencing some stage 2 logic. She believes a citizen has a duty to report an escaped convict:

> I don't think he [the tailor] would look upon it as a duty or obligation but rather do it for his own welfare really. If he saw an escaped convict, he could have been in prison for anything and that escaped convict could attack him, so it's for his own welfare, but also for others. [Should the tailor report Valjean if he were a close friend?] He wouldn't want to. You just wouldn't do that to a close friend. He could be his friend because he knows he's a good man. Not many people are friends with people because they are horrible people.

Felicity believes people who break the law should be punished:

> If they aren't punished, values and society would fall apart. If you have rules, what's the point of the rules if you don't have to obey them and if nothing is going to happen if you do break them. So definitely people should be punished who break the law.

Felicity's primarily conventional approach to morality is summed up in her final comments on the story: 'This man is good so I wouldn't punish him. He'll have to stay in line with the law, though, in future, because if he didn't, it would just break down'.

On Loevinger's Sentence Completion Test, Felicity scores at the conformist stage of ego development. Her world is structured in a conceptually simple and absolute manner; behavior is either right or wrong, governed by rules of conduct. Her responses often are generalizations or clichés. In addition to structural features of replies, content is also informative.

> RULES ARE ... enforced behavior set out by an authority.
> EDUCATION ... is probably the most important facet of life.
> THE THING I LIKE ABOUT MYSELF IS ... that I am reasonably friendly to everyone whether I like them or not.
> I FEEL SORRY FOR ... animals that don't have a home.
> IF MY MOTHER ... didn't keep writing to me, I'd be upset.

On the Hansburg Separation Anxiety Test, Felicity is rated as having a strong anxious attachment profile. Attachment and individuation responses to mild cues are nearly equal, though overall scores on these scales are in adequate ranges; painful tension and reality avoidance scale scores are in the strong range. This profile may reflect an intrapsychic organization of adolescent symbiosis.

Moratorium – Moana, aged 20

Moana is in her second year at university, at this point working towards a degree in educational psychology. She wants generally to do something 'in the social services line'. She has never been interested in 'anything medical, scientific, or clerical or anything like that'. She very much wants an occupation where 'I can use my brain'. With regard to parental influence, Moana states:

> I suppose in the social line I was influenced by Mum – she's a secondary teacher. So I've got experience in seeing what she's done. We've always been encouraged to use our brains and not do something just for the money or just because it's there.

At this point, however, Moana would definitely change career directions if something better came along:

> If something better came up, I'd grab it. [Why do you say that?] Well, there's no point. If there's something else I want to do and I'm doing another thing, then I can't see the point in doing something that's second to what I want to do.

On religion, Moana states, 'I'm not at the point where I'm ready to commit myself to one thing – I'm more open-minded in everything at the moment'. Religion has never played a big role in her parents' lives, although it matters to her. On politics, Moana mentions a number of issues she has thought about. When it comes to commitment, however, Moana balks. Asked if she has ever taken a more active political stand or if her views, instead, are things she has just been thinking about, she replies:

> Something I have really just been thinking about. It's the same sort of thing with religion. I'm in a very objective frame of mind at the moment. I'm looking around at a lot of things. There are a lot of things that concern me but as to making a definite stand – no.

She comments on the future:

> Well, sometimes I don't like being so vague. It's not that I'm not interested; it's just that I don't want to form one opinion, because if

you do, it narrows your frame of mind. By saying 'I agree with this', you have got to say a whole lot of things that you don't agree with.

It is only in the area of sex-role values that Moana appears clearly identified with and committed to those values of her mother without having undergone any decision-making process of her own.

A self able to reflect upon itself seems to be emerging in Moana's relationship to her commitments. The capacity for self-authorship comes when the self becomes unhinged from the interpersonal balance and 'moves over' to *have* rather than *be* its identifications. Now, in transit to the institutional balance, Moana's thinking is no longer categorical ('Sometimes I don't like being so vague') and she has a much greater tolerance for ambiguity as well as a reluctance to make decisive statements ('I don't want to form one opinion'). Explorations of alternatives are now possible, for there is a self able to consider and evaluate its own interests and talents; yet that very self is now becoming embedded in its psychosocial (institutional) commitments, in finding psychosocial roles 'that fit'. Moana is more conceptually complex in her thinking about the world and her place in it as she passes between the interpersonal and institutional balances.

On Kohlberg's Valjean Dilemma, Moana is rated at the Stage 4 social system orientation. In terms of reporting Valjean to the police, Moana believes that the tailor should do so, as he has no knowledge of the circumstances of the original theft.

A citizen should report an escaped convict, since he has no history of a person. The only thing he can see is an escaped convict, so I don't think he is in authority to say that person should go free or that person shouldn't go free. He should leave it up to a better authority to do it and obviously, well, in the eyes of the society, the law is the best authority.

However, later the law is considered in relation to particular circumstances.

I think every situation should be taken into account. I personally feel the law is too rigid. Should people who break the law be punished? Well, I don't necessarily think the law is the right thing in a particular circumstance. Valjean has done a positive thing for society; he's not a detriment to society and shouldn't be taken away from it.

On Loevinger's Sentence Completion Test, Moana is rated at the conscientious stage of ego development. Responding in a more conceptually complex manner than Felicity, she demonstrates an awareness of individual differences and stresses personal growth. While self-critical, Moana, at the same time, evidences self-respect.

> I FEEL SORRY ... for ignorant people who don't know what they're missing out on and don't have the incentive to find out.
> BEING WITH OTHER PEOPLE ... is a way of gaining experience and information to broaden yourself as a person.
> WHEN I AM CRITICIZED ... I feel defensive but become introspective to consider their words.

On Hansburg's Separation Anxiety Test, Moana is rated secure in her attachment profile. Scores on all psychological systems scales are in the adequate range, with an appropriate distribution of responses on mild and strong stimulus cues on attachment and individuation scales. This attachment profile may point to an intrapsychic organization disengaged from earlier internalized object ties.

Identity achievement – Anna, aged 17

Anna, too, is an intending lawyer, now in her first year of university study. She points out that statistically her chances of getting cancer are higher than her chances of passing first-year law courses, but nevertheless she wishes to pursue law as her ultimate goal. This goal, however, is approached flexibly:

> Well, I'm studying law, which is my ultimate goal, but with the pass rate being so daunting, I've considered if I don't get through the second year I'll cross-credit and do a BA majoring in English and drama and teach at a secondary school. [What appeals to you particularly about law?] Because I'm a romantic idealist it's interested me to see people get a fair deal, and I think the best way to do that is within the law. It would be lovely if I could have some influence upon changing the law, which is unrealistic but . . .

Having considered and rejected medicine as a possible career, she recalls her decision-making process: 'I'm not good at science, whereas the things I am good at – history, debating, drama – they all point towards law'. Reporting parental reaction to her vocational plans, she states:

> They've never said whether they agree or not. The only indication they have given is that they are quite proud of me in that I'm quite

academic but my father thinks that an education is perhaps wasted on me because the rest of [the women in] my family are all traditional in getting married and having children . . . he's demonstrated that to me by not giving me any money to come to varsity; that's his way of saying 'I think you're wasting your time'.

On religion, Anna is a 'devout atheist' and it plays quite a part in her life because her belief is so strong. When asked to elaborate, she replies:

I believe that people who look to God and find strength in God . . . are finding the strength from within themselves and are calling it God. There is no God. I often say this to people who are religious and they say, 'Well, you have your own religion in that sense, then'. And perhaps that's true, but I believe that people find the strength from within and call it God.

She describes herself as an agnostic in early adolescence, with her present views gradually jelling in the face of 'bad personal experiences, like death' and 'the way religious people justify God'. Religion has not been discussed much in Anna's family, and she describes her parents as uninterested agnostics. On religion, she feels certain of her views.

This probably sounds narrow-minded from someone of 17, but I think as far as religion is concerned, I know what I know and I probably won't change. I'm not intolerant of other people. In fact, a lot of my friends are probably quite religious, but we all have an understanding that we don't preach to each other. I think I will stay the same on this; I can't see anything coming along to convince me that there is a God.

On political and social issues, Anna indicates she is 'not much interested in politics anymore'. She used to be a strong supporter of Labour as opposed to National, and would still vote Labour instead of National. But she's not very interested now as 'it all seems so futile. [What's brought about the change?] Realizing they call themselves different things but neither party seems to have a better way of getting to any better goal'. Regarding parental influence, 'We've always been encouraged to listen to lots of views and draw our own conclusions'.

On sex roles, Anna states she's come from a 'chauvinist household' and has developed her own views as a result.

My dad's the classic example of a stereotypic first generation immigrant, so I've grown up with that influence and until I was about fourteen or fifteen, which is quite late, I accepted it. I thought it was quite good, Dad was lovely, and everything was fine. It was OK to run around after Dad, you know, but when I was about fourteen or fifteen I wanted to know why should we run around after Dad; what makes him better? I began to question the way my father treated my mother. [What caused you to start questioning?] I don't know, I've always thought about it, and I wanted to know what made me change, because I could very easily just have drifted along as I was going. Perhaps my friends . . . maybe a particular group introduced me to the idea of feminism or inequality. I couldn't pinpoint it. I've tried, because it interests me.

Anna's psychosocial identity commitments now *are* her self. She no longer shares Moana's search for what to *do*; rather her commitments are who she *is*. Anna's concerns are now ideological ('I am a devout atheist, and it plays quite a part in my life because I am so strong in my belief') and her vocation is a reflection of her ideological 'romantic/idealist' values ('to see that people get a fair deal'). Her thinking is conceptually complex; concerns are no longer with concrete events but rather with abstract principles. At the same time, she seems to be distancing from earlier involvements ('I'm not very interested in politics anymore. It all seems so futile'), withdrawing from earlier forms of relatedness ('Why should I run around after Dad . . . what makes him better?'). As Kegan suggests, this 'sealing up' is characteristic of a self consolidating in the institutional balance. Embedded intrapsychically in her ideological commitments, Anna may yet undergo another subject–object transition and come to *have* rather than *be* her psychosocial values.

On Kohlberg's Valjean Dilemma, Anna is rated at Stage 4(5), a mixture of the social system and social contract orientations. She finds Valjean's initial reasons for theft 'pretty justified'. Furthermore, 'punishment is all about becoming a worthwhile and acceptable member of a community', and she thinks Valjean has shown he is already such a person. Reporting would only have a negative impact on a lot of people, the ones in society he is already helping. 'I think if the tailor reported him it's upholding the law in a way but is not the true spirit of punishment'. Generally respecting the law yet recognizing its limitations, Anna believes people generally should report an escaped convict.

Taking that question on its own, yes. Because although I've just said what a wonderfully community-spirited person Valjean was, you can't always have all the information. You never know – you could be doing everyone a service by reporting somebody and I think the law must be upheld.

The closeness of the relationship between Valjean and the tailor should not affect the latter's reporting decision. Anna's predominant Stage 4 reasoning is reflected in her concluding remarks:

The laws are generally there to be upheld and they should be, because that keeps society within boundaries. That's not to say that those boundaries are perfect, but we need boundaries and hopefully the punishment would fit the crime and never be too excessive.

On the Loevinger Sentence Completion Test, Anna is rated at the conscientious/autonomous (individualistic level) transition. Responses show complex conceptions. Rather than seeing incompatible opposites, Anna sees the inherent contradictions in life and combines opposites in a single response. There is also a stress on process and change, rather than outcome.

BEING WITH OTHER PEOPLE . . . is my main source of pleasure and pain.
IF MY MOTHER . . . was less torn between her own beliefs and what is expected of her, she would be happier.
SOMETIMES SHE WISHED THAT . . . I had more influence to change situations that I find unacceptable.
THE THING I LIKE ABOUT MYSELF IS . . . my changing nature.

It is interesting that Anna's Separation Anxiety Test attachment profile is one of excessive self-sufficiency, rather than the anticipated secure attachment. An extremely high individuation scale score dominates an adequate range attachment score, with appropriate balances on mild and strong stimulus cues for these scales; all other psychological systems scales are in the adequate range. It may be that with little familial support for her own chosen values and directions, Anna has had to rely on her own resources more strongly through the second individuation process of adolescence; differentiation may have been purchased at the price of repressing attachment needs.

From these pilot interviews, several points emerge with regard to our five theoretical thoroughfares. First, identity structure, particularly beyond mid adolescence, becomes less strongly related to chronological age. Responses from adolescents in the two university age groupings of my pilot sample reflect a nearly complete range of developmental stages on all measures of identity, while a more constricted range of identity organizations characterizes the two younger age groups. Similar results have emerged from previous developmental studies of ego identity status, moral reasoning, and ego development with larger samples (see Chapters 2, 4, and 5 for reviews of such work). Reasons for structural arrest beyond early adolescence are, at present, unclear. While interaction styles of socialization agents have been associated with particular mid-to late-adolescent identity organizations on Marcia, Kohlberg, and Loevinger measures, reasons for failure by most adults to reach the highest states of structural development are in need of further study within the ranks of these theoretical persuasions. Second, while reviewed identity theorists have detailed distinct stages in their formative models of the 'I', the profiles above (along with those of other individuals in the pilot sample) frequently evidence youthful responses reflecting more than one organization within a single measurement framework. For example, Felicity shows reasoning at Stages 2, 3, and 4 on a single dilemma from the Kohlberg assessment scheme, and Daniel has sentence completion items scored at the impulsive, self-protective, and conformist stages of ego development. Moana is rated differentially across components of the Marcia ego identity status interview (moratorium/achievement on vocation, moratorium on religion and politics, and foreclosure on sex roles). While one logic often shines through, boundaries between stages may be 'fuzzier' than neatly tabled representations would indicate. The necessity to consider features of transitions between identity organizations in addition to the more clearly defined stages presented by reviewed theorists would seem to be an important research direction to further our understanding of this continuous process. Third, individuals from the pilot study do not reflect stage assessments across all identity models that would be predicted from the five theoretical approaches displayed in vertical columns of Table 7.1. Loevinger echoes a similar observation in her review of developmental identity research with larger samples:

> If the stages really reflect a common 'deep structure,' the stages of those variables should all proceed in tandem. Such bits of evidence as there are indicate only a moderate relation among the various measures. . . . If they are not all evidence of the same structure, how many structures are there, and what should be the relations among them? Those are the questions remaining to be answered in this field of research.
>
> (Loevinger 1987: 242)

Frequent failure to find empirical support for a common deep structure of identity when looking across identity measures may result, in part, from our efforts to squeeze transitional organizations into discrete stage placements. Rather than a series of distinct organizations, development may be best depicted as a series of overlapping stages which are not mutually exclusive. Erikson has attempted to convey such a concept in his portrayal of the sixty-four (rather than eight) square pattern in his stage scheme of life-cycle development. Indeed, Pine (1985, 1992) finds the concept of psychological stage, with its connotation of constant affective themes, to be misleading altogether; it may be that only key psychological 'moments' or incidents punctuate our varied existences to reflect struggles of intrapsychic development. This suggestion presents a further explanation for discrepancies observed across structural measures of identity, as any developmental period will not be completely pervaded with behavior characteristic of a given intrapsychic organization. If any common deep structure of identity exists, its form may be clouded by our understanding of the nature of stages and possible overlap of developmental organizations. When identity formation is viewed more as a continuous process (for example, the growth and loss of identity structures described by Kegan) rather than as passages through distinct organizational states, linkages across theoretical orientations may come more clearly into focus – if, in fact, any 'deep structure' of identity does exist.

THE BALANCE BETWEEN SELF AND OTHER: NEW DIRECTIONS FOR IDENTITY THEORY AND RESEARCH

In this volume, five developmental models have been presented which describe the phenomenon of identity formation during adolescence. Though each approaches the nature of the 'I' from a somewhat different direction, all models have, in some way, addressed the phenomenon of intrapsychic differentiation, a rebalance of the relationship between that considered as self and that taken to be other. Erikson and Marcia have described the structural shift of an adolescent self derived through its identificatory relationships to one incorporating yet transcending such a form to a new configuration greater than the sum of its parts; rebalancing, in Erikson's scheme, involves the loss of a self structured primarily through its identifications to be replaced by one more integrated in form, delineated in its own boundaries. Blos characterizes the second individuation process of adolescence as an intrapsychic feat in which the parental introjects, internalized and regarded as self, are gradually relinquished; an old self structure gives way to the new, with a heightened sense of distinctiveness from others emerging in the exchange. The development of moral reasoning, one subdomain of ego functioning, has been described by Kohlberg as a series of qualitatively more complex structural organizations, whereby authority becomes increasingly internalized. With each successive stage, a self more distinct from, yet at the same time concerned about, a widening circle of others comes into being. To Loevinger, ego development is again an ongoing process of rebalancing between that taken as self and that considered to be other. Earlier stages of ego organization in Loevinger's scheme reflect a self-interested self, exclusive in its attention to personal needs and impulses; a self derived from group standards and later operating according to its own authority are the hallmarks of adolescents' and adults' increasing differentiation from others. Finally, Kegan's stage sequence reflects a self embedded in a series of contexts, increasingly differentiated from the individual's own functioning; the self of the neonate, embedded in its own reflexes, gives way through successive reorganizations to the young adolescent, embedded in his or her interpersonal matrix. Progression through organizational and interpenetrating systems marks the full course of development during late adolescent and adult life. Given the evolutionary nature of the identity formation process, it is surprising that greater attention has not been directed to mechanisms involved in stage transformations; to date such important passages have been left largely to clinical observers, poets, and novelists to elucidate.

Phenomenological accounts of self–other rebalancing, the essence of the identity formation process, have been eloquently presented by many writers attempting to capture and convey the experience. Certainly Janine's poem (Chapter 6), an account of being in an intrapsychic space 'where nothing is, is now – And all that was, is no more, and that that is, isn't', conveys the sense of inner vacuum associated with such rebalancing. It is perhaps in Sartre's *Nausea* that we have one of the most brilliant first-person accounts of the breakdown in one's customary way of experiencing self and object. In this novel, Roquentin is overcome by a feeling of localized nausea in his hand as he becomes aware of a changed relationship to objects in touching a pebble on the ground.

> I think it's I who has changed: that's the simplest solution, also the most unpleasant. . . . If I am not mistaken, and if all the signs which are piling up are indications of a fresh upheaval in my life, well then, I am frightened.
>
> (Sartre 1965: 14, 15)

Less dramatic, though no less an indication of structural transformation, is a statement by Hamish, a late adolescent (moratorium) university student whom I interviewed as part of a two-year longitudinal study of identity formation:

> [What's brought about that change in your political opinions?] I would guess the reduction in the influence of my father who has a very, very strong political orientation and the realization that one doesn't have to be firmly attached to any point of view and that a 'don't know' is as good an opinion as a firm belief.

That 'reduction in the influence of my father' can be interpreted as relinquishment of the internalized father, no longer needed to provide the architecture for Hamish's self; that newly emerging self, however, has yet to clearly define its own values. Through such literary and worldly accounts, a number of questions arise regarding the nature of self–other rebalancing.

As Kegan has noted, much of our lives are spent developmentally 'out-of-balance'. Normative mechanisms at work during such transformation times have been largely unexplored by stage theorists of identity. Particularly important to illuminating transformation processes are the following: (1) delineating possible steps in structural reorganization; (2) detailing the functions of regression, mourning, and depression; (3) addressing the role of transitional objects; (4) adopting appropriate research methodologies. These issues, all of relevance to passages during the second decade of life, are also of relevance to other times of rebalancing during the life-span.

The process of structural transformation

As we have seen in Chapter 3, Margaret Mahler and her associates (Mahler *et al.* 1975) have attempted to delineate specific separation-individuation subphases in the infant's differentiation of its self from its care-taker. Blos (1967) has suggested that a second individuation process may be occurring during adolescence in the differentiation of self from an internalized other, though he has not similarly detailed movement subphases. I have suggested that the Marcia identity status framework along with measures of separation anxiety provide us with opportunities for indexing possible subphases of any adolescent separation-individuation process. Kegan and his associates (Lahey *et al.* 1987) have also proposed a sequence of steps involved in leaving an old self-other balance and creating a new one. Might we catalogue the developmental transformations of late adolescence in each of the stage models examined by this volume in terms of sequentially predictable steps? What factors are associated with engagement in and resolution of this intrapsychic feat?

Examination of a single case study by Kroger (1993c) has suggested some steps and possible factors that may be associated with successful navigation, at least, of Erikson's identity formation process. Awareness of conflict or discrepancy between personal desire and perceived role expectation begin to cause discomfort. Outward action, however, begins only at a time of readiness, when there is sufficient ego strength to withstand the withdrawal of earlier external and internal 'props' which have served to define the self. This action is assisted by a significant other who can bridge both sides of the internal dialogue but ultimately support the newly emerging self. Initial steps in this intrapsychic process are focused on desires for escape and separation, coupled with fears of dissolution. Later, desire for exploring one's own potentials, coupled with feelings of guilt, replace earlier themes. The ability to withstand both the fear of death (dissolution) and guilt appear central to successful negotiation of the identity formation process. LaVoie (1994) has further suggested that transformative learning may be active during this process of structural change. Transformative learning involves a change in one's world which necessitates one's development of a new relationship to it. Greater attention to the actual process of structural transformation implicit within each of the structural-developmental models examined here would seem a fruitful direction for future research, holding important implications for differential forms of social response.

Functions of regression, mourning, and depression

Mahler (1983: 6) has noted, 'To go forward and to reach a higher degree of integration, a temporary phase of regression, of disorganization, of outright minor crisis – a chaotic state – has to occur'. Similarly, Blos (1967: 173) has pointed to the adaptive function of regression during adolescence, though this phenomenon has generally been considered a sign of pathology during other life stages: 'Regression in adolescence is not, in and of itself, a defense, but it constitutes an essential psychic process that, despite the anxiety it engenders, must take its course'. Through times of developmental transformation, regression may operate normatively in the restructuring process. While most stage theorists would argue against the concept of structural regression, transitory retrograde movement during times of self–other rebalancing has been frequently observed and inadequately explored.

Turiel (1974) has helped to clarify the different meanings that regression may have. He notes that regression may refer to a temporary state of disorganization, not implying the return to an earlier developmental stage of functioning but rather reflecting a developmentally less advanced structure in the process of transition; or regression may also refer to the use of prior developmental structures that suggest earlier stages remain unchanged, with each succeeding organization layered on top of earlier ones. A third meaning of regression more frequently found in psychoanalytic literature connotes the re-experiencing of abandoned ego states which once constituted special ways of coping with stress; this type of regression is usually defensive in nature. Temporary disorganization may be a normative and necessary part of structural reorganization. Regression in the psychodynamic sense, however, may occur when contextual issues reactivate earlier developmental trauma and impair structural advance (Noam 1988). The possible adaptive and non-adaptive roles of regression, particularly as observed in any *rapprochement*-like subphases of identity transformation, are in need of clarification.

Lifton (1975: vii) has noted, 'there is no moving beyond loss without some experiencing of mourning. To be unable to mourn is to be unable to enter the great human cycle of death and rebirth.' Any time of self–other rebalancing involves loss – the loss of an old structure, a way of knowing and being in the world. As Kegan points out, it is only through this very process of loss and mourning that a new balance can come into being. Furthermore, he connects the phenomenon of depression to these circumstances. 'I am suggesting that depression reflects disequilibrium and the process of re-equilibration' (Kegan 1982: 271). Kegan's pilot work on depression (reviewed in Chapter 6) offers us an insightful and viable means of probing the phenomenon of loss in the restructuralization of the self. Attempts to understand different organizations of depression should provide clues regarding that self–other balance which is being shed in preparation for the new.

Role of transitional objects

Winnicott (1953) was the first writer to note the function of transitional objects – those early 'not me' physical possessions which facilitate differentiation of the self during infancy. Tolpin (1971) later pointed out the 'auxiliary soother' functions inherent in transitional objects; by symbolically recreating reunion with the primary care-taker, transitional objects ease the infant's differentiation distress. A number of psychodynamic writers have pointed towards possible uses of transitional objects during adolescence to facilitate differentiation from internalized objects; however, Kegan and his colleagues have again offered novel and insightful thoughts on natural 'bridging phenomena' used by those in different developmental transformations to facilitate change. For example, the chum for those in the imperial to interpersonal transition is '[a]nother who is identical to me and real but whose needs and self-system are exactly like needs which before *were* me, eventually [will be] a part *of* me, but now [are] something between' (Kegan 1982: 118). For those in the institutional to inter-individual transition, relationships or love affairs protected by the unavailability of the partner serve as something in between the attainment of genuine intimacy and the preservation of institutional embeddedness – 'a surrender of the identification with the form while preserving the form' (Kegan 1982: 120). An exploration of bridging phenomena or transitional objects which accompany developmental reorganizations would seem an additional fruitful area of exploration.

Research strategies

Attempts to tap any existing underlying 'deep structure' of identity are at present limited not only by our conceptions of developmental stages and our almost exclusive focus on times of equilibrium but also by our research methodology. Developmental processes, particularly those operating during times of structural transformation, are not particularly amenable to measurement. Longitudinal efforts to chart changing self–other balances through extensive in-depth interviews and clinical observations would seem the most suitable means of approaching this research challenge. Lahey *et al.*'s (1987) guide to subject–object interviews, Noam's (1985) stage-phase-and-style interview, which in part examines how a subject's self and interpersonal boundaries become set, Kegan's (1982) interview explorations of depression types, and the extended ego identity status interview outlined in this chapter are all possible starting points in this venture. Qualitative as well as empirical modes of evaluation should provide the most powerful combination of tools suited to charting such structural reorganizations.

CONCLUSIONS

Through this volume, there has been an overview of the work of five theorists who have contributed to our understanding of identity during adolescence. Each, in his or her own way, has approached the 'I' from a developmental perspective, setting forth stages through which the self differentiates and becomes 're-related' to others over the course of the life-span. Adolescence has been identified by all approaches as a time of heightened activity for most in the loss and creation of new balances. Many questions remain in attempts to tap any 'deep structure' of identity through various measurement frameworks. If such an underlying identity organization does exist, mechanisms of transformation as well as stability must be more clearly delineated to enable us to provide assistance at optimal times in optimal ways. Ultimately, however, it is only our own ease with the process of change that will allow us to aid and not hinder another on his or her own life journey.

> For this is the journey that men [and women] make: to find themselves. If they fail in this, it doesn't matter much what else they find.
>
> (Michener, *The Fires of Spring*)

References

Acklin, M. W., Bibb, J. L., Boyer, P., and Jain, V. (1991) 'Early memories as expressions of relationship paradigms: a preliminary investigation', *Journal of Personality Assessment* 57: 177–92.

Adams, G. R. (1994) 'Revised classification criteria for the Extended Objective Measure of Ego Identity Status: a rejoinder', *Journal of Adolescence* 17: 551–6.

Adams, G. R., Bennion, L., and Huh, K. (1989) 'Objective measure of ego identity status: a reference manual', unpublished manuscript, University of Guelph, Ontario, Canada.

Adams, G. R. and Fitch, S. A. (1981) 'Ego stage and identity status development: a cross-lag analysis', *Journal of Adolescence* 4: 163–71.

—— (1982) 'Ego stage and identity status development: a cross-sequential analysis', *Journal of Personality and Social Psychology* 43: 574–83.

—— (1983) 'Psychosocial environments of university departments: effects on college students' identity status and ego stage development', *Journal of Personality and Social Psychology* 44: 1266–75.

Adams, G. R. and Jones, R. M. (1983) 'Female adolescents' identity development: age comparisons and perceived childrearing experience', *Developmental Psychology* 19: 249–56.

Adams, G. R., Montemayor, R., and Brown, B. B. (1992) 'Adolescent ego-identity development: an analysis of patterns of development and the contributions of the family to identity formation during middle and late adolescence', unpublished manuscript.

Adams, G. R. and Shea, J. A. (1979) 'The relationship between identity status, locus of control, and ego development', *Journal of Youth and Adolescence* 8: 81–9.

Adelson, J. and Doehrman, M. J. (1980) 'The psychodynamic approach to adolescence', in J. Adelson (ed.) *Handbook of Adolescent Psychology,* New York: Wiley.

Albee, E. (1962) *The Zoo Story and Other Plays,* London: Jonathan Cape (First published 1958).

Alisho, K. C. and Schilling, K. M. (1984) 'Sex differences in intellectual and ego development in late adolescence', *Journal of Youth and Adolescence* 13: 213–24.

Allen, J.P., Hauser, S. T., Bell, K. L., and O'Connor, T. G. (1994) 'Longitudinal assessment of autonomy and relatedness in adolescent-family interactions as predictors of adolescent ego development and self-esteem', *Child Development* 65: 179–94.

Allison, S. (1988) 'Meaning-making in marriage: an exploratory study', unpublished doctoral dissertation, Massachusetts School of Professional Psychology.

Anderson, S. A. and Fleming, W. M. (1986) 'Late adolescents' home-leaving strategies: predicting ego identity and college adjustment', *Adolescence* 21: 453–9.

Archer, S. L. (1993) 'Identity in relational contexts: a methodological proposal', in J. Kroger (ed.) *Discussions on Ego Identity*, Hillsdale, NJ: Lawrence Erlbaum Associates.

—— (1994) *Interventions for Adolescent Identity Development*, Newbury Park, CA: Sage.

Archer, S. L. and Waterman, A. S. (1990) 'Varieties of identity diffusions and foreclosures: an exploration of subcategories of the identity statuses', *Journal of Adolescent Research*, 5: 96–111.

Armstrong, J. G. and Roth, D. M. (1989) 'Attachment and separation difficulties in eating disorders: a preliminary investigation', *International Journal of Eating Disorders* 8: 141–55.

Bagnold, E. (1972) 'The door of life', in E. D. Landau, S. L. Epstein, and A. P. Stone (eds) *Child Development through Literature*, Englewood Cliffs, NJ: Prentice-Hall (First published 1938).

Bar-Yam, M. (1991) 'Do women and men speak in different voices? A comparative study of self-evolvement', *International Journal of Aging and Human Development* 32: 247–59.

Barrett, T. C. and Harren, V. A. (1979) 'Perspectives on self-theory: a comment on Loevinger and Kegan', *The Counseling Psychologist* 8: 34–9.

Baumeister, R. F. (1986) *Identity: Cultural Change and the Struggle for Self*, New York: Oxford University Press.

—— (1987) 'How the self became a problem: a psychological review', *Journal of Personality and Social Psychology* 52: 163–76.

Bellak, L., Hurvich, M., and Gediman, H. K. (1973) *Ego Functions in Schizophrenics, Neurotics, and Normals: A Systematic Study of Conceptual, Diagnostic, and Therapeutic Aspects*, New York: Wiley.

Bellew-Smith, M. and Korn, J. H. (1986) 'Merger intimacy status in adult women', *Journal of Personality and Social Psychology* 50: 1186–91.

Benson, M. J., Harris, P. B., and Rogers, C. S. (1992) 'Identity consequences of attachment to mothers and fathers among late adolescents', *Journal of Research on Adolescence* 2: 187–204.

Berzonsky, M. D. (1994) 'Identity negotiation styles and defense mechanisms', paper presented at the Biennial Meetings of the Society for Research on Adolescence, San Diego (Feb.).

Bettelheim, B. (1969) *The Children of the Dream*, London: Macmillan.

Beykema, S. (1990) 'Women's best friendships: their meaning and meaningfulness', unpublished doctoral dissertation, Harvard Graduate School of Education.

Bilsker, D. and Marcia, J. E. (1991) 'Adaptive regression and ego identity', *Journal of Adolescence* 14: 75–84.

Blasi, A. (1980) 'Bridging moral cognition and moral action: a critical review of the literature', *Psychological Bulletin* 88: 1–45.

Blasi, A. (1988) 'Identity and the development of the self', in D. K. Lapsley and F. C. Power (eds) *Self, Ego, and Identity: Integrative Approaches,* New York: Springer-Verlag.

—— (1990) 'Kohlberg's theory and moral motivation', in D. Schrader (ed.) *The Legacy of Lawrence Kohlberg, New Directions for Child Development* 47: 51–7.

Blasi, A. and Glodis, K. (in press) 'The development of identity: a critical analysis from the perspective of the self as subject', *Developmental Review*.

Blasi, A. and Milton, K. (1991) 'The development of the sense of self in adolescence', *Journal of Personality* 59: 217–42.

Blatt, M. (1969) 'The effects of classroom discussion programs upon children's level of moral judgment', unpublished doctoral dissertation, University of Chicago.

Blatt, M. and Kohlberg, L. (1975) 'The effects of classroom moral discussion upon children's moral judgment', *Journal of Moral Education* 4: 129–61.

Blos, P. (1962) *On Adolescence: A Psychoanalytic Interpretation,* New York: Free Press.

—— (1967) 'The second individuation process of adolescence', *Psychoanalytic Study of the Child* 22: 162–86.

—— (1968) 'Character formation in adolescence', *Psychoanalytic Study of the Child* 23: 245–63.

—— (1970) *The Young Adolescent: Clinical Studies,* New York: Free Press.

—— (1971) 'The child analyst looks at the young adolescent', *Daedalus* 100: 961–78.

—— (1976) 'When and how does adolescence end?', *Adolescent Psychiatry* 5: 5–17.

—— (1979) *The Adolescent Passage: Developmental Issues,* New York: International Universities Press.

—— (1980) 'Modifications in the traditional psychoanalytic theory of female adolescent development', *Adolescent Psychiatry* 8: 8–24.

—— (1983) 'The contribution of psychoanalysis to the psychotherapy of adolescents', *Psychoanalytic Study of the Child* 38: 577–600.

—— (1985) *Son and Father: Before and Beyond the Oedipus Complex,* New York: Free Press.

—— (1989) 'The place of the adolescent process in the analysis of the adult', *Psychoanalytic Study of the Child* 44: 3–18.

Blustein, D. L., Ellis, M. V., and Devenis, L. E. (1989) 'The development and validation of a two-dimensional model of the commitment to career choices process', *Journal of Vocational Behavior* 35: 342–78.

Blustein, D. L. and Phillips, S. D. (1990) 'Relation between ego identity statuses and decision-making styles', *Journal of Counseling Psychology* 37: 160–8.

Blustein, D. L., Wallbridge, M. M., Friedlander, M. L., and Palladino, D. E. (1991) 'Contributions of psychological separation and parental attachment to the career development process', *Journal of Counseling Psychology* 38: 39–50.

Borders, L. D. (1989) 'Developmental cognitions of first practicum supervisees', *Journal of Counseling Psychology* 36: 163–9.

Borders, L. D. and Fong, M. L. (1989) 'Ego development and counseling ability during training', *Counselor Education and Supervision* 29: 71–83.

Borders, L. D., Fong, M. L., and Neimeyer, G.J. (1986) 'Counseling students' level of ego development and perception of clients', *Counselor Education and Supervision* 26: 36–49.

Bosma, H. A. (1994) 'Identity and identity processes: the application of a dynamic systems perspective', paper presented at the Biennial Meeting of the European Society for Research on Adolescence, Stockholm (June).

Bosma, H. A. and Gerrits R. S. (1985) 'Family functioning and identity status in adolescence', *Journal of Early Adolescence* 5: 69–80.

Bosma, H. A., Graafsma, T. L. G., Grotevant, H. D., and de Levita, D. J. (eds) (1994) *Identity and Development: An Interdisciplinary Approach,* Newbury Park, CA: Sage.

Bourne, E. (1978a) 'The state of research on ego identity: a review and appraisal. Part I', *Journal of Youth and Adolescence* 7: 223–51.

—— (1978b) 'The state of research on ego identity: a review and appraisal. Part II', *Journal of Youth and Adolescence* 7: 371–92.

Boyes, M. C. and Chandler, M. (1992) 'Cognitive development, epistemic doubt, and identity formation in adolescence', *Journal of Youth and Adolescence* 21: 277–304.

Boyes, M. C. and Walker, L. J. (1988) 'Implications of cultural diversity for the universality claims of Kohlberg's theory of moral reasoning', *Human Development* 31: 44–59.

Bradley, C. L. and Marcia, J. E. (1993) 'A prototype model of generativity versus stagnation', paper presented at the Annual Convention of the American Psychological Association, Toronto.

Brandt, D. E. (1977) 'Separation and identity in adolescence', *Contemporary Psychoanalysis* 13: 507–18.

Breger, L. (1974) *From Instinct to Identity: The Development of Personality,* Englewood Cliffs, NJ: Prentice-Hall.

Brenman-Gibson, M. (1986) *Clinical Implications of Erik Erikson's Work* (Cassette Recording No. 100–297–86), Washington, DC: American Psychological Association.

Brickfield, L. (1989) 'Identity development from late adolescence to adulthood: a study of ego identity status, object representation and self-esteem in women', unpublished doctoral dissertation, Adelphi University.

Broughton, J. and Zahaykevich, M. (1977) 'Review of J. Loevinger's *Ego Development: Conceptions and Theories*', *Telos* 32: 246–53.

—— (1988) 'Ego and ideology: a critical review of Loevinger's theory', in F. C. Power and D. K. Lapsley (eds) *Self, Ego, and Identity*, New York: Springer-Verlag.

Brown, B. B., Eicher, S. A., and Petrie, S. (1986) 'The importance of peer group ("crowd") affiliation in adolescence', *Journal of Adolescence* 9: 73–96.

Brown, L., Debold, E., Tappan, M., and Gilligan, C. (1991) 'Reading narratives of conflict and choice for self and moral voices: a relational method', in W. M. Kurtines, and J. L. Gewirtz, (eds) *Handbook of Moral Behavior and Development*, vol 2: *Research*, Hillsdale,NJ: Lawrence Erlbaum Associates.

Brown, L. and Gilligan, C. (1992) *Meeting at the Crossroads: Women's Psychology and Girls' Development*, Cambridge, MA: Harvard University Press.

Browning, D. L. (1987) 'Ego development, authoritarianism, and social status: an investigation of the incremental validity of Loevinger's Sentence Completion Test (Short Form)', *Journal of Personality and Social Psychology* 53: 113–18.

Bursik, K. (1991) 'Adaptation to divorce and ego development in adult women', *Journal of Personality and Social Psychology* 60: 300–6.

Campbell, E., Adams, G. R., and Dobson, W. R. (1984) 'Familial correlates of identity formation in late adolescence: a study of the predictive utility of connectedness and individuality in family relations', *Journal of Youth and Adolescence* 13: 509–25.

Candee, D. and Kohlberg, L. (1987) 'Moral judgment and moral action: a re-analysis of Haan, Smith, and Block's (1968) free speech movement data', *Journal of Personality and Social Psychology* 52: 554–64.

Caplan, P. J. (1979) 'Erikson's concept of inner space: a data-based reevaluation', *American Journal of Orthopsychiatry* 49:100–8.

Carlozzi, A. F., Campbell, N. J., and Ward, G. R. (1982) 'Dogmatism and externality in locus of control as related to counselor trainee skill in facilitative responding', *Counselor Education and Supervision* 21: 227–36.

Carlozzi, A. F., Gaa, J. P., and Liberman, D. B. (1983) 'Empathy and ego development', *Journal of Counseling Psychology* 30: 113–16.

Carpendale, J. I. and Krebs, D. L. (1992) 'Situational variation in moral judgment: in a stage or on a stage?', *Journal of Youth and Adolescence* 21: 203–24.

Carroll, J. L. and Rest, J. R. (1982) 'Moral development', in B. B. Wolman (ed.) *Handbook of Developmental Psychology,* Englwood Cliffs, NJ: Prentice-Hall.

Cebik, R. J. (1985) 'Ego development theory and its implications for supervision', *Counselor Education and Supervision* 24: 226–33.

Chapman, J. W. and Nicholls, J. G. (1976) 'Occupational identity status, occupational preference, and field dependence in Maori and Pakeha boys', *Journal of Cross-Cultural Psychology* 7: 61–72.

Christenson, R. M. and Wilson, W. P. (1985) 'Assessing pathology in the separation-individuation process by an inventory: a preliminary report', *The Journal of Nervous and Mental Disease* 173: 561–5.

Ciaccio, N. V. (1971) 'A test of Erikson's theory of ego epigenesis', *Developmental Psychology* 4: 306–11.

Colby, A. and Damon, W. (1992) *Some Do Care: Contemporary Lives of Moral Commitment,* New York: The Free Press.

Colby, A. and Kohlberg, L. (1987) *The Measurement of Moral Judgment,* vol. 1, Cambridge: Cambridge University Press.

Colby, A., Kohlberg, L., Fenton, E., Speicher-Dubin, B., and Lieberman, M. (1977) 'Secondary school moral discussion programs led by social studies teachers', *Journal of Moral Education* 6: 90–111.

Colby, A., Kohlberg, L., Gibbs, J., and Lieberman, M. (1983) 'A longitudinal study of moral judgment', *Monographs of the Society for Research in Child Development* 48: 1–124.

Colby, A., Kohlberg, L., Speicher, B., Hewer, A., Candee, D., Gibbs, J., and Power, C. (1987) *The Measurement of Moral Judgment,* vol. 2, Cambridge: Cambridge University Press.

Coleman, J. C. (1974) *Relationships in Adolescence,* London: Routledge & Kegan Paul.

—— (1978) 'Current contradictions in adolescent theory', *Journal of Youth and Adolescence* 7: 1–11.

Constantinople, A. (1967) 'Perceived instrumentality of the college as a measure of attitudes towards college', *Journal of Personality and Social Psychology* 5: 196–210.
—— (1969) 'An Eriksonian measure of personality development in college students', *Developmental Psychology* 1: 357–72.
Coonerty, S. (1989) 'An exploration of change in separation-individuation themes in the borderline disorder', paper presented at the Annual Meeting of the Division of Psychoanalysis, American Psychological Association, Boston (April).
Coor, I. F. (1970) 'The effects of grade level and motivation training on ego development', unpublished doctoral dissertation, Washington University, St Louis.
Coppolillo, H. P. (1984) 'Integration, organization, and regulation in late adolescence', in D. D. Brockman (ed.) *Late Adolescence: Psychoanalytic Studies,* New York: International Universities Press.
Costa, M. E. and Campos, B. P. (1989) 'University area of study and identity development: a longitudinal study', paper presented at the Biennial Meeting of the Society for the Study of Behavioral Development, Jyvaskyla, Finland (July).
Costa, P. T. and McCrae, R. R. (1993) 'Ego development and trait models of personality', *Psychological Inquiry* 4: 20–3.
Costos, D. (1986) 'Sex role identity in young adults: its parental antecedents and relation to ego development', *Journal of Personality and Social Psychology* 50: 602–11.
—— (1990) 'Gender role identity from an ego developmental perspective', *Sex Roles* 22: 723–41.
Côté, J. E. (1993) 'Foundations of a psychoanalytic social psychology: neo-Eriksonian propositions regarding the relationship between psychic structure and cultural institutions', *Developmental Review* 13: 31–53.
Côté, J. E. and Levine, C. (1983) 'Marcia and Erikson: the relationship among ego identity status, neuroticism, dogmatism, and purpose in life', *Journal of Youth and Adolescence* 12: 43–53.
—— (1988) 'A critical examination of the ego identity status paradigm', *Developmental Review* 8: 147–84.
—— (1989) 'An empirical test of Erikson's theory of ego identity formation', *Youth and Society* 20: 388–415.
Cummings, A. L. and Murray, H. G. (1989) 'Ego development and its relation to teacher education', *Teaching and Teacher Education* 5: 21–32.
Currie, P.S. (1983) 'Current attachment patterns, attachment history, and religiosity as predictors of ego-identity status in fundamentalist Christian adolescents', unpublished doctoral dissertation, California School of Professional Psychology, Los Angeles.
Cushman, P. (1990) 'Why the self is empty', *American Psychologist* 45: 599–611.
da Ponte, L. (1929) *Memoirs*, Philadelphia: J. S. Lippincott.
Darley, J. (1993) 'Research on morality: possible approaches, actual approaches', *Psychological Science* 4: 353–65.
Dill, D. L. and Noam, G. G. (1990) 'Ego development and treatment requests', *Psychiatry* 53: 85–91.
Dixon, J. W. (1986) 'The relation of social perspective stages to Kegan's stages of ego development', unpublished doctoral dissertation, University of Toledo.

Dolan, B. M., Evans, C., and Norton, K. (1992) 'The Separation-Individuation Inventory: association with borderline phenomena', *Journal of Nervous and Mental Disease* 180: 529–33.

Donovan, J.M. (1975) 'Identity status and interpersonal style', *Journal of Youth and Adolescence* 4: 37–55.

Douvan, E. and Adelson, J. (1966) *The Adolescent Experience*, New York: Wiley.

Dowell, C. (1971) 'Adolescents as peer counselors', unpublished doctoral dissertation, Harvard University.

Dreyer, P. H. (1994) 'Designing curricular identity interventions for secondary schools', in S. L. Archer (ed.) *Interventions for Adolescent Identity Development*, Newbury Park, CA: Sage.

Dubow, E. F., Huesmann, L. R., and Eron, L. D. (1987) 'Childhood correlates of adult ego development', *Child Development* 58: 859–69.

Dyk, P. H. and Adams, G. R. (1990) 'Identity and intimacy: an initial investigation of three theoretical models using cross-lag panel correlations', *Journal of Youth and Adolescence* 19: 91–109.

Edward, J., Ruskin, N., and Turrini, P. (1992) *Separation-Individuation: Theory and Application* (2nd edn), New York: Brunner/Mazel.

Edwards, C. P. (1986) 'Cross-cultural research on Kohlberg's stages: the basis for consensus', in S. Modgil and C. Modgil (eds.) *Lawrence Kohlberg: Consensus and Controversy*, London: Falmer Press.

Eisenberg, N. and Mussen, P. (1989) *The Roots of Prosocial Behavior in Children*, Cambridge: Cambridge University Press.

Eisenberg, N. and Strayer, J. (eds) (1987) *Empathy and its Development*, Cambridge: Cambridge University Press.

Elder, G. H. (1974) *Children of the Great Depression*, Chicago: University of Chicago Press.

Ellis, A. (1962) *Reason and Emotion in Psychotherapy*, New York: Lyle Stuart.

Enright, R. D., Lapsley, D. K., Drivas, A. E., and Fehr, L. A. (1980) 'Parental influences on the development of adolescent autonomy and identity', *Journal of Youth and Adolescence* 9: 529–46.

Erickson, V. L. (1975) 'Deliberate psychological education for women: from Iphigenia to Antigone', *Counselor Education and Supervision* 14: 297–309.

Erikson, E. H. (1956) 'The problem of ego identity', *Journal of the American Psychoanalytic Association*, 4: 56–121.

—— (1959) 'Identity and the life cycle', *Psychological Issues* 1 (Monograph no. 1).

—— (1963) *Childhood and Society* (2nd edn), New York: W. W. Norton & Co., Inc.

—— (1968) *Identity, Youth, and Crisis*, New York: W. W. Norton & Co., Inc.

—— (1970) 'Autobiographic notes on the identity crisis', *Daedalus* 99: 730–59.

—— (1975) *Life History and the Historical Moment*, New York: W. W. Norton & Co., Inc.

—— (1976) 'Reflections on Dr Borg's life cycle', *Daedalus* 105: 1–28.

—— (1977) *Toys and Reasons: Stages in the Ritualization of Experience*, New York: W. W. Norton & Co., Inc.

—— (1983) 'Concluding remarks: infancy and the rest of life', in J. D. Call, E. Galenson, and R. L. Tyson (eds) *Frontiers of Infant Psychiatry*, New York: Basic Books.

Erikson, E. H. (1984) 'Reflections on the last stage – and the first', *Psychoanalytic Study of the Child* 39: 155–65.

Esman, A. H. (1980) 'Adolescent psychopathology and the rapprochement phenomenon', *Adolescent Psychiatry* 8: 320–31.

Evans, R. I. (1967) *Dialogue with Erik Erikson,* New York: Harper & Row.

Exum, H. (1977) 'Cross-age and peer teaching', unpublished doctoral dissertation, University of Minnesota, Minneapolis.

Fasick, F. (1994) 'On the "invention" of adolescence', *Journal of Early Adolescence* 14: 6–23.

Feldberg, A. (1983) 'Adolescent separation, individuation, and identity (re)formation: theoretical extensions and modifications', unpublished doctoral dissertation, California School of Professional Psychology, Fresno.

Fitch, S. A. and Adams, G. R. (1983) 'Ego identity and intimacy status: replication and extension', *Developmental Psychology* 19: 839–45.

Flum, H. (1994) 'The evolutive style of identity formation', *Journal of Youth and Adolescence* 23: 489–98.

Frank, S. and Quinlan, D. (1976) 'Ego development and female delinquency: a cognitive-developmental approach', *Journal of Abnormal Psychology* 85: 505–10.

Frank, S. J., Pirsch, L.A., and Wright, V. C. (1990) 'Late adolescents' perceptions of their relationships with their parents: relationships among de-idealization, autonomy, relatedness, and insecurity and implications for adolescent adjustment and ego identity status', *Journal of Youth and Adolescence* 19: 571–88.

Franz, C. E. and White, K. M. (1985) 'Individuation and attachment in personality development: extending Erikson's theory', *Journal of Personality* 53: 224–56.

Friedlander, M. L. and Siegel, S. M. (1990) 'Separation-individuation difficulties and cognitive-behavioral indicators of eating disorders among college women', *Journal of Counseling Psychology* 37: 74–8.

Fromm, E. (1955) *The Sane Society,* New York: Fawcett Premier.

Furman, E. (1982) 'Mothers have to be there to be left', *The Psychoanalytic Study of the Child* 37: 15–28.

Gfellner, B. M. (1986a) 'Changes in ego and moral development in adolescents: a longitudinal study', *Journal of Adolescence* 9: 281–302.

—— (1986b) 'Ego development and moral development in relation to age and grade level during adolescence', *Journal of Youth and Adolescence* 15: 147–63.

Gilligan, C. (1982a) *In a Different Voice: Psychological Theory and Women's Development,* Cambridge, MA: Harvard University Press.

—— (1982b) 'Why should a woman be more like a man', *Psychology Today* 16: 68–77.

—— (1985) 'Response to critics', paper presented to the Biennial meeting of the Society for Research in Child Development, Toronto (April).

—— (1989) *Making Connections: The Relational Worlds of Adolescent Girls at Emma Willard School,* Cambridge, MA: Harvard University Press.

Gilligan, C. and Attanucci, J. (1988) 'Two moral orientations: gender differences and similarities', *Merrill-Palmer Quarterly* 34: 223–37.

Gilligan, C., Murphy, J. M., and Tappan, M. B. (1990) 'Moral development beyond adolescence', in C. N. Alexander and E. J. Langer (eds) *Higher*

Stages of Human Development: Perspectives on Adult Growth, New York: Oxford University Press.

Ginsburg, S. D. and Orlofsky, J. L. (1981) 'Ego identity status, ego development, and locus of control in college women', *Journal of Youth and Adolescence* 10: 297–307.

Goldberg, L. R. (1990) 'An alternative description of personality: the big-five factor structure', *Journal of Personality and Social Psychology* 59: 1216–29.

Goossens, L. (1992) 'Longitudinal trajectories of identity status development in university students', paper presented at the Fifth European Conference on Developmental Psychology, Seville, Spain (Sept.)

Goossens, L. (1994) 'Separation-individuation and the "new look" at adolescent egocentrism', paper presented at the Biennial Meetings of the Society for Research on Adolescence, San Diego (Feb.).

—— (in press) 'Identity status development and students' perceptions of the university environment: a cohort-sequential study', in A. Oosterwegel and R. Wicklund (eds) *The Self in European and North American Culture: Development and Processes,* NATO ASI Series: Kluwer.

Goossens, L. and Schillebeeks, A. (1994) 'Global versus domain-specific statuses in identity research: a comparison of two self-report measures', paper presented at the Biennial Conference of the European Society for Research on Adolescence, Stockholm (June).

Greenberg, J. R. and Mitchell, S. A. (1983) *Object Relations in Psychoanalytic Theory,* Cambridge, MA: Harvard University Press.

Grotevant, H. D. (1993) 'The integrative nature of identity: bringing the soloists to sing in the choir', in J. Kroger (ed.) *Discussions on Ego Identity,* Hillsdale, NJ: Lawrence Erlbaum Associates.

—— (1994) 'A narrative approach to identity development: examining the stories of adopted children and adolescents', paper presented at the Biennial Meeting of the International Society for the Study of Behavioral Development, Amsterdam (July).

Grotevant, H. D. and Cooper, C. R. (1985) 'Patterns of interaction in family relationships and the development of identity exploration in adolescence', *Child Development* 56: 415–28.

—— (1986) 'Individuation in family relationships', *Human Development* 29: 82–100.

Group for the Advancement of Psychiatry (1968), *Normal Adolescence,* vol. 6, Report no. 68, New York: Group for the Advancement of Psychiatry.

Haan, N. (1974) 'The adolescent antecedents of an ego model of coping and defense and comparisons with Q-sorted ideal personalities', *Genetic Psychology Monographs* 89: 273–306.

Haan, N., Smith, M. B., and Block, J. (1968) 'Moral reasoning of young adults: political-social behavior, family background, and personality correlates', *Journal of Personality and Social Psychology* 10: 255–70.

Haaré, R. (1987) 'Grammar, psychology and moral rights', in M. Chapman (ed.) *Meaning and Growth of Understanding,* Berlin: Springer-Verlag.

Habermas, J. (1975) 'Moral development and ego identity', in J. Habermas (ed.) *Communication and the Evolution of Society,* Boston: Beacon.

Hamachek, D. E. (1988) 'Evaluating self concept and ego development within Erikson's psychosocial framework: a formulation', *Journal of Counseling and Development* 66: 354–60.

(1989) 'Evaluating self-concept and ego status in Erikson's last three psycho-social stages', paper presented at the Annual Conference of the American Association for Counseling and Development, Boston (March).

Hansburg, H. G. (1980a) *Adolescent Separation Anxiety: A Method for the Study of Adolescent Separation Problems,* vol. 1, New York: Robert E. Krieger.

—— (1980b) *Adolescent Separation Anxiety: Separation Disorders*, vol. 2, New York: Robert E. Krieger.

Hartmann, H. (1958) *Ego Psychology and the Problem of Adaptation*, New York: International Universities Press.

Hauser, S. (1972) 'Black and white identity development: aspects and perspectives', *Journal of Youth and Adolescence* 1: 113–30.

Hauser, S. T. (1976) 'Loevinger's model and measure of ego development: a critical review', *Psychological Bulletin* 83: 928–55.

—— (1978) 'Ego development and interpersonal style in adolescence', *Journal of Youth and Adolescence* 7: 333–52.

Hauser, S. T., Powers, S. I., Noam, G. G., Jacobson, A. M., Weiss, B., and Follansbee, D. J. (1984) 'Familial contexts of adolescent ego development', *Child Development* 55: 195–213.

Hearn, S. and Marcia, J. E. (1994) 'Integrity status rating manual', unpublished manuscript, Simon Fraser University, Burnaby, B C, Canada.

Helson, R. and Roberts, B. W. (1994) 'Ego development and personality change in adulthood', *Journal of Personality and Social Psychology* 66: 911–20.

Henderson, A. F. and Kegan, R. (1989) 'Learning, knowing, and the self: a constructive developmental view', in K. Field, B. J. Cohler, and G. Wool (eds) *Emotions and Behavior Monographs,* Monograph no. 6, Madison, CT: International Universities Press.

Henton, J., Lamke, L., Murphy, C., and Haynes, L. (1980) 'Crisis reactions of college freshmen as a function of family support systems', *Personnel and Guidance Journal* 58: 508–11.

Hesse, H. (1980) 'Siddhartha', in Collins Collectors Choice, *Hermann Hesse. Six Novels with Other Stories and Essays,* London: Collins (First published 1950).

Hickey, L and Scharf, P. (1980) *Toward a Just Correctional System,* San Francisco: Jossey Bass.

Higgins, A. (1991). 'The just community approach to moral education: evolution of the idea and recent findings', in W. M. Kurtines and J. L. Gewirtz (eds) *Handbook of Moral Behavior and Development,* vol: 2: *Research*, Hillsdale, NJ: Lawrence Erlbaum Associates.

Higgins, R. O'C. (1985) 'Psychological resilience and the capacity for intimacy', unpublished doctoral dissertation, Harvard Graduate School of Education.

Hodgson, J. W. and Fischer, J. L. (1979) 'Sex differences in identity and intimacy development in college youth', *Journal of Youth and Adolescence* 8: 37–50.

Hodgson, T. O. (1990) 'Constructive developmental analysis of autobiographical writing', unpublished doctoral dissertation, University of Massachusetts.

Hoffer, E. (1951) *The True Believer,* New York: Harper & Row.

Hoffman, J. A. (1984) 'Psychological separation of late adolescents from their parents', *Journal of Counseling Psychology* 31: 170–8.

Holmbeck, G. N. and McClanahan, G. (1994) 'Construct and content validity of the Separation-Individuation Test of Adolescence: a reply to Levine', *Journal of Personality Assessment* 62: 169–72.

Holt, R. R. (1980) 'Loevinger's measure of ego development: reliability and national norms for male and female short forms', *Journal of Personality and Social Psychology* 39: 909–20.

Hoppe, C. (1972) 'Ego development and conformity behavior', unpublished doctoral dissertation, Washington University, St Louis.

Horner, T. M. (1985). 'The psychic life of the young infant', *American Journal of Orthopsychiatry* 55: 324–44.

Hsia, L. C. (1992) 'Learning in conflicts', unpublished doctoral dissertation, Harvard Graduate School of Education.

Hult, R. E. (1979) 'The relationship between ego identity status and moral reasoning in university women', *Journal of Psychology* 103: 203–7.

Hurtig, A. L., Petersen, A. C., Richards, M. H., and Gitelson, I. B. (1985) 'Cognitive mediators of ego functioning in adolescence', *Journal of Youth and Adolescence* 14: 435–50.

Huxley, A. (1972) 'Visionary experience', in J. White (ed.) *The Highest State of Consciousness,* New York: Archer.

Isay, R. A. (1980) 'Late adolescence: the second separation stage of adolescence', in S. I. Greenspan and G. H. Pollock (eds) *The Course of Life: Psychoanalytic Contributions toward Understanding Personality Development*, vol. II: *Latency, Adolescence, and Youth*, Washington, DC: NIMH.

Ivey, A. E. (1976) 'Counseling psychology, the psychoeducator model, and the future', *The Counseling Psychologist* 6: 72–5.

Jacobs, J. (1984) 'Holding environment and developmental stages: a study of marriage', unpublished doctoral dissertation, Harvard Graduate School of Education.

Jennings, A. G. and Armsworth, M. W. (1992) 'Ego development in women with histories of sexual abuse', *Child Abuse and Neglect* 16: 553–65.

Jennings, W. S. and Kohlberg, L. (1983) 'Effects of a just community program on the moral development of youthful offenders', *Journal of Moral Education* 12: 33–50.

Jones, R. M. (1994) 'Curricula focused on behavioral deviance', in S. L. Archer (ed.) *Interventions for Adolescent Identity Development,* Newbury Park, CA: Sage.

Jordan, D. (1970) 'Parental antecedents of ego identity formation', unpublished Master's thesis, State University of New York at Buffalo.

—— (1971) 'Identity status: a developmental model as related to parental behavior', unpublished doctoral dissertation, State University of New York at Buffalo.

Josselson, R. (1973) 'Psychodynamic aspects of identity formation in college women', *Journal of Youth and Adolescence* 2: 3–52.

—— (1980) 'Ego development in adolescence', in J. Adelson (ed.) *Handbook of Adolescent Psychology,* New York: Wiley.

—— (1982) 'Personality structure and identity status in women viewed through early memories', *Journal of Youth and Adolescence* 11: 293–9.

—— (1987) *Finding Herself: Pathways to Identity Development in Women,* San Francisco: Jossey-Bass.

—— (1988) 'The embedded self: I and thou revisited', in D. K. Lapsley and F. C. Power (eds) *Self, Ego, and Identity: Integrative Approaches*, New York: Springer-Verlag.

Josselson, R. (1992) *The Space between Us: Exploring Dimensions of Human Relationships,* San Francisco: Jossey-Bass.

Jurich, J. and Holt, R. R. (1987) 'Effects of modified instructions on the Washington University Sentence Completion Test of Ego Development', *Journal of Personality Assessment* 51: 186–93.

Kacerguis, M. A. and Adams, G. R. (1980) 'Erikson stage resolution: the relationship between identity and intimacy', *Journal of Youth and Adolescence* 9: 117–26.

Kaplan, A. and Klein R. (1985) *The Relational Self in Late Adolescent Women,* Wellesley College, Wellesley, MA: Stone Center for Developmental Services and Studies.

Kaufman, K.S. (1985) 'Parental discipline and constructive-developmental psychology', unpublished doctoral dissertation, Harvard Graduate School of Education.

Kegan, R. (1979) 'The evolving self: a process conception for ego psychology', *The Counseling Psychologist* 8: 5–38.

—— (1980) 'Making meaning: the constructive-developmental approach to persons and practice', *The Personnel and Guidance Journal* 58: 373–80.

—— (1982) *The Evolving Self: Problem and Process in Human Development,* Cambridge, MA: Harvard University Press.

—— (1983) 'A neo-Piagetian approach to object relations', in B. Lee and G. G. Noam (eds) *Developmental Approaches to the Self,* New York: Plenum.

—— (1985) 'The loss of Pete's dragon: developments of the self in the years five to seven', in R. L. Leahy (ed.) *The Development of the Self,* New York: Academic Press.

—— (1986a) 'The child behind the mask: sociopathy as developmental delay', in W. H. Reid, D. Dorr, J. I. Walker, J. W. Bonner III (eds) *Unmasking the Psychopath: Antisocial Personality and Related Syndromes,* New York: W.W. Norton & Co, Inc.

—— (1986b) 'Kohlberg and the psychology of ego development: a predominantly positive evaluation', in S. Modgil and C. Modgil (eds) *Lawrence Kohlberg: Consensus and Controversy,* London: The Falmer Press.

—— (1986c) 'Interchange: Kegan replies to Loevinger' in S. Modgil and C. Modgil (eds) *Lawrence Kohlberg: Consensus and Controversy,* London: Falmer Press.

—— (1990) 'Minding the curriculum: of student epistemology and faculty conspiracy', unpublished manuscript, Harvard Graduate School of Education.

—— (1991) 'Developmental approaches to professional development', paper presented at the conference of the Clinical-Developmental Institute, Cambridge, MA (June).

—— (1994) *In Over Our Heads: The Mental Demands of Modern Life,* Cambridge, MA: Harvard University Press.

Kegan, R., Noam, G. G., and Rogers, L. (1982) 'The psychologic of emotion: a neo-Piagetian view', in D. Cicchetti and P. Hesse (eds) *New Directions for Child Development: Emotional Development,* no. 16, San Francisco: Jossey Bass.

Keller, M., Eckensberger, L. H., and von Rosen, K. (1989) 'A critical note on the conception of preconventional morality: the case of stage 2 in Kohlberg's theory', *International Journal of Behavioral Development* 12: 57–69.

Kennedy, M. G., Felner, R. D., Cauce, A., and Primavera, J. (1988) 'Social problem solving and adjustment in adolescence: the influence of moral reasoning level, scoring alternatives, and family climate', *Journal of Clinical Child Psychology* 17: 73–83.

Kessler, G. R., Ibrahim, F. A., and Kahn, H. (1986) 'Character development in adolescents', *Adolescence* 81: 1–9.

Kirshner, L. (1988) 'Implications of Loevinger's theory of ego development for time-limited psychotherapy', *Psychotherapy* 25: 220–6.

Kishton, J., Starrett, R. H., and Lucas, J. L. (1984) 'Polar versus milestone variables in adolescent ego development', *Journal of Early Adolescence* 4: 53–64.

Kitchener, K. S., King, P. M., Davison, M. L., Parker, C. A., and Wood, P. K. (1984) 'A longitudinal study of moral and ego development in young adults', *Journal of Youth and Adolescence* 13: 197–211.

Kohlberg, L. (1958) 'The development of modes of thinking and choices in years 10 to 16', unpublished doctoral dissertation, University of Chicago.

—— (1969) 'Stage and sequence: the cognitive-developmental approach to socialization', in D. A. Goslin (ed.) *Handbook of Socialization Theory and Research*, Chicago: Rand McNally.

—— (1973) 'Continuities in childhood and adult moral development revisited', in P. B. Baltes and K. W. Schaie (eds) *Life-span Developmental Psychology: Personality and Socialization*, New York: Academic Press.

—— (1975) 'Counseling and counselor education: a developmental approach', *Counselor Education and Supervision* 14: 1975.

—— (1980a) 'Stages of moral development as a basis for education', in B. Munsey (ed.) *Moral Development, Moral Education, and Kohlberg*, Birmingham, AL: Religious Education Press.

—— (1980b) 'Educating for a just society: an updated and revised statement', in B. Munsey (ed.) *Moral Development, Moral Education, and Kohlberg*, Birmingham, AL: Religious Education Press.

—— (1981) *Essays in Moral Development*, vol. 1: *The Philosophy of Moral Development*, San Francisco: Harper & Row.

—— (1984) *Essays in Moral Development*, vol. 2: *The Psychology of Moral Development*, San Francisco: Harper & Row.

Kohlberg, L. and Gilligan, C. (1971) 'The adolescent as a philosopher: the discovery of the self in a postconventional world', *Daedalus* 100: 1051–86.

Kohlberg, L. and Kramer, R. (1969) 'Continuities and discontinuities in childhood and adult moral development', *Human Development* 12: 93–120.

Kohlberg, L. and Turiel, E. (1971) 'Moral development and moral education', in G. S. Lesser (ed.) *Psychology and Educational Practice*, London: Scott, Foresman & Co.

Kohlberg, L. and Wasserman, E. R. (1980) 'The cognitive-developmental approach and the practicing counselor: an opportunity for counselors to rethink their roles', *The Personnel and Guidance Journal* 58: 559–67.

Kowaz, A. and Marcia, J. E. (1991) 'Development and validation of a measure of Eriksonian industry', *Journal of Personality and Social Psychology* 60: 390–7.

Kraemer, S. (1982) 'Leaving home and the adolescent family therapist', *Journal of Adolescence* 5: 51–62.

Kramer, D. L. (1958) in D. L. Rubinfine, 'Problems of identity', *Journal of the American Psychoanalytic Association* 6: 131–42.

Kraus, W. and Mitzscherlich, B. (1994) ' "Normality" as a paradise lost or as a utopia? Identity development in an individualized society', paper presented at the Biennial Meeting of the European Society for Research on Adolescence, Stockholm (June).

Krebs, D. and Rosenwald, A. (1979) 'Moral reasoning and moral behavior in conventional adults', *Merrill-Palmer Quarterly* 23: 77–87.

Krebs, D. L., Vermeulen, S. C. A., Carpendale, J. I., and Denton, K. (1991) 'Structural and situational influences on moral judgment: the interaction between stage and dilemma', in W. M. Kurtines and J. L. Gewirtz (eds) *Handbook of Moral Behavior and Development*, vol. 1: *Theory*, Hillsdale, NJ: Lawrence Erlbaum Associates.

Kroger, J. (1983) 'I knew who I was when I got up this morning,' *SET Research Information for Teachers* 1: 1–6.

—— (1985a) 'Eriksonian ego identity: implications for counselling in the secondary schools', paper presented at the joint conference of the Australian/New Zealand Psychological Societies, Christchurch, New Zealand (Aug.).

—— (1985b) 'Separation-individuation and ego identity status in New Zealand university students', *Journal of Youth and Adolescence* 14: 133–47.

—— (1990) 'Ego structuralization in late adolescence as seen through early memories and ego identity status', *Journal of Adolescence* 13: 65–77.

—— (1992) 'Intrapsychic dimensions of identity during late adolescence', in G.R. Adams, T. P. Gullotta, and R. Montemayor (eds) *Adolescent Identity Formation: Advances in Adolescent Development*, vol. 4, Newbury Park, CA: Sage.

—— (1993a) 'Ego identity: an overview', in J. Kroger (ed.) *Discussions on Ego Identity,* Hillsdale, NJ: Lawrence Erlbaum Associates.

—— (1993b) 'The role of historical context in the identity formation process of late adolescence', *Youth and Society* 24: 363–76.

—— (1993c) 'On the nature of structural transition in the identity formation process', in J. Kroger (ed.) *Discussions on Ego Identity,* Hillsdale, NJ: Lawrence Erlbaum Associates.

—— (1995) 'The differentiation of "firm" and "developmental" foreclosure identity statuses: a longitudinal study', *Journal of Adolescent Research* 10: 317–37.

Kroger, J. and Green, K. (1994) 'Factor analytic structure and stability of the Separation-Individuation Test of Adolescence', *Journal of Clinical Psychology* 50: 772–9.

Kroger, J. and Haslett, S. J. (1987) 'A retrospective study of ego identity status change from adolescence through middle adulthood', *Social and Behavioral Sciences Documents* 17 (Ms. no. 2797).

—— (1988) 'Separation-individuation and ego identity status in late adolescence: a two-year longitudinal study', *Journal of Youth and Adolescence* 17: 59–81.

Kurtines, W. M. and Gewirtz, J. L. (eds) (1991a) *Handbook of Moral Behavior and Development: Theory* (vol.1), Hillsdale, NJ: Lawrence Erlbaum Associates.

—— (1991b) *Handbook of Moral Behavior and Development: Research* (vol. 2), Hillsdale, NJ: Lawrence Erlbaum Associates.

—— (1991c) *Handbook of Moral Behavior and Development: Application* (vol. 3), Hillsdale, NJ: Lawrence Erlbaum Associates.

Kurtines, W. and Greif, E. B. (1974) 'The development of moral thought: review and evaluation of Kohlberg's approach', *Psychological Bulletin* 81: 453–70.

Kutnick, P. (1986) 'The relationship of moral judgment and moral action: Kohlberg's theory, criticism, and revision', in S. Modgil and C. Modgil (eds) *Lawrence Kohlberg: Consensus and Controversy,* London: Falmer Press.

Lahey, L. L. (1986) 'Males' and females' construction of conflict in work and love', unpublished doctoral dissertation, Harvard Graduate School of Education.

Lahey, L., Souvaine, E., Kegan, R., Goodman, R., and Felix, S. (1987) 'A guide to the subject-object interview: its administration and interpretation', unpublished manuscript, Harvard Graduate School of Education.

Lapsley, D. K. (1992) 'Toward an integrated theory of adolescent ego development: the "new look" at adolescent egocentrism', *American Journal of Orthopsychiatry* 63: 562–71.

Lapsley, D. K., Enright, R. D., and Serlin, R. C. (1985) 'Toward a theoretical perspective on the legislation of adolescence', *Journal of Early Adolescence* 5: 441–66.

Lapsley, D. K. and Rice, K. (1988) 'The "new look" at the imaginary audience and personal fable: towards an integrative model of adolescent ego development', in D. K. Lapsley and F. C. Power (eds) *Self, Ego, Identity: Integrative Approaches,* New York: Springer-Verlag.

LaVoie, J. (1994) 'Identity in adolescence: issues of theory, structure and transition', *Journal of Adolescence* 17: 17–28.

Leaper, C., Hauser, S. T., Kreman, A. *et al.* (1989) 'Adolescent–parent interactions in relation to adolescents' gender and ego development pathway: a longitudinal study', *Journal of Early Adolescence* 9: 335–61.

Leming, J. S. (1986) 'Kohlbergian programs in moral education: a practical review and assessment', in S. Modgil and C. Modgil (eds) *Lawrence Kohlberg: Consensus and Controversy,* London: Falmer Press.

Levine, J. B. (1994) 'On McClanahan and Holmbeck's construct validity study of the Separation-Individuation Test of Adolescence', *Journal of Personality Assessment* 62: 166–8.

Levine, J. B., Green, C. J., and Millon, T. (1986) 'Separation-Individuation Test of Adolescence', *Journal of Personality Assessment* 50: 123–37.

Levine, J. B. and Saintonge, S. (1993) 'Psychometric properties of the Separation-Individuation Test of Adolescence within a clinical population', *Journal of Clinical Psychology* 49: 492–507.

Levitz-Jones, E. M. and Orlofsky, J. L. (1985) 'Separation-individuation and intimacy capacity in college women', *Journal of Personality and Social Psychology* 49: 156–69.

Lifton, R. J. (1975) 'Preface', in A. Mitscherlich and M. Mitscherlich, *The Inability to Mourn,* New York: Grove Press.

Loevinger, J. (1976) *Ego Development: Conceptions and Theories,* San Francisco: Jossey-Bass.

—— (1979a) 'The idea of the ego', *The Counseling Psychologist* 8: 3–5.

—— (1979b) 'Reply to Kegan', *The Counseling Psychologist* 8: 39–40.

—— (1979c) 'Construct validity of the sentence completion test of ego development', *Applied Psychological Measurement* 3: 281–311.

—— (1980) 'Some thoughts on ego development and counseling', *Personnel and Guidance Journal* 58: 389–90.

Loevinger, J. (1982) 'Confessions of an iconoclast', invited address to symposium sponsored by Psi Chi and American Psychological Association Committee on Women, Washington, DC (Aug.).

—— (1983) 'On ego development and the structure of personality', *Developmental Review* 3: 339–50.

—— (1984) 'On the self and predicting behavior', in R. A. Zucker, J. Aronoff, and A. I. Rabin (eds) *Personality and the Prediction of Behavior,* Orlando, FL: Academic Press.

—— (1985) 'Revision of the Sentence Completion Test for ego development', *Journal of Personality and Social Psychology* 48: 420–7.

—— (1987) *Paradigms of Personality,* New York: W. H. Freeman.

—— (1991) 'Personality structure and the trait-situation controversy: on the uses of low correlations', in W. M. Grove and D. Cicchetti (eds) *Thinking about Psychology*, vol.2, Minneapolis: University of Minnesota Press.

—— (1993a) 'Conformity and conscientiousness: one factor or two stages?' in D.C. Funder, R. D. Parke, and C. Tomlinson-Keasy (eds) *Studying Lives through Time: Personality and Development,* Washington, DC: American Psychological Association.

—— (1993b) 'Measurement of personality: true or false?' *Psychological Inquiry* 4: 1–16.

—— (1994) 'Has psychology lost its conscience?' *Journal of Personality Assessment* 62: 2–8.

Loevinger, J. and Blasi, A. (1991) 'Development of the self as subject', in J. Strauss and G. R. Goethals (eds) *The Self: Interdisciplinary Approaches,* New York: Springer-Verlag.

Loevinger, J., Cohn, L. D., Redmore, C. D., Bonneville, L. P., Streich, D. D., and Sargent, M. (1985) 'Ego development in college', *Journal of Personality and Social Psychology* 48: 947–62.

Loevinger, J. and Wessler, R. (1970) *Measuring Ego Development,* vols. 1 and 2, San Francisco: Jossey-Bass.

Loevinger, J., Wessler, R., and Redmore, C. (1970) *Measuring Ego Development,* vol. 2, San Francisco: Jossey-Bass.

Logan, R. D. (1986) 'A reconceptualization of Erikson's theory: the repetition of existential and instrumental themes', *Human Development* 29: 125–36.

Lyons, N. P. (1983) 'Two perspectives: on self, relationships, and morality', *Harvard Educational Review* 53: 125–45.

McCammon, E. P. (1981) 'Comparison of oral and written forms of the sentence completion test for ego development', *Developmental Psychology* 17: 233–5.

McClanahan, G. and Holmbeck, G. N. (1992) 'Separation-individuation, family functioning, and psychological adjustment in college students: a construct validity study of the Separation-Individuation Test of Adolescence', *Journal of Personality Assessment* 59: 468–85.

McCullers, C. (1946) *Member of the Wedding,* Boston: Houghton Mifflin.

Mahler, M. S. (1983) 'The meaning of developmental research of earliest infancy as related to the study of separation-individuation', in J. D. Call, E. Galenson, and R. L. Tyson (eds) *Frontiers of Infant Psychiatry,* New York: Basic Books.

Mahler, M. S., Pine, F., and Bergman, A. (1975)*The Psychological Birth of the Human Infant,* New York: Basic Books.

Mansfield, K. (1972) 'Prelude', in E. Bowen (ed.) *34 Short Stories,* London: Collins (First published 1918).

Marcia, J. E. (1966) 'Development and validation of ego identity status', *Journal of Personality and Social Psychology* 3: 551–8.

—— (1967) 'Ego identity status: relationship to change in self-esteem, "general maladjustment", and authoritarianism', *Journal of Personality* 35: 118–33.

—— (1976a) 'Identity six years after: a follow-up study', *Journal of Youth and Adolescence* 5: 145–60.

—— (1976b) 'Studies in ego identity', unpublished research monograph, Simon Fraser University, Burnaby, BC, Canada.

—— (1979) 'Identity status in late adolescence: description and some clinical implications', Identity Development Symposium, Gröningen: The Netherlands (June).

—— (1980) 'Identity in adolescence', in J. Adelson (ed.) *Handbook of Adolescent Psychology,* New York: Wiley.

—— (1983) 'Some directions for the investigation of identity formation in early adolescence', *Journal of Early Adolescence* 3: 215–23.

—— (1986) 'Clinical implications of the identity status approach within psychosocial developmental theory', *Cadernos de Consulta Psicologica* 2: 23–34.

—— (1989) 'Identity diffusion differentiated,' in M. A. Luszez and T. Nettelbeck (eds), *Psychological Development: Perspectives across the Life-Span,* North-Holland: Elsevier Science.

—— (1993) 'The relational roots of identity', in J. Kroger (ed.) *Discussions on Ego Identity,* Hillsdale, NJ: Lawrence Erlbaum Associates.

—— (1994) 'Ego identity and object relations', in J. Masling and R. F. Bornstein (eds) *Empirical Perspectives on Object Relations Theory,* Washington, DC: American Psychological Association.

Marcia, J. E. and Friedman, M. (1970) 'Ego identity status in college women', *Journal of Personality* 38: 249–63.

Marcia, J.E. , Waterman, A. S., Matteson, D. R., Archer, S. L., and Orlofsky, J. L. (1993) *Ego Identity: A Handbook for Psychosocial Research,* New York: Springer-Verlag.

Markstrom-Adams, C., Ascione, F. R., Braegger, D. and Adams, G. R. (1993) 'Promotion of ego identity development: can short-term intervention facilitate growth?', *Journal of Adolescence* 16: 217–24.

Markstrom-Adams, C., Sabino, V., Turner, B., and Berman, R. (1994) 'Adolescent ego resiliency: the Eriksonian measure of ego strengths', paper presented at the Biennial Meeting of the International Society for the Study of Behavioral Development, Amsterdam.

Maslach, C., Stapp, J., and Santee, R. T. (1985) 'Individuation: conceptual analysis and assessment', *Journal of Personality and Social Psychology* 49: 729–38.

Masterson, J. F. (1986) 'Creativity as a vehicle to establish a real self: Jean Paul Sartre, Edvard Munch, Thomas Wolfe', in J. F. Masterson (ed.) *The Real Self: A Developmental and Object Relations Approach* (Cassette Recording 4), New York: The Masterson Group.

Masterson, J. F. and Costello, J. L. (1980) *From Borderline Adolescent to Functioning Adult: The Test of Time,* New York: Brunner/Mazel.

Mazor, A., Alfa, A. and Gampel, Y. (1993) 'On the thin line between connection and separation: the individuation process, from cognitive and object-relations perspectives, in kibbutz adolescents', *Journal of Youth and Adolescence* 22: 641–69.

Meeus, W. and Dekovic, M. (1994) 'Identity development, parental and peer support in adolescence: results of a national Dutch survey', unpublished manuscript, Utrecht University, The Netherlands.

Michener, J. (1949) *The Fires of Spring*, New York: Random House.

Miller-Tiedeman, A. and Tiedeman, D. V. (1972) 'Decision-making for the 70s', *Focus on Guidance* 1: 1–15.

Millis, S. R. (1984) 'Separation-individuation and intimacy status in young adulthood', unpublished doctoral dissertation, University of Cincinnati.

Mirsky, J. and Kaushinsky, F. (1989) 'Migration and growth: separation-individuation processes in immigrant students in Israel', *Adolescence* 24: 725–40.

Mitchell, V. (1993) 'The synthetic function in the study of personality', *Psychological Inquiry* 4: 37–40.

Modgil, S. and Modgil, C. (1986) *Lawrence Kohlberg: Consensus and Controversy,* London: Falmer Press.

Moore, D. and Hotch, D. F. (1981) 'Late adolescents' conceptualizations of home leaving', *Journal of Youth and Adolescence* 10: 1–10.

—— (1982) 'Adolescent-parent separation: the role of parental divorce', *Journal of Youth and Adolescence* 11: 115–19.

—— (1983) 'The importance of different home-leaving strategies to late adolescents', *Adolescence* 18: 413–16.

Moustakas, C. E. (1974) *Portraits of Loneliness and Love*, Englewood Cliffs, NJ: Prentice-Hall.

Neill, A. S. (1972) *Summerhill: A Radical Approach to Child Rearing*, Harmondsworth: Penguin.

Nelson, J. R., Smith, D. J., and Dodd, J. (1990) 'The moral reasoning of juvenile delinquents: a meta-analysis', *Journal of Abnormal Child Psychology* 18: 231–9.

Nettles, E. J. and Loevinger, J. (1983) 'Sex role expectations and ego level in relation to problem marriages', *Journal of Personality and Social Psychology* 45: 676–87.

Nin, A. (1978) *Linotte: The Early Diary of Anaïs Nin,* New York: Harcourt Brace Jovanovich.

Noam, G. (1985) 'Stage, phase, and style: the developmental dynamics of the self', in M. Berkowitz and F. Oser (eds) *Moral Education,* Hillsdale, NJ: Lawrence Erlbaum Associates.

—— (1988) 'The self, adult development, and the theory of biography and transformation', in D. K. Lapsley and F. C. Power (eds) *Self, Ego, and Identity: Integrative Approaches,* New York: Springer-Verlag.

—— (1990) 'Beyond Freud and Piaget: biographical worlds – interpersonal self' in T. E. Wren (ed.) *The Moral Domain,* Cambridge, MA: MIT Press.

—— (1992) 'Development as the aim of clinical intervention', *Development and Psychopathology* 4: 679–96.

Noam, G. G., Kohlberg, L. and Snarey, J. (1983) 'Steps towards a model of the self', in B. Lee and G. G. Noam (eds) *Developmental Approaches to the Self,* New York: Plenum.

Noam, G. G., Powers, S. I., Kilkenny, R., and Beedy, J. (1991) 'The interpersonal self in life-span developmental perspective: theory, measurement and longitudinal case analyses', in P. B. Baltes, D. L. Featherman, and R. M. Lerner (eds) *Life-span Development and Behavior* 10: 59–104.

Noam, G. G., Recklitis, C. J., and Paget, K. F. (1991) 'Pathways of ego development: contributions to maladaptation and adjustment', *Development and Psychopathology* 3: 311–28.

Novy, D.M. (1993) 'An investigation of the progressive sequence of ego development levels',*Journal of Clinical Psychology* 49: 332–8.

Novy, D. M., Gaa, J. P., Frankiewicz, R. G., Liberman, D., and Amerikaner, M. (1992) 'The association between patterns of family functioning and ego development of the juvenile offender', *Adolescence* 105: 25–35.

Offer, D. (1969) *The Psychological World of the Teenager*, New York: Basic Books.

—— (1991) 'Adolescent development: a normative perspective', in S. I. Greenspan and G. H. Pollock (eds) *The Course of Life*, vol. IV: *Adolescence*, New York: International Universities Press.

Offer, D. and Offer, J. (1975) *From Teenage to Young Manhood*, New York: Basic Books.

Orlofsky, J. L. (1976) 'Intimacy status: relationship to interpersonal perception', *Journal of Youth and Adolescence* 5: 73–88.

—— (1978) 'Identity formation, achievement, and fear of success in college men and women', *Journal of Youth and Adolescence* 7: 49–62.

Orlofsky, J. and Frank, M. (1986) 'Personality structure as viewed through early memories and identity status in college men and women', *Journal of Personality and Social Psychology* 50: 580–6.

Orlofsky, J. L., Marcia, J. E., and Lesser, I. M. (1973) 'Ego identity status and the intimacy versus isolation crisis of young adulthood', *Journal of Personality and Social Psychology* 27: 211–19.

Osgood, C. (1991) 'Readiness for parenting teenagers: a structural-developmental approach', unpublished doctoral dissertation, University of Massachusetts.

Palmer, T. B. (1974) 'The youth authority's community treatment project', *Federal Probation* 38: 3–14.

Papini, D. R., Micka, J. C., and Barnett, J. K. (1989) 'Perceptions of intrapsychic and extrapsychic functioning as bases of adolescent ego identity status', *Journal of Adolescent Research* 4: 462–82.

Peskin, H. (1972) 'Multiple prediction of adult psychological health from preadolescent and adolescent behavior', *Journal of Consulting and Clinical Psychology* 38: 155–60.

Phinney, J. S. (1989) 'Stages of ethnic identity development in minority group adolescents', *Journal of Early Adolescence* 9: 1–2, 34–49.

Phinney, J. S. and Chavira, V. (1992) 'Ethnic identity and self-esteem: an exploratory longitudinal study', *Journal of Adolescence* 15: 271–81.

Phinney, J. S. and Rosenthal, D. A. (1992) 'Ethnic identity in adolescence: process, content, and outcome', in G.R. Adams, T. P. Gullotta, and R. Montemayor (eds), *Adolescent Identity Formation: Advances in Adolescent Development*, vol. 4, Newbury Park, CA: Sage.

Piaget, J. (1932) *The Moral Judgment of the Child*, London: Kegan Paul.

—— (1967) 'On the nature and nurture of intelligence', invited address delivered at New York University (March).

Picano, J. J. (1987) 'Automatic ogive scoring rules for the short form of the Sentence Completion Test of Ego Development', *Journal of Clinical Psychology* 43: 119–22.

Pine, F. (1985) *Developmental Theory and Clinical Process,* New Haven, CT: Yale University Press.

—— (1990) *Drive, Ego, Object, and Self,* New York: Basic Books.

—— (1992) 'Some refinements of the separation-individuation concept in light of research on infants', *Psychoanalytic Study of the Child* 45: 179–94.

Pipp, S., Shaver, P., Jennings, S., Lamborn, S., and Fischer, K. (1985) 'Adolescents' theories about the development of their relationships with parents', *Journal of Personality and Social Psychology* 48: 991–1001.

Podd, M. H. (1972) 'Ego identity status and morality: the relationship between two developmental constructs', *Developmental Psychology* 6: 497–507.

Podd, M. H., Marcia, J. E., and Rubin, B. M. (1970) 'The effects of ego identity and partner perception on a prisoner's dilemma game', *Journal of Social Psychology* 82: 117–26.

Pollack, S. and Gilligan, C. (1982) 'Images of violence in Thematic Apperception Test stories', *Journal of Personality and Social Psychology* 42: 159–67.

—— (1983) 'Differing about differences: the incidence and interpretation of violent fantasies in women and men', *Journal of Personality and Social Psychology* 45: 1172–5.

—— (1985) 'Killing the messenger', *Journal of Personality and Social Psychology* 48: 374–5.

Power, C. (1991) 'Lawrence Kohlberg: the vocation of a moral psychologist and educator. Part 1', in W. M. Kurtines and J. L. Gewirtz (eds) *Handbook of Moral Behavior and Development,* volume 1: *Theory,* Hillsdale, N J: Lawrence Erlbaum Associates.

Prager, K. J. (1982) 'Identity development and self-esteem in young women', *The Journal of Genetic Psychology* 141: 177–82.

Prager, K. J. and Bailey, J. M. (1985) 'Androgyny, ego development, and psychosocial crisis resolution', *Sex Roles* 13: 525–36.

Pratt, M. W., Diessner, R., Hunsberger, B., Pancer, S. M., and Savoy, K. (1991) 'Four pathways in the analysis of adult development and aging: comparing analyses of reasoning about personal-life dilemmas', *Psychology and Aging* 6: 666–75.

Quintana, S. M. and Kerr, J. (1993) 'Relational needs in late adolescent separation-individuation', *Journal of Counseling and Development* 71: 349–54.

Quintana, S. M. and Lapsley, D. K. (1990) 'Rapprochement in late adolescent separation-individuation: a structural equations approach', *Journal of Adolescence* 13: 371–85.

Rappaport, H., Enrich, K., and Wilson, A. (1985) 'Relation between ego identity and temporal perspective', *Journal of Personality and Social Psychology* 48: 1609–20.

Raskin, P. M. (1994) 'Identity and the career counseling of adolescents: the development of vocational identity', in S. L. Archer (ed.) *Interventions for Adolescent Identity Development,* Newbury Park, CA: Sage.

Redmore, C. D. (1983) 'Ego development in the college years: two longitudinal studies', *Journal of Youth and Adolescence* 12: 301–6.

Redmore, C. D. and Loevinger, J. (1979) 'Ego development in adolescence: longitudinal studies', *Journal of Youth and Adolescence* 8: 1–20.

Rest, J. R. (1979a) *Development in Judging Moral Issues,* Minneapolis: University of Minnesota Press.

Rest, J. (1979b) *Revised Manual for the Defining Issues Test*, Minneapolis: Minnesota Moral Research Projects.

Rest, J., Turiel, E., and Kohlberg, L. (1969) 'Relations between level of real judgment and preference and comprehension of the moral judgments of others', *Journal of Personality* 37: 225–52.

Rhodes, B. and Kroger, J. (1992) 'Parental bonding and separation-individuation difficulties among late adolescent eating disordered women', *Child Psychiatry and Human Development* 22: 249–63.

Rice, K. (1990) 'Attachment in adolescence: a narrative and meta-analytic review', *Journal of Youth and Adolescence* 19: 511–38.

Rice, K. G. (1991) 'Attachment and separation-individuation: a time-sequential study of late adolescents', paper presented at the Biennial Meeting of the Society for Research in Child Development, Seattle (April).

Rice, K. G., Cole, D. A., and Lapsley, D. K. (1990) 'Separation-individuation, family cohesion, and adjustment to college: measurement validation and test of a theoretical model', *Journal of Counseling Psychology* 37: 195–202.

Richmond, M. B. and Sklansky, M. A. (1984) 'Structural change in adolescence', in D. D. Brockman (ed.) *Late Adolescence: Psychoanalytic Studies*, New York: International Universities Press.

Rogers, C. R. (1983) *Freedom to Learn for the 80's*, Columbus, OH: Charles E. Merrill.

Roker, D. and Banks, M. H. (1993) 'Adolescent identity and school type', *British Journal of Psychology* 84: 297–300.

Rosenthal, D. A., Gurney, R. M., and Moore, S. M. (1981) 'From trust to intimacy: a new inventory for examining Erikson's stages of psychosocial development', *Journal of Youth and Adolescence* 10: 526–37.

Rowe, I. and Marcia, J. E. (1980) 'Ego identity status, formal operations, and moral development', *Journal of Youth and Adolescence* 9: 87–99.

Rubin, K. H. and Trotter, K. T. (1977) 'Kohlberg's moral judgment scale: some methodological considerations', *Developmental Psychology* 13: 535–6.

Rustad, K. and Rogers, M. (1975) 'Promoting psychological growth in a high school class', *Counselor Education and Supervision* 14: 277–85.

Sabatelli, N. R. and Williams, D. E. (1993) 'A factor analytic examination of the adolescent individuation measure', paper presented at the Biennial Meeting of the Society for Research in Child Development, New Orleans (April).

Sartre, J. P. (1964) *Words*, London: Hamish Hamilton.

—— (1965) *Nausea*, Harmondsworth: Penguin (first published 1938).

—— (1976) *No Exit*, New York: Vintage Books (first published 1947).

Schafer, R. (1973) 'Concepts of self and identity and the experience of separation-individuation in adolescence', *Psychoanalytic Quarterly* 42: 42–59.

Schenkel, S. and Marcia, J. E. (1972) 'Attitudes toward premarital intercourse in determining ego identity status in college women', *Journal of Personality* 3: 472–82.

Schwarz, K. and Robins, C. J. (1987) 'Psychological androgyny and ego development', *Sex Roles* 16: 71–81.

Selles, T., Markstrom-Adams, C., and Adams, G. R. (1994) 'Identity formation and risk for suicide among older adolescents', paper presented at the Biennial Meetings of the Society for Research on Adolescence, San Diego (Feb.).

Seymour, R. D. (1991) 'Constructing a personal future time perspective', unpublished doctoral dissertation, Harvard Graduate School of Education.

Shaw, G. B. (1966) 'Major Barbara', in R. Cohn and B. Dukore (eds) *Twentieth Century Drama: England, Ireland, and the United States,* New York: Random House (first published in 1907).

Shulkin, A. (1990) 'Separation-individuation and identity status among late adolescent college students', unpublished doctoral dissertation, University of Minnesota.

Sieg, A. (1971) 'Why adolescence occurs', *Adolescence* 6: 337–48.

Silverberg, S. B. and Steinberg, L. (1987) 'Adolescent autonomy, parent-adolescent conflict, and parental well-being', *Journal of Youth and Adolescence* 16: 293–312.

Simmons, D. D. (1983) 'Identity achievement and axiological maturity', *Social Behavior and Personality* 11: 101–4.

Simpson, E. L. (1974) 'Moral development research: a case study of scientific cultural bias', *Human Development* 17: 81–106.

Skoe, E. E. (1993) 'The ethic of care interview manual', unpublished manuscript, University of Tromsø, Norway.

Skoe, E. E. and Diessner, R. (1994) 'Ethic of care, justice, identity, and gender: an extension and replication', *Merrill-Palmer Quarterly* 40: 272–89.

Skoe, E. E. and Gooden, A. (1993) 'Ethic of care and real-life moral dilemma content in male and female early adolescents', *Journal of Early Adolescence* 13: 154–67.

Skoe, E. E. and Marcia, J. E. (1991) 'A measure of care-based morality and its relation to ego identity', *Merrill-Palmer Quarterly* 37: 289–304.

Slugoski, B. R., Marcia, J. E., and Koopman, R. F. (1984) 'Cognitive and social interactional characteristics of ego identity statuses in college males', *Journal of Personality and Social Psychology* 47: 646–61.

Smolak, L. and Levine, M. P. (1993) 'Separation-individuation difficulties and the distinction between bulimia nervosa and anorexia nervosa in college women', *International Journal of Eating Disorders* 14: 33–41.

Snarey, J. (1985) 'Cross-cultural universality of social-moral development: a critical review of Kohlbergian research', *Psychological Bulletin* 97: 202–32.

Snarey, J., Friedman, K., and Blasi, J. (1986) 'Sex role strain among kibbutz adolescents and adults: a developmental perspective', *Journal of Youth and Adolescence* 15: 223–42.

Snarey, J. and Keljo, K. (1991) 'In a *Gemeinschaft* voice: the cross-cultural expansion of moral development theory', in W. M. Kurtines and J. L. Gewirtz (eds.) *Handbook of Moral Behavior and Development,* vol. 1: *Theory,* Hillsdale, NJ: Lawrence Erlbaum Associates.

Snarey, J. Kohlberg, L., and Noam, G. (1983) 'Ego development in perspective: structural stage, functional phase, and cultural age-period models', *Developmental Review* 3: 303–38.

Soldz, S. (1988) 'The construction of meaning: Kegan, Piaget, and psychoanalysis', *Journal of Contemporary Psychotherapy* 18: 46–59.

Souvaine, E., Lahey, L. L., and Kegan, R. (1990) 'Life after formal operations: implications for a psychology of the self', in C. N. Alexander and E. J. Langer (eds) *Higher Stages of Human Development: Perspectives on Adult Growth,* New York: Oxford University Press.

Speicher, B. (1992) 'Adolescent moral judgment and perceptions of family interaction', *Journal of Family Psychology* 6: 128–38.

Spitz, R. (1959) *No and Yes: On the Beginnings of Human Communication,* New York: International Universities Press.

Sprinthall, N. A., Hall, J. S., and Gerler, E. R. (1992) 'Peer counseling for middle school students experiencing family divorce', *Elementary School Guidance and Counseling* 26: 279–394.

Stephen, J., Fraser, E., and Marcia, J. E. (1992) 'Moratorium-achievement (Mama) cycles in lifespan identity development: value orientations and reasoning system correlates', *Journal of Adolescence* 15: 283–300.

Sterling, C. M. and Van Horn, K. R. (1989) 'Identity and death anxiety', *Adolescence* 23: 321–6.

Stern, D. N. (1985) *The Interpersonal World of the Infant,* New York: Basic Books.

Stevens, R. (1983) *Erik Erikson: An Introduction,* Oxford: Open University Press.

Streitmatter, J. (1993) 'Gender differences in identity development: an examination of longitudinal data', *Adolescence* 28: 55–66.

Sullivan, E. V. (1977) 'A study of Kohlberg's structural theory for moral development: a critique of liberal social science ideology', *Human Development* 20: 352–76.

Sullivan, H. S. (1953) *The Interpersonal Theory of Psychiatry,* New York: W. W. Norton.

Sullivan, K. and Sullivan, A. (1980) 'Adolescent-parent separation', *Developmental Psychology* 16: 93–9.

Swensen, C.H. (1980) 'Ego development and a general model for counseling and psychotherapy', *Personnel and Guidance Journal* 58: 382–8.

Tamashiro, R. T. (1979) 'Adolescents' concepts of marriage: a structural-developmental analysis', *Journal of Youth and Adolescence* 8: 443–52.

Tan, A. L., Kendis, R. J., Fine, J. T., and Porac, J. (1977) 'A short measure of Eriksonian ego identity', *Journal of Personality Assessment* 41: 279–84.

Tesch, S. A. and Cameron, K. A. (1987) 'Openness to experience and development of adult identity', *Journal of Personality* 55: 615–30.

Tiedeman, D. V. and Miller-Tiedeman, A. (1977) 'An "I" power primer', *Focus on Guidance* 9: 1–16.

Tolpin, M. (1971) 'On the beginning of the cohesive self', *Psychoanalytic Study of the Child* 26: 316–54.

Tomlinson-Keasey, C. and Keasey, C. B. (1974) 'Formal operation in females from eleven to fifty-four years of age', *Developmental Psychology* 6: 364.

Tupuola, A. M. (1993) 'Critical analysis of adolescent development – a Samoan women's perspective', unpublished master's thesis, Victoria University of Wellington, New Zealand.

Turiel, E. (1966) 'An experimental test of the sequentiality of developmental stages in the child's moral judgments', *Journal of Personality and Social Psychology* 3: 611–18.

—— (1969) 'Developmental processes in the child's moral thinking', in P. H. Mussen, J. Langer, and M. Covington (eds) *Trends and Issues in Developmental Psychology,* New York: Holt, Rinehart & Winston.

—— (1974) 'Conflict and transition in adolescent moral development', *Child Development* 45: 14–29.

—— (1990) 'Moral judgment, action, and development', in D. Schrader (ed.)

The Legacy of Lawrence Kohlberg. New Directions for Child Development 47: 31–49.

Vaillant, G. E. and McCullough, L. (1987) 'The Washington University Sentence Completion Test compared with other measures of adult ego development', *American Journal of Psychiatry* 144: 1189–94.

Vaillant, G. E. and Milofsky, E. (1980) 'Natural history of male psychological health: IX. Empirical evidence for Erikson's model of the life cycle', *American Journal of Orthopsychiatry* 137: 1348–59.

van Hoof, A. (1994) 'Structural integration of identity', paper presented at the Biennial Meeting of the European Society for Research on Adolescence, Stockholm (June).

Walker, L. (1980) 'Cognitive and perspective taking prerequisites for moral development', *Child Development* 51: 131–9.

—— (1984) 'Sex differences in the development of moral reasoning: a critical review', *Child Development* 55: 677–91.

—— (1989) 'A longitudinal study of moral reasoning', *Child Development* 60: 157–66.

—— (1991) 'Sex differences in moral reasoning', in W. M. Kurtines and J. L. Gewirtz (eds) *Handbook of Moral Behavior and Development: Research*, vol. 2, Hillsdale, NJ: Lawrence Erlbaum Associates.

Warren, M. Q. (1969) 'The case for differential treatment of delinquents', *Annals of the American Academy of Political and Social Science* 381: 47–59.

Waterman, A. S. (1982) 'Identity development from adolescence to adulthood: an extension of theory and a review of research', *Developmental Psychology* 18: 341–58.

—— (1984) *The Psychology of Individualism*, New York: Praeger.

—— (1993) 'Finding something to do or someone to be: a Eudaimonist perspective on identity formation', in J. Kroger (ed.) *Discussions on Ego Identity*, Hillsdale, NJ: Lawrence Erlbaum Associates.

Waterman, A. S. and Archer, S. (1979) 'Ego identity status and expressive writing among high school and college students', *Journal of Youth and Adolescence* 8: 327–41.

Waterman, A. S., Geary, P.S., and Waterman, C. K. (1974) 'Longitudinal study of changes in ego identity status from the freshman to the senior year at college', *Developmental Psychology* 10: 387–92.

Waterman, A. S. and Goldman, J. A. (1976) 'A longitudinal study of ego identity development at a liberal arts college', *Journal of Youth and Adolescence* 5: 361–9.

Waterman, A. S. and Whitbourne, S. K. (1981) 'The Inventory of Psychosocial Development: a review and evaluation', *JSAS Catalog of Selected Documents in Psychology* 11 (Ms. no. 2179).

Weinmann, L. L. and Newcombe, N. (1990) 'Relational aspects of identity: late adolescents' perceptions of their relationships with parents', *Journal of Experimental Child Psychology* 50: 357–69.

Welker, J. N. (1971) 'Observations and comments concerning young children in a preschool', unpublished manuscript, University of California, Davis.

Willemsen, E. W. and Waterman, K. K. (1991) 'Ego identity status and family environment: a correlational study', *Psychological Reports* 69: 1203–12.

Winnicott, D. W. (1953) 'Transitional objects and transitional phenomena: a study of the first not-me possession', *International Journal of Psychoanalysis* 34: 89–97.

Wires, J. W., Barocas, R., and Hollenbeck, A. R. (1994) 'Determinants of adolescent identity development: a cross-sequential study of boarding school boys', *Adolescence* 29: 361–78.

Name index

Subject index